1992

THE GOOD LIFE
AND THE HUMAN GOOD

THE GOOD LIFE
AND THE HUMAN GOOD

Edited by

**Ellen Frankel Paul, Fred D. Miller, Jr.,
and Jeffrey Paul**

CAMBRIDGE
UNIVERSITY PRESS

Published by the Press Syndicate of the University of Cambridge
The Pitt Building, Trumpington Street, Cambridge CB2 1RP, England
40 West 20th Street, New York, NY 10011, USA
10 Stamford Road, Oakleigh, Melbourne, Victoria 3166, Australia

First published 1992

Printed in the United States of America

Library of Congress Cataloging-in-Publication Data

The good life and the human good / edited by Ellen Frankel Paul, Fred D. Miller, Jr.,
and Jeffrey Paul.   p.   cm.
Includes bibliographical references and index.
ISBN 0-521-43759-8 (pbk.)
1. Ethics.   2. Social ethics.
I. Paul, Ellen Frankel.   II. Miller, Fred Dycus, 1944–
III. Paul, Jeffrey.
BJ1012.G655   1992
170–dc20   92-13361
CIP

ISBN 0-521-43759-8 paperback

CONTENTS

	Introduction	vii
	Acknowledgments	xvi
	Contributors	xvii
L. W. SUMNER	Two Theories of the Good	1
LAWRENCE C. BECKER	Good Lives: Prolegomena	15
AMÉLIE OKSENBERG RORTY	The Advantages of Moral Diversity	38
JOHN KEKES	On There Being Some Limits to Morality	63
WARREN QUINN	Rationality and the Human Good	81
JUDITH JARVIS THOMSON	On Some Ways in Which a Thing Can Be Good	96
JAMES GRIFFIN	The Human Good and the Ambitions of Consequentialism	118
JULIA ANNAS	The Good Life and the Good Lives of Others	133
THOMAS HURKA	Virtue as Loving the Good	149
SHELLY KAGAN	The Limits of Well-Being	169
FRANK I. MICHELMAN	Legalism and Humankind	190
	Index	209

INTRODUCTION

Socrates (469–399 B.C.) held that the unexamined life was not worth living, and dedicated himself to an examination of the good life. Aristotle (384–322 B.C.) saw this topic as closely tied to the study of the human good:

> If, then, there is some end of the things we do, which we desire for its own sake (everything else being desired for the sake of this), and if we do not choose everything for the sake of something else (for at that rate the process would go on to infinity, so that our desire would be empty and vain), clearly this must be the good and the chief good. Will not the knowledge of it, then, have a great influence on life? Shall we not, like archers who have a mark to aim at, be more likely to hit upon what we should? If so, we must try, in outline at least, to determine what it is, and of which of the sciences or capacities it is the object.[1]

These two questions—"What is the good life?" and "What is the human good?"—defined the basic subject matter for the ethics and politics of the competing schools of ancient philosophy. These issues ought to be no less compelling today. As Aristotle observed, to enquire about the good life is to ask, not about proper conduct in a particular situation, but about the proper course of an entire life. It is to ask what we ought to make of ourselves as moral beings, what standards we ought to follow, and to what goals we ought to aspire. The answers to these questions will have profound ramifications for how we live together and govern ourselves.

The essays in this volume address fundamental and longstanding disputes concerning the good life and the human good. Does it make sense to talk about *the* good life or *the* human good, or are there many human goods and many ways of leading a good life? If there are many goods, then how are they related, and how are we to determine whether one good outweighs another? Does living one's life well leave room for concern for the well-being of others? Are there other, nonmoral concerns that may sometimes take precedence over moral values?

Roughly, theories of the good divide into two kinds: monistic and pluralistic. A monistic theory holds that there is a single good or value, a *summum bonum*, at which all our actions (ultimately) ought to aim. A plu-

---

[1] *Nicomachean Ethics* I.2.1094a18–24; translated by W. D. Ross (and J. O. Urmson), revised by J. Barnes (Revised Oxford Translation; Princeton: Princeton University Press, 1984).

ralistic theory holds that there are two or more values that ought to guide our actions, and that those values are not reducible to a single value. Like the quest for a unified field theory in physics, the search for a monistic theory of value has a certain appeal. Such a theory would justify and explain a range of ethical practices in terms of the promotion of a single good, and in so doing it would satisfy those who believe that simplicity and broad explanatory power are marks of a theory's truth.

The possibility of a monistic theory of the good is the focus of the first essay of this collection. In "Two Theories of the Good," L. W. Sumner considers whether a single value could play a foundational role in an ethical theory. He proceeds by examining two values which have historically been put forward as candidates for that role: welfare and perfection. He evaluates the candidates on the basis of four criteria. A foundational value must be an intrinsic value: it must be worth pursuing for its own sake, not merely for the sake of some further value which it brings about. It must be broad or generic, encompassing all lesser values and explaining their appeal. It must be important; that is, the case for its pursuit must be compelling. Finally, it must be capable of underlying and justifying a wide range of ethical judgments and practices. Sumner argues that one of the two candidates, perfection, fails to meet these criteria, especially the first. Perfectionist value is measured according to an objective standard; a thing has perfectionist value when it exhibits the excellences characteristic of things of its nature, when it is a good specimen of its kind. Perfection lacks subjectivity: the preferences or goals of particular agents or subjects do not enter into the calculation of perfectionist value. A course of action may be valued on perfectionist grounds even if its pursuit would not be in the agent's interests. Welfare, on the other hand, takes into account the preferences and goals of agents—their point of view. From the standpoint of welfare, the good is what is good *for the agent*. Sumner concludes that welfare may plausibly be viewed as an intrinsic good, while perfection may not; perfection may sometimes be worth pursuing instrumentally, when it contributes to an agent's well-being, but does not seem to be worth pursuing for its own sake. The full case for welfare as a foundational value for ethics has yet to be made, but Sumner maintains that, at the very least, welfare is the most likely candidate for such a role.

Lawrence C. Becker approaches the monistic/pluralistic question from a different perspective and arrives at a different conclusion. In "Good Lives: Prolegomena," he argues against a monistic account of the good by describing seventeen distinct goods that are all, in some sense, criteria of a good life. Among these "criterial goods" are understanding, self-command, benevolence, self-love, achievement, and integrity. Becker proceeds by reviewing a number of monistic accounts of the good life and considering how well each manages to incorporate the criterial goods. In addition to Sumner's candidates for *the* good, welfare and perfection

(Becker's terms are "well-being or fulfillment" and "human excellence"), Becker evaluates accounts based on conformity to an external order (for example, living in harmony with nature or doing God's will), on autonomous activity (formulating and living out one's own conception of the good life), and on rationality (basing one's plans and choices on rational deliberation). Becker's aim is to show that none of the forms of life which these accounts describe is clearly superior to all the others; each form of life can accommodate most or all of the criterial goods which he has described. The strength of each proposed monistic account undermines the claim of any of the others to be an account of *the* good life.

Becker's treatment of the various accounts of the good life suggests that — whatever the appeal of a monistic account — a plurality of good lives is not necessarily a bad thing. The idea that lives which differ greatly from one another can nevertheless all be good lives has its own appeal. Indeed, in "The Advantages of Moral Diversity," Amélie Oksenberg Rorty argues that a kind of symbiosis can develop among those who pursue different visions of the good life. All moral systems, Rorty writes, address the question "How should we live?" — and different moral systems find different answers. Expressed in terms of norms and values, a moral system influences those who live in accordance with those norms and pursue those values. As a result of this influence, individuals who follow different moral systems tend to develop different types of ethical character. Ethical character is, roughly, a collection of traits and dispositions which shape an individual's beliefs and desires, and affect his choices and actions. People with different types of ethical character tend to have significantly different goals and priorities; they tend to pursue different ethical projects. This can lead to difficulties, if the various projects conflict. Fortunately, Rorty claims, those who have different types of ethical character also have different strengths; some are better at solving certain types of problems than others. People with different types of ethical character may be able to compensate for one another's weaknesses. Just as a diversity of talents and skills can lead to a division of labor in the field of production, a diversity of ethical character types can lead to a *moral* division of labor. This division of labor, like the other, can produce important advantages; it can greatly facilitate the pursuit of various ethical projects. The key to attaining these advantages, Rorty writes, is to encourage constructive cooperation and coordination among those with different types of ethical character. She concludes by emphasizing the importance of moral education in the development of ethical character; she suggests that the educative institutions of a society can be designed to promote that development and the cooperation it makes possible.

While Rorty considers the advantages of pluralism, John Kekes focuses on pluralism's dark side. "On There Being Some Limits to Morality" offers a discussion of conflicts among different values, and of how those conflicts ought to be resolved. Kekes's essay differs from those of the previous authors in that, while they concentrate on the question of the plurality of moral values, he is concerned with conflicts between moral values and nonmoral ones. Assuming that all values derive from benefits and harms for human beings, Kekes draws the distinction between the moral and the nonmoral in this way: moral values involve benefits and harms agents cause for others; nonmoral values involve benefits and harms agents cause for themselves. Thus, nonmoral values include (among others) beauty, creativity, humor, charm, adventure, and peak physical condition. The question Kekes seeks to address is whether nonmoral values may ever override moral ones; his approach is to consider a number of cases in which nonmoral values appear to be overriding. He notes that a common response to such cases is to broaden the notion of moral value in order to encompass putative nonmoral values. Indeed, a common view holds that moral considerations are just those considerations which have overriding force. To challenge this view, Kekes attempts to formulate examples in which agents undertake unambiguously immoral actions for the sake of some nonmoral value. There must be a limit to how far the notion of moral value can be broadened, he reasons; surely it cannot include *immoral* actions. After setting out his examples, Kekes concludes that there are some cases in which moral values may be overridden by at least one particular nonmoral value: the value of having a minimally acceptable life. The value of having a life worth living can be overriding, he argues, because having such a life is normally a precondition of the pursuit of any moral values.

The conflict between morality and rationality is at the heart of the next essay in this collection. In "Rationality and the Human Good," Warren Quinn explores the tension between the recommendations of practical rationality and the dictates of morality. The conception of rationality that concerns Quinn is a neo-Humean one; it is a practical rationality which aims at the satisfaction of an agent's desires and preferences, without regard for whether those desires and preferences are moral or immoral. Practical rationality, on this view, is concerned with discovering the best means to a certain end, but not with evaluating ends; it does not count the immorality of an action as a reason for not performing it. If we conceive of rationality this way, it is easy to envision cases in which agents desire and take pleasure in shameful and evil ends, such as telling lies or harming innocent people. Neo-Humean rationality can tolerate or even recommend the pursuit of such ends. The tension that Quinn is interested in arises when we consider that on most accounts, rationality is taken to be the primary excellence (or at least one important excellence) of human beings as agents. How can the status of rationality as an excellence be compatible with the fact that rationality can sometimes recommend shameful ends? Quinn considers a number of strategies for reconciling the excellence of practical rationality with its shamefulness, but he suggests that, ultimately, it may be necessary to abandon the idea that practical rationality is an excellence of human beings. He leaves open the possibility, however, that some other form of rationality (construed in different terms) may enjoy that status.

As Quinn's essay illustrates, it is possible for questions to arise about the proper construal of a pivotal concept (such as 'rationality'). "On Some Ways in Which a Thing Can Be Good," Judith Jarvis Thomson's contribution to this collection, is an examination of the concept of 'the good' itself. What is it for a thing to be good? One plausible answer, Thomson suggests, is that every good thing is good in a way: someone can be good at an activity; or a thing can be good for use in achieving some purpose, or good aesthetically; or an event or state of affairs can be good for an agent (meaning, roughly, in that agent's interest). Is the concept of 'moral goodness' captured by any of these ways of being good? One view is that morally good states of affairs are those which are themselves intrinsically good or are related to intrinsically good states of affairs. But this just brings us to another question: What is it for a state of affairs to be intrinsically good? Is being intrinsically good a way of being good, or is it something else? Some of the terms traditionally used in defining 'intrinsic goodness'—"good in itself," "valued for its own sake"—suggest that being intrinsically good is not being good in a way. A review of traditional attempts to explicate 'intrinsic goodness' leaves us with the impression that the concept is, in Thomson's words, "in dire need of clarification." Yet it is difficult to deny the importance of the concept of 'intrinsic goodness'; it plays a central role in consequentialist moral theories. Consequentialism is standardly defined as the thesis that one ought to maximize intrinsic goodness. The basis of its appeal is the intuition that it can never be right to prefer an intrinsically worse state of affairs to an intrinsically better one. As an alternative to standard consequentialism, Thomson proposes *interest* consequentialism, a theory which calls for the maximization of what is good for (in the interest of) agents. Interest consequentialism shares much of the intuitive appeal of the standard version; it is also subject to many of the same objections. Yet its strength lies in the fact that it does not rely on the ill-defined concept of 'intrinsic goodness'.

James Griffin's essay is also concerned with the human good and the role it plays in consequentialist moral theories. Griffin's aim is to explore the central tenet of consequentialism: the idea that a characterization of the good can be used to derive the right, that is, to derive norms which guide human action. In "The Human Good and the Ambitions of Consequentialism," he questions whether this derivation can be carried out. Consequentialist theories pick out certain goods and call for their promotion. The difficulty for consequentialists lies in giving content to the idea of promoting the good, especially when their characterization of 'the good' includes a wide range of goods. If, for example, such goods as promise-keeping, respect for rights, and equality are included in the characterization, then it is hard to see how the injunction to "promote" these goods translates into specific norms for guiding action. To complicate matters, there are other forces at work shaping human norms. Griffin contends that our commitments to those who are close to us set limits on the kinds of actions we can choose to undertake; such ties limit our capacity for being impartial in our dealings with others. But even if we were able to overcome these commitments and choose to promote some collection of goods impartially — and even if we could give solid content to the idea of "promoting the good" — we would still need to determine which set of rules would best achieve that end. Griffin maintains that there are limits to our knowledge in this area. It is difficult, perhaps impossible, to know what the results of implementing a particular set of norms will be. Since our knowledge is limited, there will be a certain amount of arbitrariness in the set of norms that we settle on. A strict derivation of the right from the good is perhaps too ambitious a goal.

The issue of impartiality, which Griffin touches on briefly, is the focus of "The Good Life and the Good Lives of Others," Julia Annas's contribution to this volume. Annas discusses a challenge raised against modern "virtue ethics" and ancient eudaimonistic ethical theories. What these theories have in common is their emphasis on the virtues and the idea that every agent has an ultimate goal or "final end" which the virtues help him to achieve. The role of ethics, on these views, is to help individuals to specify their final ends, and to provide guidance in achieving them. The concern that eudaimonistic theories demonstrate for individual virtue, and for the course of individual lives, sometimes leads to the charge that such theories are egoistic, that they leave no room for concern about how others' lives are going. For those who believe that some degree of impartiality in one's dealings with others is crucial to morality, the charge of egoism calls into question the status of eudaimonistic theories as *moral* theories. Annas answers the charge by drawing a distinction between the framework of a theory and its content. Eudaimonistic theories have an egoistic framework; their starting point is the individual agent's reflections about his own life and values; but such theories need not be egoistic in content. Annas illustrates this point by examining the ethical theory of the Stoics. Impartiality, for the Stoics, is a crucial part of the moral point of view; they present a theory of moral development in which the agent is initially concerned only for himself, but gradually broadens the scope of his concern to include others. At first, his concern extends only to his family and those to whom he has made particular commitments; ultimately, however, it extends to every other human being. The Stoics did not hold that an agent must have the *same* level of concern for every other human being, but they did believe that an agent should not attribute weight to his own particular interests and commitments merely because they are *his*. And this, Annas suggests, is plausibly what impartiality requires. As the case of the Stoics makes clear, then, a eudaimonistic ethical theory is compatible with varying levels of concern for others.

The Stoics and other ancient eudaimonists reserved a prominent place for virtue in their ethical thought, but the nature of virtue itself is a matter of some dispute. Thomas Hurka addresses this issue with his essay "Virtue as Loving the Good." Some philosophers question whether virtue is an intrinsic good, that is, good for itself and not merely for its consequences. If it is an intrinsic good, they ask whether it is the only intrinsic good or one of many. Hurka suggests that we should treat virtue as one of many intrinsic goods. He proposes an account which defines virtue by its relation to other goods (for example, pleasure or knowledge). The key to his account is the idea that if x (pleasure, knowledge) is intrinsically good, then loving x for itself is intrinsically good. If virtue is defined in terms of "loving the good," then on this account virtue is an intrinsic good. "Loving the good," on Hurka's view, takes three forms: desiring the good, pursuing the good, and taking pleasure in the good when it is attained. The advantages of this view, he argues, are that it provides a unified account of virtue and that it conforms to traditional beliefs about virtue. Hurka closes his essay by considering several issues raised by the account, including the question of whether one form of loving the good (for example, desiring it without pursuing it) is enough to constitute virtue.

While Hurka is concerned with the nature of virtue, Shelly Kagan is concerned with the nature of well-being. In "The Limits of Well-Being," Kagan explores two key questions: What constitutes an individual's well-being? What sorts of facts are relevant to a judgment of whether someone is well-off? Kagan distinguishes three traditional views of well-being — *mental state* theories, which equate well-being with the presence of certain kinds of mental states; *desire* or *preference* theories, which account for well-being in terms of the satisfaction of desires; and *objective* theories, which maintain that some things are good for individuals whether or not individuals desire them. A consideration of hedonism, which equates well-being with certain pleasant mental states, suggests that the traditional classification is inadequate. When asked to describe what all pleasant mental states have in common, the hedonist is forced to retreat to a theoretical position which incorporates aspects of either the desire theory or the objective theory. Kagan proposes a new scheme of classification which would divide theories of well-being according to two criteria: the source of the value of well-being, and the kinds of facts which are relevant to well-being. The source of well-being's value may be either *subjective* or *objective*, depending on whether or not the individual's subjective preferences bear on the determination of what is good for him. The facts which are relevant to well-being may be either *internal* or *external*, depending on whether they are facts about the agent considered in isolation (his physical and mental states) or facts about the agent's relations to other agents and objects. In the light of these new classifications, Kagan suggests that external facts may be irrelevant to determining whether an agent is well-off, and that, if those facts are irrelevant, the moral importance of well-being may be surprisingly limited.

The final essay in this volume examines the relationship between theories of human nature and institutional arrangements. Frank I. Michelman's "Legalism and Humankind" concerns the relationship between two kinds of beliefs: beliefs about what human beings are like and what serves their good, and beliefs about how they ought to act or be governed. The former are judgments about human nature, the latter, moral judgments. It is commonly supposed that a particular view of human nature leads to particular judgments about how people ought to act. Michelman's objective is to consider whether this relationship runs both ways. Do intuitively appealing moral judgments lend support to specific judgments about human nature? Michelman argues that strong beliefs about what actions are permissible, and what social institutions are just, can support beliefs about the nature of humankind. He is especially interested in beliefs about legal institutions; he argues that a certain conception of law leads us to reject a certain view of human nature. If we conceive of law as a body of antecedently binding and highly general principle, and if we believe that it is right for people to conform their actions to law, then we are led to reject any view of human nature that denies substantial human commonality and treats plasticity, or the capacity for self-revision, as the essence of being human. Indeed, a strong sense that people are bound by moral law suggests the possibility that a propensity for principled action is a component of human nature.

The good life and the human good are perennial concerns of moral philosophy. Using a wide range of perspectives and methods, the contributors to this volume offer important new insights regarding these concerns.

ACKNOWLEDGMENTS

The editors wish to acknowledge several individuals at the Social Philosophy and Policy Center, Bowling Green State University, who provided invaluable assistance in the preparation of this volume. They include Mary Dilsaver, Terrie Weaver, and Jennifer Lange.

We wish to thank Executive Manager Kory Tilgner, for his tireless administrative support; Publication Specialist Tamara Sharp, for her patient attention to detail; and Managing Editor Harry Dolan, for editorial assistance above and beyond the call of duty.

CONTRIBUTORS

L. W. Sumner is Professor and Chair at the Department of Philosophy, University of Toronto. He was educated at the University of Toronto and Princeton University, and is the author of *Abortion and Moral Theory* (1981) and *The Moral Foundation of Rights* (1987). He is currently working on a book on the nature of welfare and its place in ethical theory.

Lawrence C. Becker is Professor of Philosophy and Kenan Professor of Humanities at the College of William and Mary. He is the editor, with Charlotte Becker, of the forthcoming *Encyclopedia of Ethics*, and the author of several books, including *Property Rights* (1977; 1980) and *Reciprocity* (1986; 1990).

Amélie Oksenberg Rorty is the Matina Horner Visiting Distinguished Professor at Radcliffe College and Professor of Philosophy at Mt. Holyoke College. She has published widely in the philosophy of mind, the history of philosophy, and moral psychology. Many of her articles appeared in a collection, *Mind in Action* (1988). She has edited *The Identities of Persons* (1976), *Essays on Aristotle's Ethics* (1980), and *Essays on Aristotle's Poetics* (1992). She was the recipient of a John S. Guggenheim Fellowship in 1990–91.

John Kekes is Professor of Philosophy and Public Policy at the State University of New York at Albany. He is the author of *A Justification of Rationality* (1976), *The Nature of Philosophy* (1980), *The Examined Life* (1987), *Moral Tradition and Individuality* (1989), and *Facing Evil* (1990).

Warren Quinn served as Professor of Philosophy and Chair of the Philosophy Department at the University of California, Los Angeles. He wrote numerous articles on topics in meta-ethics, ethical theory, and normative ethics. Some of his papers appeared in *The Philosophical Review*, *Philosophy & Public Affairs*, and *Philosophical Studies*.

Judith Jarvis Thomson is Laurance S. Rockefeller Professor of Philosophy at the Massachusetts Institute of Technology. Her essay in the present volume is part of a longer work in progress on the metaphysics of moral requirement. Her earlier books include *Acts and Other Events* (1977), *Rights, Restitution, and Risk* (1986), and *The Realm of Rights* (1990).

CONTRIBUTORS

James Griffin is Reader in Philosophy, Oxford University, and Fellow of Keble College. He is the author of *Well-Being* (1986) and is now working on various subjects, including moral realism, consequentialism, and human rights.

Julia Annas is Professor of Philosophy at Columbia University. She has published widely in ancient philosophy and is the author of *An Introduction to Plato's Republic* (1981), *Aristotle's Metaphysics: Books M and N* (1976), and (with Jonathan Barnes) *The Modes of Scepticism: Ancient Texts and Modern Interpretations* (1985). She is working on a book on ancient ethical theory. For ten years she has been the editor of *Oxford Studies in Ancient Philosophy*.

Thomas Hurka is Associate Professor of Philosophy at the University of Calgary. His main research interest is moral theory, especially perfectionist moralities. He has published articles in *Ethics*, *The Journal of Philosophy*, *Mind*, and *Social Theory and Practice*; his book *Perfectionism* is forthcoming from Oxford University Press. He is also part of a multidisciplinary research team working on the ethics of global warming. Since 1989, he has written a weekly philosophy column for *The Globe and Mail*, Canada's national newspaper.

Shelly Kagan is Associate Professor of Philosophy at the University of Illinois at Chicago. He works primarily on the foundations of normative ethics and is currently writing an introductory textbook for this area. His first book, *The Limits of Morality* (1989), attacked the widely held view that there are limits to the sacrifices that morality can demand of us, and that certain acts are morally off-limits, even if performing them would lead to better results overall. His essay in this collection is an initial foray into a larger project on the nature of well-being. He has taught previously at the University of Pittsburgh.

Frank I. Michelman is Professor of Law, Harvard University. He has published extensively on constitutional law, property law, general legal theory, and connections among these fields and those of political and moral theory.

The editors deeply regret
the death of Warren Quinn on September 18, 1991.
This volume is dedicated to his memory.

TWO THEORIES OF THE GOOD

By L. W. Sumner

Suppose that the ultimate point of ethics is to make the world a better place. If it is, we must face the question: better in what respect? If the good is prior to the right—that is, if the rationale for all requirements of the right is that they serve to further the good in one way or another—then what is this good? Is there a single fundamental value capable of underlying and unifying all of our moral categories? If so, how might it defeat the claims of rival candidates for this role? If not, is there instead a plurality of basic goods, each irreducible to any of the others? In that case, how do they fit together into a unified picture of the moral life?

These are the questions I wish to address, in a necessarily limited way. To many the questions will seem hopelessly old-fashioned or misguided. Some deontologists will wish to reverse my ordering of the good and the right, holding that the right constrains acceptable conceptions of the good. For many contractarians, neither the good nor the right will seem normatively basic, since both are to be derived from a prior conception of rationality. Finally, some theorists will reject the classification of moral theories in terms of their basic normative categories, arguing that the whole foundationalist enterprise in ethics should be abandoned.

In the face of these challenges to the priority of the good, and in light of the many current varieties of moral skepticism and relativism, I cannot provide a very convincing justification for raising the questions I intend to discuss. It is not enough to say that through much of the history of ethics they have seemed to be worth asking, or that to me they still seem so. The idea that the unifying—and justifying—function of all of our ethical categories is ultimately to make our lives go better, or to make the world a better place, is one that I find utterly compelling. If that is not the point of the whole business of moral thinking, then I find it difficult to imagine what the point might be. What else could morality be *for*? And if it is not *for* anything—if it has no point—what claim can it have on our allegiance?

I recognize that these are not arguments, only rhetorical questions raised to camouflage the absence of arguments. Those who espouse the alternative theoretical models I have mentioned—deontologists, contractarians, anti-foundationalists—all claim to underwrite the importance of ethics by some means other than pointing to the good it does, and I cannot show that they are all mistaken. If you belong to one of these camps, you will find my questions less urgent than I do. Nevertheless, I can still ask you to entertain them as hypotheticals. Imagine that your favorite deity decides to settle this much of human philosophical controversy: she reveals that the good is prior to the right, but does not tell us what the good is. Then you will need to ask my questions.

In the history of ethics, at least in its modern period, these questions have been raised most insistently by utilitarians, or, more broadly, consequentialists. However, they are not peculiar to this tradition. Affirming the priority of the good is a necessary condition for being a consequentialist, but it is not a sufficient one. The idea that the good is prior to and constrains the right is shared by many theorists whose anti-consequentialist credentials are above suspicion.[1] Once a menu of basic values has been adopted, the distinctive consequentialist move is to affirm their commensurability and treat them as factors in an overall cost/benefit analysis.[2] The idea that the right consists in maximizing the good is peculiarly consequentialist, but the more primitive idea that the right is to be derived from the good is not. Consequentialists are welcome to keep the particular structure of their moral theory in mind as we proceed, but I will be working at a prior stage of ethical theory-building.

The questions with which I began are unruly, and would be overwhelming if I tried to address them all within the compass of a brief discussion. As a simplifying device, therefore, I want to explore the possibility of a foundational theory of the good which is simple or monistic. Is it possible that all of our ethical thinking and action might have as its point the furthering of just one particular kind of value? Even to those who accept the priority of the good, the monistic story may seem implausible. After all, the world throws a bewildering array of values at us (or we project such an array on it); how could it be that just one of these is the fundamental good for ethics? Perhaps it cannot be, but it seems to me worth finding out, at least as a first step in a longer inquiry. If we find a successful monistic account of the good, then we will have answers to all of our questions. If not, then we may still have on hand some of the pieces which we will need to fit together a more complex, pluralistic picture.

I. The Contenders

I have resolved my initial questions into one: Is there anything capable of serving as the sole fundamental value for ethics? Even now it is difficult to know how to proceed. Who are the candidates? Do we need to check the credentials of every distinct variety of goodness? How many

[1] See, for example, John Finnis, *Natural Law and Natural Rights* (Oxford: Clarendon Press, 1980), chs. 3–5.
[2] I have outlined my conception of the nature of consequentialism in *The Moral Foundation of Rights* (Oxford: Clarendon Press, 1987), section 6.1.

such varieties are there? How are they to be individuated? Where do we start?

Any value capable of occupying the theoretical niche which we have identified must have a number of important features. First, it must be a mode of intrinsic value: it must be worth having or pursuing for its own sake, not merely by virtue of some further good with which it is somehow connected. This condition eliminates anything whose value is merely instrumental or contributory. Second, it must be abstract or generic. Our ethical deliberations and evaluations cover a myriad of contexts from the larger issues of law or politics, through questions of community and personal relations, to our own individual aspirations and actions. In these different realms, we pursue or promote many goods: liberty, equality, sociality, loyalty, intimacy, security, health, achievement, and so on. It is not credible that any one of these could somehow turn out to be the point of the whole enterprise, or the deep justification of the rest; they are all too parochial for that. If there is a single fundamental value, it must be broad enough to encompass all local goods, and to support and explain their appeal. Nothing short of an abstract category or mode of value will have the requisite degree of generality.

Third, the value in question must be important. What is characteristic of morality, across most of its domains, is its peremptory or insistent tone. Moral considerations are advanced as constraints on our wishes or desires, as demands we must heed even when we would prefer not to. If these constraints and demands all serve some single fundamental good, then the case for promoting this good had better be pretty compelling. Finally, the good we are seeking must be ethically salient. We are not merely asking for an inventory of intrinsic values. We also want to know which of these values might count as foundational *for an ethical theory*. Now an ethical theory has a certain distinctive content and function, dealing as it does with such matters as the distribution of rights and duties, the assessment of motives and dispositions, the assignment of responsibility, the allocation of blame and punishment, the appropriateness of guilt and shame, and so on. If there is a fundamental value in ethics, then it must not only be something worth pursuing for its own sake, but also something capable of grounding all of these judgments and practices. Not all values, however central they may be to their own domain, can bear this weight. Aesthetic value, for example, is (arguably) intrinsic, abstract, and important, but it can provide at best the materials for building an aesthetic theory; it seems out of the question as a foundation for ethics.

These four prerequisites in the job description will serve to screen potential candidates and to narrow our search to a short list of genuine contenders. I suggest that this list contains only two candidates which merit serious consideration: welfare and perfection. It seems to me that, throughout the long history of ethics, virtually all theorists who have affirmed the priority of the good have grounded their moral structure on one or the other of these categories. In any case, these are the candidates which I intend to take seriously as possible fundamental goods for ethics. First, however, we must be clear about what they are and how they differ from one another.

Common sense tells us that a person's welfare, or well-being, is a matter of how well she is doing, or how well her life is going, or how well-off she is. To speak of a person's welfare is therefore plainly to evaluate her life. Lives, however, are complex things whose value can be assessed from a number of standpoints. Welfare assessments concern what we may call the prudential value of a life,[3] namely how well it is going *for the individual whose life it is*. This relativization of prudential value to the proprietor of the life which it modifies is one of the deepest features of the language of welfare: however valuable something may be in itself, it can promote someone's well-being only if it is also good or beneficial *for her*.

The best way to highlight this feature is to contrast the prudential value of a life with its perfectionist value.[4] To say that something has perfectionist value is to say that it is a good instance or specimen of its kind, or that it exemplifies the excellences characteristic of its nature. Perfectionist evaluation assesses a life by means of standards derived from the species, or other natural kind, to which the subject of that life belongs. The traits or abilities selected by those standards will count as personal excellences for each member of the species, regardless of their contribution to the well-being of their bearer. Assuming that we can determine which traits count as excellences for creatures of our nature, there is no logical guarantee that the best human specimens will also be the best off, or that their underdeveloped or pathological rivals will not fare better.

An example may serve to make this contrast between welfare and perfection more concrete. Since the development of talents or abilities generally ranks high on a perfectionist's agenda, imagine that you possess unusually acute philosophical skills. As an undergraduate you stumble into philosophy by accident and, once having sampled its wares, decide to pursue it seriously, both because you quickly discover how good you are at it and because you find this exercise of your intellectual capacities intrinsically satisfying. As a prodigy you progress rapidly, formulating dazzling new theories of truth and reference, and eventually taking a position at a prestigious university. For a while all is well, until you begin to discern a nagging feeling of unease. Your talents have not abated, indeed you are just now beginning to hit your stride, but you are no longer certain that this is the activity to which you wish to dedicate your life.

---

[3] I borrow this useful expression from James Griffin, *Well-Being* (Oxford: Clarendon Press, 1986), part one.

[4] The most developed contemporary account of the nature of perfectionist value is to be found in Thomas Hurka, *Perfectionism* (New York: Oxford University Press, forthcoming).

Other possibilities now begin to seem tempting: perhaps organic farming or building yourself a cabin in the north woods. For a while you persist in your career, but your mood gradually darkens into irritability and depression, and you begin to feel trapped and driven by your own talents. Finally, you leave the academic life to pursue an alternative direction. One discovery you find saddening: you do not have the talent for farming or cabin-building that you have for philosophy. You therefore do not feel challenged in quite the old way, but, by way of compensation, you do feel relaxed and at peace with yourself. What you are now doing may develop your capacities less, but it leads to a more satisfying and fulfilling life for you.

What this story illustrates is that welfare is subjective in a way that perfection is not. The kind of subjectivity I have in mind here is the dependence of the prudential value of a life on the feelings, or aims, or preferences — what I shall generically call the attitudes or concerns — of the person whose life it is.[5] Welfare is subjective because the prudential value of a life is the value it has *for its subject*, and the subject's hierarchy of attitudes or concerns defines her evaluative point of view. For this reason, a person's well-being has to do with the extent to which her life is in the way of satisfying her authentic aims or aspirations — in short, the extent to which she is happy.

Perfection, by contrast, is objective; the criteria which determine the perfectionist value of a life are derived entirely from the natural kind to which the subject of the life belongs, and not at all from her own choices or preferences. Therefore, while happiness is constitutive of welfare it is only incidental to perfection. In the story told above, it is evident that continuing your brilliant philosophical career will produce a more excellent life — a better, more fully realized specimen of a human life — than pursuing any alternative career. Your life as a philosopher will meet the demands of perfection even if it fails to be rewarding for you. It would be easier for us all if the world were so ordered that prudential and perfectionist value could not diverge in this way. In fact, they often do remain together, since our own self-development is typically a source of satisfaction for us. Sadly, however, the fit is an imperfect one.

II. PERFECTIONISM

Both welfare and perfection seem initially well suited to playing a foundational role in ethics. The value of each appears to be intrinsic; at least, it seems odd to ask of either what it is valuable for. Each is abstract, em-

---

[5] Welfare is subjective as long as the subject's attitudes or concerns are an essential ingredient in the analysis of her good; they need not be the only ingredients. In this sense, welfare is analogous to secondary qualities, which count as subjective even though an account of their nature may also refer to some nonsubjective items, such as physical properties and normal conditions of perception.

bracing many local goods within its general category, and each is, seem-
ingly, important. Finally, we can imagine that the pursuit of either mode
of value might be the deep story which underlies our diverse moral practices. Each therefore has a *prima facie* claim to the role. Which claim, if either, can be sustained?

We are supposing that all rules of right—all assignments of duties,
rights, responsibilities, and so on—ultimately aim at achieving the good.
But we must ask, *whose* good? Who are the bearers of the kind of value
which is the point of it all? This question opens up a clear gap between
our two contenders. If welfare is subjective, then it can inhere only in
subjects, in beings capable of a certain kind and level of consciousness.
This is why it seems so natural to think of prudential value as belonging
to lives: what else could it belong to? As we have seen, a life, or the subject of a life, is also capable of possessing perfectionist value, but so are
many other things. In order for something to be a potential bearer of perfectionist value it seems to require only a nature—some answer to the
question: what kind of thing is it? An account of the nature of a thing will
presumably identify certain properties which are essential to it, and perhaps also distinctive of it.[6] From this account it will then be possible to
extract criteria for determining how well a particular thing measures up
to the standards of its kind. However this abstract schema comes to be
filled in, it will clearly apply across the full range of natural kinds. Inevitably, therefore, many things will be potential bearers of perfectionist
value which could not possibly have a welfare.

While it is tempting to think that the good which is foundational to ethics must be the human good, this restriction must be defended, lest it
seem a mere unthinking speciesism (or, more broadly, natural-kindism).
Philosophical debates in environmental ethics have shown how difficult
it is to provide the needed defense. For a perfectionist ethics it would
surely be impossible. Perfectionism begins by telling us that excellence,
by the standards of one's kind, is a good thing. What reason could perfectionism have for narrowing this claim to one particular kind? Why
should human excellence be worth promoting for its own sake, but not
the excellence of any other kind of thing? The logic of perfectionism
drives it in the direction of holding that the good of the members of any
natural kind is intrinsically valuable, and that furthering that (general category of) good is the ultimate point and rationale of ethics.

For those who take their environmental ethics seriously this may seem
a welcome result. Although individual entities remain the sole (or primary)
bearers of value—which will displease the more holistically minded—at

---

[6] Thomas Hurka's account of human nature (in *Perfectionism*) is constructed in terms of
properties essential to human beings, but not in terms of properties distinctive of them. Presumably, he would generalize this approach to other natural kinds.

least this is a step beyond the reflex human chauvinism which characterizes most traditional ethical frameworks. Indeed, it is a long step beyond anthropocentrism, since it extends moral consideration to every natural object in the world. In this it quite outstrips welfarism, which can confer such consideration only on creatures who are the subjects of lives (and not even on all of them). Such a dramatic overturning of the old paradigms can be refreshing, but perhaps it should also induce caution. For consider what perfectionism threatens to commit us to.

The perfectionist programme requires the idea of a natural kind. Let us suppose that this idea is coherent, and that we can assemble some intelligible account of it. Then every particular thing which counts as natural will belong to at least one such kind. This will not only include all organisms, but also inanimate objects such as rocks, oil deposits, bodies of water, mountains, planets, and stars. The objects which belong to each of these kinds, we are to suppose, are capable of being evaluated in terms of their own standards of excellence. Now I do not think that this notion is crazy, however difficult it might be to give it a satisfying philosophical explication. I think I have a rough working sense of what it might mean to say that the Rockies are superior to the Laurentians *as mountains*, where this comparison just points to the fact that they are, well, more mountainous, as opposed to being more scenic or more interesting to climb. And I suppose I can also make sense of thinking that one strain of virus is superior to another *as a virus* if it does better whatever viruses typically do: invades cells more efficiently, or mutates more readily, or whatever. So I think that we can make some sense of natural objects being more or less ideal specimens of their kind, and thus of their having more or less perfectionist value. What is unclear to me is why we should think ourselves morally obliged in general to make things better examples of their kind.

In the case of human beings, the idea that we should promote their good surely owes at least part of its appeal to the fact that we can do so for their sake or on their behalf. In doing good for someone, we are therefore not merely increasing the world's stock of that kind of value but also doing something for that particular person. The notion of furthering someone's good for her own sake can be generalized beyond the boundaries of our species; I have a perfectly good sense of what it means to take my cat to the veterinarian for her sake. But it cannot be generalized indefinitely, since not all natural objects have a "sake" for which we can do things. Therefore, although I can make sense of preserving a mountain as a good specimen of its kind, and might actually be prepared to contribute some time or money to such a project, my doing so would be for the sake, not of the mountain, but of those creatures whose lives will be enhanced by its preservation. Our ethical sensibilities seem to have much to do with our ability to see things from the point of view of potential victims and beneficiaries. I am prepared to think that mountains and stars can fare better or worse on some objective scale of perfection, but this fact does not give them a point of view on behalf of which I can marshal my services. Having a point of view in this sense seems to require being a subject, but perfectionist value is not confined to subjects.

So far I have assumed that what matters — what must matter — for perfectionists is the good of any object belonging to a natural kind. If anything, however, this may lead us to underestimate the number of potential bearers of perfectionist value. We also classify artifacts into kinds and evaluate them in terms of criteria drawn from these kinds. In fact, our paradigmatic bearers of perfectionist value are things with clearly delineated functions; on the natural side, we readily think of items such as organs (one of Aristotle's favorite examples), but the world of functional objects also includes such things as tools and machines. Although I have to stretch somewhat to imagine the criteria for assessing the perfectionist value of a mountain, I have no such problem in the case of a hammer or a dishwasher. On the other hand, if we have difficulty with the idea of promoting the good of mountains for their own sake, what will we say about artifacts? There are, of course, many good reasons for building better (cheaper, more efficient, less wasteful) machines, but the fact that doing so will be better *for the machines*, or will add to the sum total of perfection in the world, does not seem to be among them.

In environmental debates, the unwelcome extension of moral standing to lawn mowers and oil rigs has sometimes been blocked by pointing out that, while such things have a good, they do not have a good of their own.[7] The point being made is that our standards of excellence for artifacts are determined by our purposes in making them, thus by something external to the things themselves. It is not clear that this distinction really makes any ethical difference (would we lose our standing if it turned out, as many seem to believe, that we were created by a deity for some obscure purpose of her own?). Even if the distinction does make a difference, the lesson to be learned does not seem to be a perfectionist one. Artifacts plainly have a nature from which norms can be derived. Since that is all that perfectionist value requires, why isn't that sufficient? What difference could the genesis of such things make, from a perfectionist standpoint? Of course, it is crazy to count the good of tools or machines as mattering in its own right, independently of the contribution they make to our good (or the good of other sentient creatures). But the best explanation of why it is crazy seems to be available only to welfarism.

Part of the problem with perfection as a fundamental value for ethics is that as a category of the good it applies to just about everything. It is

---

[7] See, for example, Robin Attfield, *The Ethics of Environmental Concern* (New York: Columbia University Press, 1983), and Paul W. Taylor, *Respect for Nature* (Princeton: Princeton University Press, 1986). Both Attfield and Taylor use this move to justify limiting moral standing to living beings.

not easy to imagine what it would be like to set about trying to increase it, or to protect it wherever it happens to be. This problem of scope, as serious as it is in its own right, also exacerbates a further difficulty. Excellence or perfection is, as we have seen, relative to kinds. It is possible, at least in principle, to compare things belonging to the same kind in terms of their perfectionist value. However, we have no resources for carrying out comparisons across kinds. Unless different kinds belong to some common super-kind (what would it be? the category *thing*?), it is difficult to see how such comparisons could ever get started. In that case, perfectionism threatens to be mute regarding all conflicts among different varieties or locations of perfectionist value. When a category of value is distributed so widely, such conflicts will be legion. How are any of them to be adjudicated?

How, indeed, are they even to be conceptualized? So far I have assumed that each particular thing, whether natural or artificial, belongs to exactly one kind. This assumption was necessary in order to ensure that the perfectionist value of each thing would be measured against one determinate set of criteria. But the assumption is patently false. Even if we have adequate rules for determining what is to count as a kind, it is obvious that every particular thing belongs to many, perhaps infinitely many, such kinds. I am a human being, to be sure, but I am also a spatiotemporal object, an organism, an animal, a vertebrate, a biped, a parent, a philosopher, a baseball fan, and heaven knows what else. Presumably, each of these kinds generates its own standard of evaluation, in which case I can be better or worse as a human being, animal, parent, and so on. Is my level of perfection to be determined by just one favored standard? If so, how is this to be selected? Or is it to be determined by all of them? But then the conflict problem looms again: what makes me a better parent may make me a worse philosopher. The problem with perfectionist value is not just that it is borne by everything; there is also too much of it in each particular bearer.

The superabundance of perfectionist value entails that there will often be no ethical point to promoting or protecting it. This still leaves open the possibility that a particular domain of such value, circumscribed by some extraneous factor, might be foundational for ethics. Perhaps *only* perfection is germane to ethics, even if not *all* of it is.[8] This possibility would be undercut, however, if there were a reason to think that there is *never* any ethical point to promoting perfection for its own sake. Is there such a reason? In pursuing this question, I shall confine myself to the core case of human good, so as to ensure that the issues at stake stand out as

---

[8] Thomas Hurka has suggested that only the perfection of living things matters. Even if this scope restriction turned out to be intuitively plausible, it would still be helpful to have some account of why being alive makes this kind of difference. The line of argument explored earlier—that only organisms have a good of their own—seems unlikely to do the job.

starkly as possible, and that we are not distracted by the distinct problem of scope.

We know from the example in Section I that you can face a choice between your perfection and your welfare, between being an unhappy philosopher and a happy farmer. When you are choosing between such options for yourself, the sacrifice of either to the other seems intelligible; we can understand the point of the choice in either case, and we may take the view that it is simply your decision to make. (On the other hand, if you continue your philosophical career at a mounting emotional cost, we may stop being so supportive.) In cases of personal choice, where people are determining the array of goods within their own lives, we assume that individuals enjoy a broad prerogative. Within certain limits, they may strike their own balance between perfection and welfare (and other goods as well). To stipulate any rigid priority among these goods, whether it favors perfection over welfare or vice versa, seems an unwarranted intrusion into the sphere of individual autonomy.

But we must also make choices whose impact will fall on the lives of others. If the good is to be pursued or promoted wherever it occurs, and if we have adopted a perfectionist theory of the good, then we will systematically prefer other people's perfection to their welfare. Imposing that priority on them also seems presumptuous on our part, but this time in a more troublesome way than if we imposed the priority of welfare. To see why this is so, recall that perfection is objective; the perfectionist value of your life is in no way determined by your own interests or concerns. Perfectionist evaluation imposes on an individual standards derived from the species as a whole; it enforces the hegemony of the natural kind. But then my preferring your perfection to your welfare involves completely overriding any say you might have in the matter. However you may feel about it, whatever the impact on your aims or aspirations, you will be compelled to live up to an ideal reflecting the standpoint of the species. (Imagine raising a child this way.) To put it mildly, this accords little recognition or respect to your individuality, or to your say over the management of your own life.

Objective values are quite literally alien to us because they emanate from a standpoint which is external to us as individuals, and because their status as values requires no acceptance or endorsement of them on our part. The problem for perfectionism can therefore be generalized: promoting any objective value as the fundamental good for ethics will infringe autonomy or individuality. Perfectionists can soften the impact of their theory of value by making autonomy one of the items in their conception of the human good, but this is at best only a partial solution. The importance assigned to autonomy, in relation to other perfectionist goods, will still be determined from outside the individual and with no reference to her own priorities. The deep problem for any objective theory lies in its implication that personal concerns should play no role in determining why something (anything) counts as a good for an individual, or why one thing counts as a greater good than another. Any such theory will be committed in principle to overriding the autonomous choices of individuals concerning their own lives and imposing on them what they themselves may value less. Only a subjective theory, which incorporates the individual's point of view into its account of the good, is capable of acknowledging the status of human agents as determiners of the priorities for their own lives.

III. WELFARISM

Like perfection, welfare may be conceived of in different ways: as pleasure and the absence of pain, the satisfaction of desires or preferences, and so on. Without attempting to defend my choice, I shall take welfare to consist in happiness, and I shall interpret happiness as a felt satisfaction with one's life or an endorsement of its conditions. Assessments of welfarism as a theory of the good are often compromised by assuming an inadequate or defective conception of welfare (crude hedonism, for example). The conception of welfare as happiness is, to my mind, the best available, and presupposing it therefore allows us to consider the best case for welfarism.

Because it is subjective rather than objective, welfare is in many ways the mirror image of perfection. The weaknesses of the latter are therefore the strengths of the former (and vice versa?). Since welfare is restricted to subjects, there is no worry that moral standing might be attributable indiscriminately to everything. Of course, we still need an account of what makes something a subject, but this will flow from a developed account of the nature of welfare. Roughly speaking, what is required in order to count as a subject will be determined by whatever is taken to be constitutive of welfare: if pleasure and pain then the capacity for these feelings, if the satisfaction of preference then the ability to form and order preferences, and so on. If welfare is taken to be happiness, then the necessary wherewithal will be the capacity to be satisfied or dissatisfied, fulfilled or unfulfilled, by the conditions of one's life. Without further specification, the precise distribution of this capacity is uncertain: does it extend as far as shellfish? But this much, at least, is clear: ethical consideration will be accorded only to living things (and not to all of them), and there will be no justification, on a welfarist theory, for focusing attention exclusively on the human good.

From the vantage point of environmental ethics, the welfarist result lies halfway between anthropocentrism, on the one hand, and views which aim for a wider attribution of moral standing, on the other. That it decisively rejects human chauvinism counts strongly in favor of welfarism (as it did for perfectionism). The only serious question is whether welfarism draws the circle too narrowly, excluding too many things from consideration. There are two problems here. First, welfarism is inherently individualistic, since the sole (or, at any rate, primary) bearers of welfare are individuals. Second, welfarism counts as subjects only those individuals who are capable of having interests. Regarding the second problem, when one considers the groups of réfusés (animals lacking the requisite subjectivity, plants, natural inanimate objects, artifacts), it is difficult to see any ground for complaint. After all, not all value need be intrinsic and fundamental, and we will generally have (derivative) welfarist reasons for protecting and preserving many of these things. In any case, if we want a more generous distribution of moral standing the only way I can see to obtain it is to return to perfectionism. There appears to be no viable intermediate position: we may either grant moral consideration only to those creatures with interests or accept the idea that consideration may be merited by just about everything.

The issue of individualism is more difficult. For one thing, we do not know just how individualistic welfarism is until we work out whether the welfare of groups is logically dependent on that of their members. Then, if it is true (as I believe) that individuals are the sole ultimate bearers of welfare, we need to determine whether that is a strength or a weakness of welfarism. I am inclined to think that it is a strength, since the central claim of welfarism — and the source, I believe, of its enormous intuitive appeal — is that nothing which requires ethical notice has occurred unless someone's (or something's) life has been made to go well or badly, or has been affected for better or worse. The localization of welfare in individuals provides a clear (well, a tolerably clear) criterion for determining the scope of the ethical domain and differentiating it from other realms of value (such as aesthetics). Perhaps axiological individualism is not necessary for this, but it seems to me a promising way of explaining both the range and the motivating force of ethics. Moral considerations matter because it matters how well lives are going, and how well the lives of other creatures are going must matter to us *because* it matters (from the inside) to those creatures.

In this latter respect, the subjectivity of welfare is once again a crucial factor. One of the problems with perfectionism is its propensity to override the concerns and priorities of individuals in the name of an external standard of the good. Since an assessment of an individual's welfare must take her own point of view into account, welfarism cannot suffer from the same weakness, at least not to the same extent. However, the point must not be overstated. Since individuals often have ends other than their own well-being (we are not psychological egoists), welfare cannot simply be identified with whatever we aim at: what someone wants for herself and what is best for her may still diverge. In such cases, welfarism sides with welfare against individual preference. The defense of this stand must be that there is no (ethical) value in the satisfaction of preference as such, but only in the contribution it makes to the quality of life. In this, welfarism is in accord with perfectionism. However, there is a major difference: welfare, but not perfection, already takes into account the individual's assessment of the quality of her life. The promotion of perfection might require extensive infringement of autonomy; the promotion of individual welfare would likely require far less.

There are many conditions which we take to be good for a human life: health, security, companionship, freedom, meaningful work, accomplishment, self-esteem, autonomy, and so on. The central question for assessing welfarism, as a foundational theory of the good, is this: Are all these things valuable from the moral point of view only insofar as their possession contributes to making people's lives go better (prudentially)? This seems to me one of those ground-floor, bedrock questions in ethics which can be answered only by facing it in a good strong light and reflecting very carefully. When I carry out this reflection my answer is yes.[9]

The great strength of welfare as a candidate for the fundamental good for ethics is its subjectivity. This may also be its great weakness. A person's well-being is ultimately assessed from her own point of view: it is constituted by the way she feels about her life. But points of view are not handed down from a Platonic heaven; they are socially constructed and, therefore, profoundly affected by the external circumstances of one's life. The way I feel about the conditions of my life—how satisfying I find them—will depend in part on my expectations for myself and my sense of my own worth. It is notoriously possible for people to be so demoralized—by poverty, domination, manipulation, brainwashing, socialization, and so on—that they internalize their oppression in their self-assessments. Other factors can also cloud perception or judgment: mood or emotion, for example, or mind-altering drugs. A conception of welfare which identifies it with happiness must take care, lest it be committed to advancing as paragons the blissed-out druggies of *Brave New World*.

Some constraint is needed on the standpoint which is taken as authoritative in determining an individual's well-being. Subjective accounts of welfare have typically fulfilled this need by requiring that subjects be informed and/or rational.[10] The point of some such condition is obvious: it

---

[9] It must be acknowledged that reflection on the part of some others has led them to the opposite conclusion. Amartya Sen's critique of welfarism has been particularly influential; see, for example, "Utilitarianism and Welfarism," *The Journal of Philosophy*, vol. 76, no. 9 (September 1979), and "Well-Being, Agency and Freedom," *The Journal of Philosophy*, vol. 82, no. 4 (April 1985).

[10] The prototype of this approach is, of course, John Stuart Mill's criterion for the quality of pleasure in *Utilitarianism*, ch. 2. A good recent treatment may be found in Griffin, *Well-Being*, chs. 1 and 2.

is to guarantee that the individual's self-assessment is reliable. However, merely saying that some such qualification is necessary if welfarism is to be attractive is not the same as providing it; nor is it the same as giving it a rationale compatible with maintaining the subjectivity of welfare. There are some deep and dark questions here, for subjectivism and for welfarism.[11] Exploring them will, however, have to wait for another occasion.

IV. Conclusions

My question has been: What, if anything, might serve as the sole fundamental good for ethics? In considering perfection as a candidate for this role, I have urged ("argued" would be too strong a term) both the weaker point that it is not always worth promoting in its own right (since the capacity for it is too widely distributed) and the stronger point that it is never worth promoting in its own right (since it threatens individual autonomy). Both points suggest that perfection should influence our ethical deliberations only when it contributes to some other value, such as well-being.

As for welfare, a final verdict on its candidacy will require successful resolution of the standpoint problem. We must find some way of determining when an individual's assessment of her own happiness is to be taken as authoritative. If such a way is found, welfare will have a solid claim to being counted as one of the goods foundational to ethics. Could it be the sole foundational good? The exclusiveness of welfarism—its displacement or absorption of all competing goods—is difficult either to defend or to attack. The issue is so fundamental that it is hard to find ground on which to stand. Perhaps the best interim conclusion about welfarism is hypothetical: if any good proves capable of playing a unique foundational role in ethics, it will be welfare. Conversely, if the argument for welfarism does not succeed, those of us committed to the priority of the good will need to explore other, more complex, theoretical options.

Philosophy, University of Toronto

---

[11] They have been nicely exposed in Arthur Ripstein, "Preference," forthcoming in *Value, Welfare, and Morality*, ed. R. G. Frey and C. W. Morris.

GOOD LIVES: PROLEGOMENA*

By Lawrence C. Becker

A philosophical essay under this title faces severe rhetorical challenges. New accounts of the good life regularly and rapidly turn out to be variations of old ones, subject to a predictable range of decisive objections. Attempts to meet those objections with improved accounts regularly and rapidly lead to a familiar impasse—that while a life of contemplation, or epicurean contentment, or stoic indifference, or religious ecstasy, or creative rebellion, or self-actualization, or many another thing might count as *a* good life, none of them can plausibly be identified with *the* good life, or the *best* life. Given the long history of that impasse, it seems futile to offer yet another candidate for the genus "good life" as if that candidate might be new, or philosophically defensible. And given the weariness, irony, and self-deprecation expected of a philosopher in such an impasse, it is difficult for any substantive proposal on this topic to avoid seeming pretentious.

Unfortunately, it is only the effort to contribute to a detailed, defensible, substantive account of the good life that sustains my interest in writing on the topic. So I will offer a modest proposal. Stated as a set of ordinal[1] precepts for individuals, it is simply that we should first immunize ourselves against bad fortune by acquiring the power to detach ourselves from harm. (The object is not to *become* detached, but to acquire the ability to detach; not to have the ability to ignore events or deceive ourselves about them, but rather, by means of understanding them, to be able to control the damage they do.) Second, we should construct and follow a schematic, practicable, revisable plan for our whole lives[2]—a plan

---

* My main intellectual debts for the ideas in this paper, beyond the obvious ones to the history of philosophy and the people cited in the footnotes, are to three groups: the Social Philosophy and Policy Center's conference on the good life, which both prompted and refined this paper; my seminar on the subject, offered in the fall of 1990 at the College of William and Mary, where some of these ideas were distilled from a long list of possible topics; and the Social and Political Philosophy Discussion Group, which gave me advice on a draft of the paper. Individuals who deserve mention include George Harris for discussion of the nature of integrity; Todd Davidson on the criterial good of unity; Eric Foster on the criterial good of action; Sebastian Dunne on (against) the notion of having a good life by accident; Mark Fowler on examples of good but miserable lives; and George Harris, Alan Fuchs, Sharon Rives, Wayne Sumner, and Todd Davidson for criticism of the list of precepts.

[1] The precepts are meant to be ordinal (not lexical) in the sense that any momentary conflict between two of them must be resolved in favor of the one prior to the other on the list.

[2] I call attention below to the importance of a whole-life frame of reference in assessing the goods realized in a life. This precept simply acknowledges that importance and proposes a modest amount of schematic planning. Those who find the notion of a life-plan either empty or wrongheaded may yet be able to assent to the proposal here.

© 1992 Social Philosophy and Policy Foundation. Printed in the USA.

15

which, if followed successfully, will accomplish the following things (in lexical order[3]): it will create and sustain the exercise of the deontic virtues (traits that issue in actions required for a productive social life: reciprocity, justice, fidelity, and so on); it will create and sustain in us a high level of goal-directed activity; it will leave open at least one possibility, consistent with the above, for having a fulfilling and beautiful life; it will create and sustain the prudence required to minimize the need for detachment (especially the sort of detachment that flattens affect, reduces expectations, and induces passivity). Third, within the framework of such a plan, we should (in the following nonlexical order) cultivate loving relationships and make them just and beautiful; find a vocation and follow it; act as if the Aristotelian principle[4] were true; stay calm; be passionate; be convivial; and, ultimately, stop trying to have a good life and get on with it. Then if our lives are not good by accident, or not good as a by-product of the activity bounded by those precepts, we will be able to make them good, in at least one robust sense of that term, under almost any circumstances.

The preliminary material assembled in the following sections is meant to make those precepts plausible. But the precepts are not themselves meant to be, or to imply, a particular account of *the* good life — or even of *a* good one. If one labels the rest of the paper theoretical, then the precepts are meta-theoretical. They define a way of managing the pluralistic results of the theoretical inquiry. The *modus vivendi* they define is plausible, I believe, in the light of those results, when one considers the uncertainty of life, its vulnerability to reversals, its resilience (in either a good or bad direction), the multiplicity of ways in which a bad life can become a good one, and the self-defeating gap between a contrived life and a good one. For rhetorical reasons, I will say no more about my substantive aims, lest they appear ignorant, self-indulgent, and embarrassingly autobiographical. I will also hide, as best I can, the disappointingly limited consequences of this inquiry for the rest of ethics and social and political philosophy. Such deception calls for a disgracefully misleading introduction.

I. WHOLE LIVES

Commercial speech encourages the belief that "the good life" is something like a good vacation, or a good house, or a good meal — at best a long stretch of happiness. One can have (and lose) the good life repeat-

---

[3] "This is an order which requires us to satisfy the first principle in the ordering before we can move on to the second, the second before we consider the third, and so on. A principle does not come into play until those previous to it are either fully met or do not apply." John Rawls, *A Theory of Justice* (Cambridge: Harvard University Press, 1971), p. 43.

[4] "Other things begin equal, human beings enjoy the exercise of their realized capacities (their innate or trained abilities), and this enjoyment increases the more the capacity is realized, or the greater its complexity." *Ibid.*, p. 426.

edly; whether one has it at a given moment will be determined by the quality of one's life at that moment.

There is a more interesting line to take for present purposes: Living is the process of creating a single, unitary, spatiotemporal object—a life. A life has a value *as* an object, as a whole. It is not always the case that its value as an object will be a function of the value of its spatiotemporal parts considered separately. But it is always the case that an evaluation of the parts will be incomplete until they are understood in the context of the whole life. What seems so clearly valuable (or required, or excellent) when we focus on a thin temporal slice of a life (or a single, long strand of a life) may turn out to be optional, or awful, or vicious when we take a larger view. And it is the life as a whole that we consider when we think about its value in relation to other things, or as part of the cosmos.

This focus on the entire life is explicit in Aristotle and, in more or less elaborated versions, is to be found in a long succession of texts in the history of ethics. It is my impression of that history, however, that despite the efforts of some major philosophers the whole-life frame of reference has gradually receded into the background under systematic pressure from Christian theology (with its emphasis on the universal availability of redemption), consequentialism (with its forward-looking, fluctuating summations of expected value), and deontological theories (with their "antecedentialist" emphasis).

Whatever the cause, the focus on the parts, or on the sum of the parts of a life, obscures some important features of the inquiry here.[5] One of them is the extent to which one's own estimate of the value of one's life is necessarily inconclusive. (For example, others will have to judge my life as a whole, because its character as a whole is not likely to be predictable while I am around to judge it, and because many important holistic considerations—such as its beauty, excellence, justice, and net effect—are things that I am either not well-situated to judge or at least not in a privileged position to judge.) Something else obscured by the focus on parts of a life is the range of ways in which a single event or characteristic, without wide causal connections to other elements of one's life, can nonetheless ruin it (for example, the possibility that a monstrously unjust act can indelibly stain a whole life[6]). Also, focusing on the parts of a life tends to obscure the roles played by aesthetic criteria and the notion of excellence in the evaluation of a life.

II. Unitary Conceptions of the Good Life

It is useful to divide conceptions of the good life into pluralist and unitary ones. A pluralist conception holds (a) that the goods realizable in a

---

[5] Compare Robert Nozick's remarks on this subject in his *Philosophical Explanations* (Cambridge: Harvard University Press, 1981), pp. 411ff.

[6] One of the themes of Costa-Gavras's 1989 film, *The Music Box*.

human life are genuinely diverse, that is, not reducible to a single species, (b) that genuinely diverse combinations of goods are sufficient to make a life a good one, and thus that good lives may differ in kind as well as degree, and (c) that any theoretical explanation to be found for the diverse array of good lives will be purely formal, or schematic, or perhaps merely heuristic. A unitary (or monistic) conception, by contrast, holds either (d) that goods are not diverse, and thus good lives differ only in degree, or (e) that whether goods are diverse or not, there is only one set of them sufficient for making a life a good one, or (f) that though there may be more than one sufficient set, all of them have in common the same ordered subset of necessary goods, a subset rich enough, or ordered rigidly enough, to ensure that all good lives will be remarkably similar.

The history of philosophical accounts of the good life can plausibly be written as the history of failed unitary conceptions, with footnotes to pluralist ones. Would it be profitable to extend this history by putting forward yet another unitary account? The following considerations suggest that such a course would be futile.[7]

III. Criterial Goods

Assume that attempts to construct an account of the final good are either vacuous or unsound. That is, assume that we cannot specify, in a nonvacuous way, a final or ultimate intrinsic good (for example, happiness) such that every other thing we value as good is valued ultimately only as a means to the final good. Then consider the range of things that might plausibly be regarded as (a) distinct goods, not reducible to others on the list, (b) intrinsic, necessary, or widely instrumental goods,[8] and (c) definitive, at least in part, of a good life. We may call goods falling into this range "criterial" ones with respect to a good life. Here is a reasonably full list of them.

1. *The material conditions necessary for sustaining life and consciousness.* On the assumption that a vegetative existence is not a life in any sense rele-

---

[7] A deflective remark may be in order here. The *prima facie* diversity of goods is a commonplace. A recital of the obvious candidates would be pointless if the result were to leave open the possibility that they could all be generated and nicely ordered by some one overarching good (say, rationality or self-realization). It will be my contention, though, that an "inclusive" account of the good life — one which defines such a life as the realization (through some overarching aim) of a maximal array of goods — is only plausible when we jump too quickly over the lists to follow. I hold a similar view of the contention (which one assumes is almost audible by now in the minds of those interested in Aristotelian accounts of these matters) that lists of the goods that might be realized in a life are pointless — that the real issue is which, among the various good lives that are possible, is the best. I will argue that this issue, too, does not look fruitful against a reasonably full set of lists.

[8] The idea here is to limit the list by excluding the indefinitely large number of things that have only limited, contingent, and instrumental worth. Intrinsic goods are those desired for their own sake, and not (only) as a means to something else; necessary goods are those without which no (other) goods are realizable in a life; widely instrumental goods are those which, while not necessary, are useful as means to all (or almost all) other goods.

vant to this discussion, the material conditions for life and consciousness are bedrock necessary goods. Since they are so obvious, and so far from being sufficient for any sort of life that has been put forward as a good one, they are typically relegated to the background and not treated as definitive "criteria" of a good life. But given the prevalence of war, famine, disease, and natural disaster, this reminder does not seem pointless.

2. *The quality of consciousness.* Here the definitive criterion is a certain state or states of consciousness (sensation, pleasure, desire, serenity, passion, compassion, active contemplation, and so on). The good life is defined, at least in part, as one in which such a state of consciousness is actually achieved — either by design or by default — to a degree sufficient to warrant describing a whole life as a good one.

3. *Understanding.* Here the definitive criterion is a form of knowledge or comprehension of the nature, value, and meaning of things, events, and experience. The good life is then defined as one in which, among other things, soundness and completeness in such matters are to some extent achieved. Note that the criterion is an epistemic one, and that the good defined here is not reducible to a state of consciousness in which one merely believes things or has a simulacrum of understanding.

4. *Self-command.* Here the definitive criterion is the possession of a sound self-concept and the ability to resolve states of consciousness into acts of will: decision, choice, and action. As a practical ability, then, this is not reducible to criterial goods 2 or 3 above. It defines the good life, at least in part, as one of will and action. It is a (nearly) universal instrumental good and is arguably both an intrinsic and a necessary one.

5. *The harmonization of reason, desire, and will.* Here the definitive criterion is not the quality of consciousness achieved (though that may be a byproduct), or the soundness and completeness of one's understanding, or action alone, but rather the unification of the multiple and often conflicting elements of action. Roughly speaking, there are three elements to be unified or harmonized: (a) the dispositions, motives, desires, needs, appetites, drives, impulses, raw energy, and intentions antecedent to action (say, for short, *desire*); (b) the knowledge, practical wisdom, and deliberation characteristic of deliberative rationality (or, for short, *reason*); and (c) the sort of self-command (or *will*) that resolves itself in choice. Unity may be understood in terms of an appropriate hierarchy of elements, in which, for example, desire and will are subordinated to reason (Plato, Freud); or in terms of the purification of one or more elements, for example, the purification of reason by the elimination of false beliefs (Epicurus, Marcus Aurelius), or the purification of desire (Epictetus), or the elimination of mixed motives (Kant). Or unity can be understood in terms of the ecstatic convergence of all these elements in a single, triumphant, and definitive aim (Nietzsche). Lives are good, by this criterion, insofar as they achieve such unity. As a special sort of combination of the quality of consciousness (2), understanding (3), and self-command (4), this fifth criterion is not simply reducible to the conjunction of them.

6. *The exemplification of goodness-of-a-kind*. Here the definitive criterion is the excellence or perfection of a certain type of thing, for example, an individual human being, a human community, the natural order, a divine order, a tradition, or a narrative. A good life is defined as one that realizes (or contributes to) goodness-of-a-kind. Aristotelian accounts of excellence are examples. Such accounts may be unitary — for example, by stressing the perfection of a single element, such as reason, which is thought to be the essential defining characteristic of the species — or they may be (more) inclusive, stressing the perfection of one or more sets of diverse elements characteristic of members of the species.

7. *Meaningful opportunity*. Here the definitive criterion lies in the liberty (either negative or positive) and autonomy to choose and carry out projects that are valuable, valuable enough to warrant the claim that the mere potential to pursue projects gives value to one's whole life. Claims that autonomous human lives have a dignity that is immeasurable, incommensurable, infinite, beyond price — and that the loss of autonomy forecloses all possibility for a good life — embody this criterion. Note that this criterion is not reducible to a "sense" or "experience" of freedom or autonomy; it is not, that is, reducible to a version of the quality of consciousness (criterial good 2). Nor is it reducible to mere self-command (good 4). The happy slave or prisoner-unaware, who may be blissful and able to act, has lost the chance for a genuinely free and autonomous life. Moreover, what is at stake here is potential alone. The potential to choose and carry out valuable projects is sufficient to give life dignity and make it good, even if that potential is never actualized. This criterion is not a consequentialist one.

8. *Meaningful activity*. Here the definitive criterion lies in the effort to achieve valuable ends, that is, in the active pursuit of projects valuable enough to warrant the claim that their mere pursuit (regardless of success or potential for success) has made one's whole life valuable. We may think of Socrates, here, for whom doing philosophy was apparently both necessary and sufficient for the good life, and perhaps also of Camus's rebel, in perpetual, creative revolt against the absurdity of the human quest for meaning in an indifferent universe.

9. *Meaningful necessity*. Here the definitive criterion is found in being required for, or compellingly called to a role in, something apart from one's own life — something good enough to make carrying out that role (whatever the result) sufficient for a good life. Note again that this criterion is distinct from the attendant experience of happiness or exhilaration which sometimes comes from recognizing such necessity. It is also distinct (or at least it is meant to be distinct) from the value of the activity or the outcome.[9] Religious vocations, or immersion in politics, a profession, an organization, or a family can be goods of this sort. These goods are thought

---

[9] See Kazuo Ishiguro, *The Remains of the Day* (New York: Knopf, 1990).

to be sufficient to give one's whole life meaning no matter how small the role one plays or how remote or ambiguous the consequences.[10]

10. *Self-love*. Here the definitive criterion lies in the self-esteem required to avoid self-destructive acts, the self-respect required to defend one's liberty and integrity, and the concern for one's own interests that gives shape to rational deliberation. Without self-love, no other goods in one's life can be sustained long enough, or realized completely enough, to make one's whole life good. Self-love is a distinct sort of widely instrumental good.

11. *Benevolence*. Here the definitive criterion lies in the direct concern or affection one person may have for the being and well-being of another. This concern or affection is measured not by the giver's state of consciousness or acts of will alone, and not by what the giver produces in the recipient, but by the congruence between the other's well-being and the giver's desire for it. This is held by some to be an intrinsic good, since people express it in self-sacrificial ways (implicitly valuing it for its own sake?). But of course, its instrumental connection to the vast array of goods that can only arise from stable, cooperative social relationships (from families to international organizations) gives us a warrant for regarding it as a widely instrumental good.

12. *Mutual love*. Here the definitive criterion is the reciprocal desire, affection, benevolence, empathy, and conviviality that might be thought to be the source of the most deeply rewarding states of consciousness we can have; the matrix in which we can achieve the most perfect harmony of reason, desire, and will; the characteristic through which we can best exemplify what is good of our kind, or the most meaningful kinds of opportunity and necessity; the source of the only sustainable form of self-love, and hence all of the goods for which it is necessary; or a necessary condition for the sort of self-sustaining cooperation that makes productive social life (and hence all good lives) possible. Thus, in addition to being an intrinsic good, it has a strong claim to being necessary.

13. *Sexuality*. Here the definitive criterion is the expression, in consciousness and conduct, of the sexual aspect of our human nature, in erotic love (mutual or not), sexual behavior, and reproduction. Erotic experience and sexual desire are intrinsic goods as states of consciousness, of course, and important forms of mutual love are erotically charged or otherwise sexual. Moreover, our sexuality may be necessarily linked to our self-concept, will, and self-love. But it seems plausible to hold that there is a species of intrinsic good, here, that is not reducible to one or the other of those other goods (states of consciousness, self-command, self-love, mutual love) or to a simple conjunction of them. Like the unity of reason, desire, and will, the intrinsic good of sexuality lies in its unique

---

[10] See Walt Harrington, "The Mystery of Goodness," *The Washington Post Magazine*, January 6, 1991. The article is about Bryan Stevenson, director of the Alabama Capital Representation Project.

fusion of compelling, sensuous activity (not necessarily acts of will) aimed
at the satisfaction of egoistic, other-directed, specifically (though not necessarily overtly) sexual desires. We have reason to believe that sexuality
suffuses, and contributes powerfully to the good of, a great area of our
lives. Its connection to reproduction, and hence to the necessary material
conditions of life, is a warrant for calling it a widely instrumental good.

14. *Achievement.* Here the definitive criterion lies in the results, rather
than the antecedent elements, of action, in the product rather than the
opportunity or necessity of the project, in the external outcome rather
than the inner experience. The good life is thus one of productive activity, intentional or otherwise—good because, and to the extent that, its
products are good. (Even a miserable wretch may have a good life in this
sense.) It seems a safe empirical generalization to say that for most humans productive activity is an intrinsic good. Given the scarcity of resources, the perils of the natural environment, and the limitations of
human nature, achievement must be on this list as an instrumental value
as well.

15. *Rectitude.* Here the element that is definitive of a good life is morally right conduct. The good life is the morally correct one, the just one,
the one that fulfills moral requirements. Moral requirements can be distinguished from the normative implications of the other criterial goods in
a variety of familiar ways. For example, moral requirements are typically
held to include (a) a universalization principle that bars purely egoistic
pursuits and requires similar action in similar circumstances, and (b) either a value-optimization principle (under which the right is defined as
the option that realizes the higher net balance of good) or a principle that
makes the right independent of the good in some important way (such
as by making it independent of consequences). Philosophers are divided
about whether this is an intrinsic good or a widely instrumental one.

16. *Integrity.* Here the thing definitive of a good life is an intact, coherent identity as a particular kind of life—for example, noble or ignoble,
courageous or cowardly, honorable or dishonorable. The contention is
that in order to have a good life, one must first have *a* life. That life must
be something identifiable, in terms of essential defining characteristics,
as a life of a certain sort. Integrity, in this nonmoral sense, is a necessary
condition for *every* sort of good life and may perhaps be sufficient for one.

17. *A life as an aesthetic object.* Here the thing definitive of a good life is
the extent to which, considered as an object, the life has intrinsic aesthetic
value. Is the life beautiful, sublime, or a work of art? This good, while often coupled with those of understanding (3), self-command (4), and integrity (16), is in principle distinct from them, since there is no necessary
conceptual connection between a unified, coherent, intact, or exemplary[11] life and an aesthetically valuable one. Chaos can be beautiful; so
can ruins.

---

[11] The trivial exception is the life that exemplifies an aesthetically valuable object.

Most of these criterial goods (perhaps all but the last) are intuitively plausible as partial criteria of the good life. Any attempt to select only one, to the exclusion or lexical subordination of all the others, will be very difficult to defend. In fact, standard unitary accounts of the good life rarely attempt to do that. Instead, they attempt to show that one or another of these criteria, when properly satisfied, will generate a life that necessarily satisfies (most of) the other criteria as well. Since attempts to show this inevitably involve some redescription and reorganization of the other criteria, it is useful to briefly survey the major ones.

IV. UNITARY ACCOUNTS OF THE GOOD LIFE

Suppose we catalog the most influential accounts of the good life under these headings: congruence, inner unity, human excellence, personal excellence or achievement, personal well-being or fulfillment, right conduct, autonomous activity, vocation, aesthetic value, and rationality.

Congruence theories measure a good life by the degree to which it conforms to, or fits into, or is attuned to a given external order. Injunctions to follow nature, or to do God's will, or to accept one's place in a given social order fall under this heading, and under criterial goods 6 (exemplification of goodness-of-a-kind) and 9 (meaningful necessity) described above. Stoicism is a leading example. But it is crucial to notice that the various Stoic and religious disciplines (detachment, resignation, humility) designed to achieve such congruence are also offered as routes to rectitude, personal happiness, human excellence, inner harmony, meaningful freedom and activity, and (occasionally) beauty and/or achievement. It is obvious that many modern readers reject all congruence accounts on the grounds that none of them can actually achieve all of this, or even very much of it. The connection between doctrines of congruence and the sort of indoctrination that produces prejudice, reinforces injustice, and perpetuates oppression is clear; clear too is the danger that conformity to an external order will suppress individual excellence. Thus, it is highly implausible to accept any ordering of priorities compatible with a unitary account of the good life based on congruence. In order to meet the obvious objections to a congruence theory, we need to have an independent criterion of rectitude to rule out conformity to an unjust social order, and we need to preserve autonomy in some sense—for example, by insisting that conformity be either voluntary and reversible, or hypothetically rational, or both. However, adding these conditions to congruence yields a pluralist account, not a unitary one.

Accounts based on *inner unity* measure a good life by its inner harmony, unity, integrity, or wholeness—particularly with respect to reason, passion, and will. Here good 5 (the harmonization of reason, desire, and will) has been given pride of place. Advocates of this view—for example, Plato, Butler, Nietzsche, and Freud—insist that it is also the route to satisfying other criteria. Thus, Plato makes inner unity's compatibility with individual happiness, ideal communities, and human excellence central to his discussion; Butler is concerned to reconcile self-love and benevolence; Nietzsche puts inner unity forward as a measure of human excellence and aesthetic value; Freud connects it to personal happiness and the conditions for civilization. Again, however, it is fair to say that the monism is insupportable. A moral monster can have inner unity, and justice surely should not be subordinated to that sort of unity. A consciousness flickering just above the level of extinction can be unified, but surely we think a fuller version of human excellence is better than a near-vegetative one, even if some degree of unity has to be sacrificed to get it. The goods of mutual love, achievement, meaningful opportunity, meaningful necessity, and meaningful activity all support this conclusion. They cannot all plausibly be subordinated, all of the time, to inner unity. No account of the good life seems defensible if it is unitary in that sense. Or rather, if we insist that unity is sufficient for a good life, we must be prepared to conclude that some "good" lives are not good all-things-considered.

A unitary theory based on *human excellence* measures a good life by the degree to which it exemplifies, or realizes, generic human characteristics. This is a version of criterial good 6 (exemplification of goodness-of-a-kind). Aristotelian accounts of human flourishing fall under this heading. But some other accounts of self-realization belong here as well, whether grounded in metaphysics (for example, Idealism, dialectical materialism, existentialism), evolutionary biology, or developmental physiology and psychology; accounts that emphasize achievements measured against generic human capacities rather than personal potential also fall under this rubric. The fundamental problem with unitary accounts along these lines is that they are insupportable without independent guarantees that human excellence is compatible with inner unity, integrity, congruence, rectitude, and mutual love. After all, if our consciousness is by nature as chaotic as Freud thought, or as plastic as Skinner thought, then the perfection of it will be perfect chaos or perfect plasticity, not unity; if we are by nature more selfish than righteous, then the perfection of that nature will lead to injustice. Of course, it may be that the perfection of human nature *is* compatible with the other goods on the list. But the recognition that it *must* be so, if human excellence is to be the leading measure of a good life, is tantamount to the recognition that other goods cannot be subordinated to human excellence.

Personal excellence or achievement measures a good life by the extent to which it realizes one's personal potential, given one's particular circumstances and talents. The standard here is individual (rather than generic) human excellence, but the objections to using it as a unitary account are the same as those for the generic account.[12] The temptation to use it (as

---

[12] This will, perhaps, be evident enough from a brief outline of David Norton's case for a eudaimonistic account of ethics and the good life, in his *Personal Destinies* (Princeton: Prince-

opposed to a generic standard) may come in part from an egalitarian desire to have an account of the good life that makes it available, in principle, to everyone.

Personal well-being or fulfillment provides an account of the good life in terms of the degree to which (a) the cup of one's experience is filled with pleasure (or at least is free from pain), (b) one's needs and desires are satisfied (or at least not frustrated), and (c) the conditions under which one experiences the world are conducive to pleasure, satisfaction, and the absence of pain and frustration. Hedonism and Epicureanism belong here, as do various psychological theories of "adjustment" that look similar to Stoic, Buddhist, or Christian disciplines for the transformation, diminution, or elimination of desire, but stripped of their metaphysical doctrines. It is notorious that such doctrines, to be plausible at all as accounts of the good life, must not be compatible with a purely passive existence in which nothing is achieved, or with a contrived existence in which (as in a Nozickian experience machine)[13] fulfillment is achieved through illusion, or with a stunted existence in which one's generic human capacities are deliberately allowed to wither, or with a ruthless disregard for justice.

A much more robust version of this candidate for the good life is possible. It centers on the nature of positive personal experience and the material conditions necessary for such experience; it acknowledges diversity in the types of good experience; it recognizes that circumstances may make personal fulfillment or well-being (defined in terms of such experience) impossible, and that certain sorts of efforts to guarantee such experience are self-defeating. It then makes the case that (viewed from

---

ton University Press, 1976). Norton understands the "daimon" in eudaimonism to refer to one's innate, individual "ideal possibility." This possibility is understood as having normative force. Thus, the basic imperatives are to know oneself (one's daimon) and to choose to approximate it, that is, to turn it, as completely as possible, from an ideal possibility into an actuality. The life one thus chooses to live will be dominated by the virtue of integrity, the pursuit of one's unique destiny. This defines the notion of moral necessity. But justice and benevolence are implicit in this moral necessity, since one will refuse to consume (or exclude others from) things that are not necessary for self-actualization, will take delight in others' achievements, and will be rewarded by their reciprocal justice and benevolence. Norton's account is pluralistic in two senses. First, each person's daimon in unique, and thus there are as many definitions of the good life as there are persons. Second, each person goes through a developmental process that has distinct stages (childhood, adolescence, maturity, and old age), correlated with incommensurably distinct phases of that unique daimon. But in my terms Norton's is a unitary account, since it unambiguously insists that working out one's personal destiny (that is, finding and taking the self-actualizing path from one's actuality to one's daimon or ideal possibility) is *the* good (or best) life for everyone.

[13] The allusion here is to a thought-experiment introduced by Robert Nozick in *Anarchy, State, and Utopia* (New York: Basic Books, 1974), pp. 42–45. The question is this: If our only ultimate concern about the quality of our lives is about the way our experience "feels from the inside," then if there were a machine that could (reliably) stimulate one's brain to produce any felt-experience imaginable, what objection could there be to defining the sort of experience one wants to have and then living one's whole life in the machine?

"inside" one's life, so to speak) personal well-being, broadly conceived, must be the ultimate measure of a good life.[14]

What these powerful descriptions of well-being lack, it seems to me, is something that comes easily when we adopt a whole-life frame of reference. From that standpoint it is not hard to see how figures like Sardanopolis, Lucrezia Borgia, Catherine the Great, or de Sade (without the difficulties they encountered) might have had lives characterized by a high level of personal well-being, and yet had lives which, as a whole, were so unjust, ugly, or pointless as to preclude our describing them as good. And from that standpoint it is not hard to see how Joan of Arc, Kierkegaard, Virginia Woolf, or Albert Schweitzer might have had lives so desolate as not to qualify as ones of personal well-being, and yet had lives which, as a whole, were so noble, profoundly creative, courageous, or self-sacrificial that we are compelled to describe them as good. If these judgments are right, as I believe, then personal well-being or fulfillment is not a plausible candidate for a unitary account of the good life.

Right conduct measures a good life by the extent of its conformity to moral requirements, where those requirements are defined under some special conception of morality.[15] Such a special conception might be defined, for example, in terms of universalizable, rationally justifiable rules of conduct directed by concern for the welfare of others. Alternatively, it might be defined in terms of a single, supreme principle held to be determinative for all conduct. Either way, right conduct is very often thought to be a constraint on conceptions of the good life, in the sense that pleasure, or congruence, or achievement will be required to stay

---

[14] See James Griffin, *Well-Being* (Oxford: Clarendon Press, 1986). Griffin lists five "prudential values" for well-being (pp. 67–68): accomplishment, the components of human existence or agency, understanding, enjoyment, and deep personal relations. He states that "being moral enters [this] list only in a limited way: only by being part of what it is to be at peace with one's neighbour and with oneself" (p. 70). In considering the necessity of moral rectitude for the good life, Griffin considers the claim that a certain sort of moral failure might make a good life impossible:

> It is an extravagant claim, and . . . rests on a confusion. We need to split "the good life" into two. There is a sense in which moral failure, being a failure to act for the best reasons, is a falling off from an ideal — and not just in the trivial, circular sense that it is not the most moral or most rational life. It is not the finest life: the life one would hope to lead. But there is another conception of a good life, a life one would hope to lead. It is the sense that appears in judgments such as that it is better to be moral *and* alive than to be moral and thereby lose one's life, or that it is sometimes better to fail morally and stay alive than not to fail and thereby lose one's life. And it is this second conception that should be the base for judgments of well-being in moral theory. (p. 69)

It is my contention that while this is plausible in an account of well-being made from "inside" one's life, its very plausibility makes well-being defective as a candidate description of the good life.

[15] As opposed to one in which whatever one ought to do or be all-things-considered is morally required.

(mostly)[16] within the boundaries defined by moral duty and obligation. Some basic level of justice or right conduct may thus be thought to be a necessary condition of a good life. But how basic? How necessary? Does unjust conduct foreclose the possibility of a good life? Is it possible for people to foreclose the possibility of good lives for themselves by being fundamentally, dispositionally unjust, even though they restrain themselves from unjust conduct? The answers to these questions are by no means obvious. What does it mean, for example, to say that a murderer might have lost forever the possibility for a good life? It amounts to making claims such as the following:

> People who have acted unjustly, and by so doing have unforgivably and irreparably destroyed the good life of another, have also necessarily destroyed or foreclosed the possibility of a good life for themselves.

One assumes that if wrongdoers repair the damage they do, and/or are properly forgiven, their injustice has been rectified, and no obstacle (from a criterion of right conduct) remains in the way of their having good lives. But suppose neither condition can be met because the wrong involved is unforgivable and the damage cannot possibly be repaired. The wrongdoers can never, in that respect, rectify the wrong they have done. Then one of the following must be true: (a) any unforgivable and irreparable wrong will stain one's entire life, such that no antecedent or subsequent conduct, and no other good ever realized in one's life, can make that life a good one; or (b) the stains such wrongs introduce are merely local ones, whose effects on one's prospects for a good life are minimized over time, or canceled by past and future goods;[17] or (c) only wrongs of a certain magnitude foreclose all possibility of a good life.[18] I suggest that (a) is wholly implausible. It entails that one's life as a whole can never be redeemed from the minor short- and long-term damage done by (for example) an unforgivable and irreparable act of petty cruelty. If that were true, we could never hope to find an example of a good life, unless we defined "unforgivable and irreparable" in such a way as to collapse this category into either (b) or (c). But that would be no help, because both (b) and (c) entail that rectitude is not a necessary condition for a good life; both entail that, under certain conditions, a good life is possible without recti-

---

[16] I say "mostly" because it is usually conceded that injustice is an inescapable part of the human condition, that all of us are to some degree culpable, and yet that even fairly extensive, persistent culpability is not a bar to having a good life.

[17] An issue raised pointedly in Woody Allen's 1990 film, *Crimes and Misdemeanors*.

[18] For example, one might say that the stain on the wrongdoer's life is proportional to the harm to the victim's life, so that to destroy the victim's good life is to destroy one's own, to destroy ten years of it is to destroy ten years of one's own, etc.

tude. This generates an unpalatable story, but I do not readily see how that can be avoided.

Leaving aside the question of whether right conduct is a necessity of the good life, it remains to be seen whether such conduct is ever *sufficient* to make a life a good one. The usual objection here is that the quality of consciousness, self-love, mutual love, liberty, and various nonmoral forms of excellence will often get unjustifiably damaged in a life dominated by rectitude. Whatever we think about the sufficiency of rectitude in lives bereft of these other important goods, surely their absence is cause for great regret. Albert Schweitzer reportedly said that by no stretch of the imagination could he be called a happy man. Did he nonetheless have a good life? Perhaps. Could we imagine a better life for him, without altering his rectitude, by imagining that his reason, desire, and will had been more unified? Or that he had had more meaningful opportunity, or mutual love, or pleasure in his life? Certainly. Thus, it seems that even if rectitude is necessary and sufficient for a good life it is only *minimally* sufficient, never desirable by itself, and only tolerable alone when all other forms of the good life are impossible. It may be, as I shall urge below, that while nothing is *more* important to the good life than rectitude, there are other things which are *as* important. If that is so, we will have to give up the effort to make our account a unitary one.

Autonomous activity measures a good life by the extent of one's ability to direct one's own affairs, to construct and live out one's own conception of a good life. The idea here, drawn from good 4 (self-command), is that the essence of a good life lies in the dignity, or nobility, that comes from being the author of one's own story, the creator of one's own good life. Autonomous activity requires opportunity or liberty, both negative and positive, and agency: the ability to conceive of goals, to deliberate about their worth and about means to them, and to choose to pursue them. Obviously, there are antecedent necessary conditions for the exercise of autonomy; such conditions include life itself, the requisite cognitive, conative, and physical abilities, the availability of resources, and the cooperation of others. But without autonomy life is mere existence; conduct is mere reflex or conditioned response; knowledge, ability, and resources are mere inputs; and cooperative social life is akin to what is found among the social insects. The nature and extent of such autonomy in human lives is disputed, but the notion that it is central to a good life is now very generally held.

It is tempting to think that autonomy, so conceived, bears roughly the same relation to a good life as does right conduct: that it is a necessary condition for it, and perhaps just barely sufficient in extreme circumstances. It seems impossible to argue for anything stronger, since autonomous agents may be desperately unfulfilled and unhappy, have lives full of inner turmoil, be decidedly mediocre, be bereft of loving relationships, act with great cruelty and injustice, and achieve virtually nothing good. The claim that autonomy is sufficient to make all of that into a good life is just barely credible. It is credible only for circumstances so reduced (a state of nature, solitary confinement) that nothing more is possible. At most autonomy is like right conduct, that is, necessary and occasionally, under extreme circumstances, sufficient. But if that is true of both, neither can be a *unitary* account of the good life; if we are committed to such an account, we must choose one or the other. And if we suppose that autonomy is a *precondition* for morally right conduct, then it appears that we must choose autonomy.

There is, however, some reason to doubt that liberty (and hence autonomy) is a necessary condition of a good life.[19] Consider the following line of argument about the value of liberty, which begins with a distinction between negative and positive sorts. Negative liberty is the absence of impediments to action.[20] Positive liberty is the presence of the means necessary for effective choice and action. Conceived in this way, negative liberty is not a "thing," but rather the absence of something. It is like the hole in a doughnut; take away the doughnut and it is hard to see the hole at all, let alone regard it as valuable; take away the impediments to action, and negative liberty, as an "object," vanishes with them. It may be wise, then, to organize a discussion of the value of negative liberty by beginning with *things*, rather than the spaces they leave, by looking at the impediments rather than at the elbowroom those impediments define.

When we do that, it is clear that among impediments, as among doughnuts, some are good and some are bad, from the agent's point of view. The friction caused by an obstacle is sometimes a necessary condition for doing what we want to do, and, when it is, we see the obstacle as valuable. In fact, valuable impediments provide us with another sort of liberty: positive or material liberty. If the impediment is a good one, the corresponding negative liberty — or absence of the impediment — is derivatively bad. We should be able to learn all we need to know about the derivative values of derivative things (such as holes and elbowroom) by immediate inference from the things that define them.

Positive liberty, by contrast, is not the absence of something but rather the presence of it: the presence, indeed the possession, of the means necessary for action. It is the "stuff" we require in order to act in the space provided by negative liberty. The presence of social and political institu-

---

[19] The remainder of this section on autonomous activity is adapted from an unpublished conference comment presented in response to a paper by William Ruddick and James Rachels, "Lives and Liberty." Their revised version was published in *The Inner Citadel: Essays on Individual Autonomy*, ed. John Christman (New York: Oxford University Press, 1989), pp. 221–33.

[20] Negative liberty should not be equated with the absence of coercion or active interference. Liberty can be limited by passive, even accidental impediments, as well as by active, intentional, or coercive ones. Negative political liberty should be defined quite generally as the absence of impediments imposed or legitimated by political institutions. Other sorts of negative liberty — social, interpersonal, physical — may be defined correspondingly.

tions gives us the means—the liberty—to lead lives that we could not otherwise have. So do friends, courage, and physical strength. Individualist political theory tends to resist labeling such things as "liberty." But the description of economic resources, education, and many other things as "liberating" is surely a warrant for calling them liberties, and it is unassailable that negative liberty alone is of very little importance unless one can or might be able to use it. For using it, some resources (psychological and physical) are necessary, and we may plausibly speak of them as constituting our positive or material liberty.

The question, then, is whether liberty of either sort is a necessary condition for a good life. Since we know that various criterial goods that might make a life a good one are possible without genuine liberty (one can be happy and feel free in a room one does not know to be a locked cell), and since advocates of autonomy connect it to the very nature of human action itself, perhaps the question is whether, without liberty of some sort, we can have anything describable as a *life* at all, good or bad, as opposed to physical existence.[21] Why not? Suppose my name is Calvin, and suppose that my creator has predestined every detail of my life, every nuance of my thought and action, including the fact that through theological study I have now discovered that my life is predetermined. Does this mean that I have not had a (good) life to this point, or that I cannot continue to have one? I have no genuine liberty at all to do anything other than what God has planned for me. I am, in effect, a total slave to God. But I certainly *think* I have a life. I remember, and feel, and feel joy, anticipation, fear, responsibility, pride, guilt, shame, and obligation. I fear judgment. I do not know how things will turn out for me, but I suspect I am one of the elect and am glad for that. In any case, I know that whatever happens, it will be exactly as God has planned. In the meantime, I will live the life that I have been given. Given God's will, nothing else could have happened. I was never at liberty to do other than I did in fact do. I had a life without liberty. But I rejoice in it, and affirm it anew every day.

End of story. Now what is wrong with it? It surely does not suggest that we cannot have (good) lives without liberty. Negative liberty, in general terms, is the space left to us by the political, social, personal, and metaphysical impediments that surround us; positive liberty is the stuff that enables us to act in that space. What Calvin imagines is that the space and stuff available to him are enough for exactly one life: the one God has given him to live, without liberty. If so, then liberty is not a necessary condition for having a good life.

Vocation measures a good life by the extent to which one is drawn into a necessary role in something good enough so that playing one's part in

---

[21] See Ruddick and Rachels, "Lives and Liberty," for a developed analysis of this distinction.

it promises to yield a better life than one could reasonably hope to construct for oneself. The plausibility of this vision of a good life rests on showing that participation in the role to which one is drawn or called is either morally right, licit, or sufficiently good to justify participation and to warrant the loss of autonomy involved in surrendering to it. How can this be shown?

We may begin with the observation that autonomy often undermines inner harmony—the unity of reason, desire, and will described under criterial good 5. Autonomy inevitably separates the autonomous subject from all its objects—other people, projects, achievements, and even most states of consciousness (all but one of which—self-consciousness—are experienced as things separable from the self). And autonomy systematically undermines the perceived value of opportunity, activity, and achievement by insisting that their worth as elements of a good life is ultimately subjective in the sense that it is legislated by the self. Some defenders of autonomy (for example, Kant) have in effect responded to such charges by arguing that the legislative activity of the autonomous self is generic, that is, it follows a path identical to that followed by every other autonomous agent. Autonomous action can thus be seen as a form of participation in something greater than oneself, and thus may itself be a kind of vocation. Other defenders of autonomy may choose to attack the very idea of vocation as defined here, for example, by insisting on the necessity of autonomy as the source of human dignity, moral rectitude, human excellence, and self-love. Insofar as vocations undermine autonomy, then, they undermine something necessary for a good life. Defenders of vocation may reply either by denying the possibility of genuine autonomy (for example, by arguing for a strong notion of the social self), or by denying that autonomy is damaged by living out a vocation.[22] This last reply seems sufficient to save a place for vocation in a pluralist account of the good life. Vocations are, after all, compatible with autonomy in the sense that they can in principle be autonomously chosen, and many pursuits involve the cultivation of traits that systematically foreclose whole regions of autonomous choice by changing one's dispositions, or traits of character. (Becoming a thoroughly honorable person, for example, means that many options faced by someone with a more fluid character simply will not present themselves as live options in deliberation.) Unless we are prepared to say that all such foreclosures are incompatible with the level of autonomy required for a good life, we will have to acknowledge the legitimacy of vocations into which people are willingly drawn and within which they are changed in such a way that the vocation becomes integral to their lives. It is evident from the history of modern philosophy that the attempt to remove the possibility or centrality of this sort of vocation to

[22] Or, of course, by reiterating the charges against, or against the necessity of, autonomy.

the good life leads directly to a struggle with the problems of nihilism, despair, and anomie that can only be solved (as Camus solved them)[23] by showing that creative activity is an acceptable substitute for a vocation.

Aesthetic value measures a good life, considered as an object, by the extent to which it has some superordinate aesthetic value. I say "superordinate" here to emphasize the fact (which could as well be said of any other attempt at a unitary account) that the sort of aesthetic value at issue is only the sort that could plausibly dominate moral rectitude, inner harmony, and all the other criterial goods, that is, the sort that might by itself be sufficient for a good life. It is fairly clear that making one's life a work of art or achieving some sort of narrative unity in one's life will not suffice unless one aims at a rather exalted form of art. A soap opera has narrative unity; there are forms of art barely discernible as works, or as art; there are works of art meant to be self-negating, repellent, or disgusting. A life exhibiting such qualities may be a good one, in part because it has such aesthetic value, but I have not been able to find a way of describing such qualities as either necessary or sufficient for a good life. As for more exalted forms of art, three objections come to mind. First, they are artifacts in the most thoroughgoing sense imaginable. A whole life that exhibited such a degree of artifice would surely seem objectionably contrived. Second, the artificiality aside, it is not clear at all that we can justify (all-things-considered) a *recommmendation* that life be lived so as to make it high art. (Shall we say, "Go make a life like Iago's"? or Desdemona's? or Medea's?) It seems very odd for a theory of the good life to recommend against making one's life good, and, of course, if it sorts aesthetically good lives by some other criterion (say the quality of consciousness, or rectitude) and recommends only those that meet both criteria, it is no longer a unitary account. Finally, even if we were to take the bit in our teeth and recommend making life an exalted work of art, to whom could we reasonably give such advice? Who is capable of carrying it out? And what will we say of the failures?[24] In short, life as a work of art seems a nonstarter.

What about beauty, and sublimity?[25] Is a beautiful life necessarily a good one? The temptation to say so is dependent, it seems to me, on the claim that a beautiful life necessarily realizes many of the goods described in the other criteria: inner unity and integrity, excellence of a kind, mean-

---

[23] See esp. Albert Camus, *The Rebel* (1951; reprint, New York: Vintage, 1956).

[24] An artist once remarked, overhearing a spectator's outrage at a silly piece in the Hirshhorn Museum, that at this museum of modern art, people are often angered by the failures they see, but that at the Air and Space Museum they find the failed flying machines hilarious.

[25] Nobility, which might also be thought of in aesthetic terms, is probably best treated under the exemplification of goodness-of-a-kind. Integrity, which can also be brought under the heading of aesthetic value in various ways, is probably better regarded as an altogether separate candidate. In my view, it fails as a unitary account for reasons parallel to the ones I note for beauty and sublimity.

ingful activity, meaningful necessity, or (sometimes) an exalted state of consciousness and/or moral rectitude. Suppose, as a rough approximation, we give something like the following analysis. To say that a life is *beautiful* is to say (a) that perception or contemplation of it is both pleasant and attractive, that is, that to experience a life as beautiful is to have certain affective responses to one's *cognition* of it; and (b) that the nature of the life as a whole—as an object—is the cause of our pleasure in it and attraction to it; and, more particularly, (c) that the cause of our pleasure and attraction lies in the fact that the life embodies a combination of aesthetic properties such as unity, completeness, fullness, magnitude, narrative form, originality, uniqueness, balance, simplicity, purity, variability, contrasts (internal and against a ground), fittingness, proportion, profundity, memorability, immediacy, transcendence, excellence of execution, difficulty of execution, and fragility. Then suppose a sublime life is defined as one that has a terrible or dangerous or awesome beauty.

The question, then, is whether any sort of beauty or sublimity definable in these ways (or plausible alternatives) can credibly be either necessary or sufficient for a good life. If it is true that rectitude and perhaps autonomy are necessary conditions, then beauty or sublimity obviously cannot be sufficient. If (as seems highly probable) any combination of other criteria, absent aesthetic ones, is sufficient for a good life, then beauty or sublimity is not necessary either. (Think of trying to defend the thesis that an ugly little life, characterized by right conduct, personal achievement, personal fulfillment, meaningful opportunity, meaningful action, and meaningful necessity, is not a good one. Rule out the transparently *ad hoc* attempt to argue that no such life could be ugly or little.) In short, it seems plausible to go only this far: that beauty or sublimity can be fundamental and sufficient for a good life when (enough) other goods are realized through it. That modest result, however, falls far short of the claim that one could plausibly advance a unitary account of the good life in terms of such aesthetic values. The same is true of integrity.

A unitary account based on *rationality* measures a good life by the extent to which one's plans and choices are the product of rational deliberation. The idea here is not to unify reason and other elements of action in order to achieve inner harmony, nor is it to require only that a life in principle be rationally justifiable (though perhaps lived out impulsively, or passionately, or through habit). Rather, the idea is to make rational deliberation a necessary and sufficient condition for a good life, and to organize a unitary account in terms of it.

Rawls has given such an account.[26] For him, a "person" is an individual life lived according to a plan. If the plan is rational, and if one has drawn up such a plan under favorable circumstances and believes oneself to be "in the way of realizing it" with good prospects of success, then

---

[26] Rawls, *A Theory of Justice*, ch. 7.

one is happy.[27] A plan is rational if and only if it meets the conditions for rational choice and would be chosen under conditions of full deliberative rationality. The principles of rational choice are those of finding effective means, choosing the more over the less inclusive good, and choosing the goods with greater over lesser likelihood of realization.[28] The conditions of full deliberative rationality are full information, careful consideration under favorable circumstances, awareness of the genesis of wants and desires, and the application of rational choice principles with particular attention to (a) a whole-life frame of reference, (b) no discounting for the future, (c) the advantages of rising expectations throughout life, (d) the consequences of the "Aristotelian" principle that "other things equal, human beings enjoy the exercise of their realized capacities . . . and this enjoyment increases the more the capacity is realized, or the greater its complexity," and (e) a concern for continuity, unity, and a dominant theme in one's life.[29] Summarizing, Rawls says:

> The guiding principle [is] that a rational individual is always to act so that he need never blame himself no matter how his plans finally work out. Viewing himself as one continuing being over time, he can say that at each moment of his life he has done what the balance of reason required, or at least permitted. Therefore any risks he assumes must be worthwhile, so that should the worst happen that he had any reason to foresee, he can still affirm that what he did was above criticism.[30]

Note that rationality is proposed solely for its instrumental value in producing a whole life that is both just[31] and as full of goods (other than rationality) as it can be. Unless rationality yields these things it is not defensible as a unitary account. Whether rationality of the sort described yields moral rectitude is a much disputed point. Suppose it does, and that it yields *only* rectitude, not pleasure, or inner unity, or achievement, or something else. Then if rectitude is sufficient for a good life, rationality will be. But the sufficiency of rectitude is questionable. Suppose, then, that in addition to rectitude, rationality yields important goods described in the list of criteria: unity, for example, and peace of mind, a variety of pleasures and achievements, excellence. Then it seems that the plausibility of this unitary vision of the good life rests on the extent to which we can be confident that the persistent, thorough deliberation rationality re-

---

[27] *Ibid.*, p. 409.

[28] *Ibid.*, pp. 411–16.

[29] *Ibid.*, pp. 416–33. Quoted material is from p. 426.

[30] *Ibid.*, p. 422.

[31] Rawls believes, of course, that rationality will give *the right* priority over *the good*, and presumably yield a life-plan that is *just* as well as *good*. This implies that for any account of the good life based on this notion of rationality, right conduct will be a necessary component.

quires will not be self-defeating, that is, will not defeat the pursuit of rationally desirable goods that are necessary for a good life. This is comparable to the question of whether living on act-utilitarian principles will necessarily force one to cultivate traits of character (habits of thought and conduct, dispositions) that gradually diminish the extent to which one is able to apply the utilitarian principle, even at the most abstract level.

I suggest that rationality is self-defeating in this sense. After all, it recommends something like Rawls's full deliberative rationality *as a way of life*.[32] I submit that, under all but the most reduced circumstances, it is rational to cultivate dispositions regarding mutual love, risk, personal achievement, integrity, and perhaps aesthetic values and unity, which will grow, become self-reinforcing, and gradually erode the extent of the areas of life in which one is prepared to deliberate seriously (that is, as between live alternatives) and the extent to which one is willing to count a life free of rational regret sufficient for a good life. I imagine, in other words, that in a very wide range of life-circumstances it will be rational for us to cultivate deeply internalized commitments (to family, friends, institutions) which thereafter will typically block the pursuit of full deliberative rationality in important areas of our lives. Once we have acquired such commitments, we will no longer be able to pursue full deliberative rationality as a comprehensive way of life. Rather, we will find ourselves unwilling or unable to deliberate about some matters that, considered objectively, would be genuinely open questions. We will, for example, find ourselves saying, with Bernard Williams, that when we have thought about why we should save our families from death rather than save strangers in similar peril we have had one thought too many.[33]

V. THE BEST LIFE

It might be objected that there is virtually nothing to be learned, at this late date, from a recital of the various ways in which a life may be said to be a good one. Philosophers have always acknowledged plural possibilities for good lives. What has concerned them is finding the best one from among those possibilities — the one sort of life that, given the requisite abilities and favorable circumstances, we ought to strive for, all-things-considered. That is the only unitary account of these matters worth having, and indeed the only one that philosophers who have considered

---

[32] If all it means to adopt rationality as an account of the good life is that a good life must be hypothetically justifiable in terms of full deliberative rationality, then the inquiry into the nature of such a life is equivalent to philosophical inquiry (as I understand it) into the nature of the good life.

[33] Bernard Williams, "Persons, Character, and Morality," in *The Identities of Persons*, ed. Amélie O. Rorty (Berkeley: University of California Press, 1976), p. 215. Reprinted in Williams, *Moral Luck* (New York: Cambridge University Press, 1981).

them deeply have tried to get. Nothing in what has been said so far precludes or even casts doubt on the possibility of getting a unitary account of the best life. My reply to this is a flat denial. At this late date, what a recital of the range of possibilities for a good life does above all else is to remind us of how preposterous it is to suppose that there is only one best sort of life. Each of the candidates for a good life has its own better and best versions, defined in large part by how completely other important goods are realized in it. When the candidates are defined so as to look their best, the contention that a life of personal fulfillment is either inferior or superior to a life of human excellence, or achievement, or rationality at a comparable level is barely worth considering. Consider how such forms of life can be compared:

1. They can be ranked according to achievability and likelihood of success on their own terms, but it is obvious that that is a function of the circumstances in which they are pursued. The best, then, means merely the best under the circumstances. It does not seem plausible to suppose that only one form of life would turn out to have the "most likely to succeed" rating for all individuals under conditions defined broadly enough to cover most human lives.

2. Forms of life can be ranked according to sustainability and self-sufficiency, but that too is a function of circumstance. Every *best* version of a form of good life is vulnerable to disastrous misfortunes. (The sort of invulnerability recommended by Epictetus is arguably sufficient for a minimally good life, but hardly a plausible candidate for the best life possible for a stoic.)

3. Forms of life can be ranked according to necessity, that is, according to their compatibility with all the things necessary for a good life, and their ability to guarantee those necessities. If it turned out that only one form of good life were genuinely compatible with all the necessary goods, then the best version of that form would necessarily be the best life. But I take it that the discussion of criterial goods and candidate definitions of the good life implies that all of the influential candidates are fully compatible with the necessities, at least in the sense that each defines a kind of life that is both good and achievable, in a fairly wide range of circumstances. As for the ability of each candidate to guarantee the necessary goods, that is a question of achievability and likelihood of success, which is, as already noted, a function of circumstance.

4. Forms of life can be ranked in terms of preference, that is, in terms of which candidate is preferred by all or most suitably situated agents. The very persistence of the candidates described above, each apparently ranked by many thoughtful people as the best form of life, is evidence that this procedure will not yield a unitary result. Of course, the conditions of choice could be rigged to force one candidate to the top. If ancient Athenian philosophers—the ones past forty, perhaps, with money and slaves—were the only voters, that would narrow the range considerably.

But that is not a worthwhile exercise. Turning the choice over to a Millean panel of experts[34] is not likely to narrow the field. (Certainly Mill's liberalism is premised on the conviction that it will not.) Nor will it help to turn the choice over to hypothetical rational agents, unless they are defined so schematically as to render the result uninteresting. (*If* I were not a particular person, in a particular time and place . . . then . . . ?)

5. Forms of life can be ranked according to inclusiveness, that is, in terms of the quantity and quality of goods of diverse sorts that they can coexist with, make possible, create, or sustain. The diversity of criterial goods and the way in which most of them show up (in one guise or another) in all candidate descriptions of the good life suggests that the best life will be replete with diverse goods. It will be one in which all the necessities, and as many as possible of the other criteria, are as fully realized as possible. If it turns out that one of the candidates defines the sort of life that is the most inclusive in this way, it will be the best (in one important sense of "best"). Presumably, this idea could be tested by asking of each candidate in turn: (a) whether it is compatible with each of the criterial goods, considered separately, even though it may not be compatible with all at once; and (b) whether, given favorable conditions and a dominant role in defining a life, it will typically generate all the necessary goods and a more robust set of goods overall than any other candidate.

Given the length of the lists involved and the technical difficulties of the hypothetical comparisons to be made, there is no hope of carrying out this analytical task in a mere essay. And I am not aware of any more sustained attempt to do it, or something like it. It appears to me that inclusive accounts of the good life typically proceed by picking just one candidate definition and showing that, under favorable conditions, a life lived in accord with it will be inclusive enough to fend off the obvious objections from advocates of other candidates. But we now have developed philosophical accounts of this sort for rationality, human excellence, right conduct, congruence, unity, and personal fulfillment. Taken together, these accounts constitute an argument for pluralism, and that is a result I am happy to let stand.

Philosophy, College of William and Mary

---

[34] If indeed one could be convened. It is clear enough that people can have genuine "inside" experience of a succession of diverse ways of life. But it is not clear whether they can hold them all in mind in such a way that their preferences would be "expert."

THE ADVANTAGES OF MORAL DIVERSITY*

By Amélie Oksenberg Rorty

> Those who are careful, fair and conservative — those of a moderate temperament — are not keen; they lack a certain sort of quick active boldness. The courageous on the other hand are far less just and cautious, but they are excellent at getting things done. A community can never function well . . . unless both of these are present and active . . . woven together by the ruler.
>
> Plato, *The Statesman*, 311B–C (my translation).

We are well served, both practically and morally, by ethical diversity, by living in a community whose members have values and priorities that are, at a habit-forming, action-guiding level, often different from our own. Of course, unchecked ethical diversity can lead to disaster, to chaos and conflict. We attempt to avoid or mitigate such conflict by articulating general moral and political principles, and developing the virtues of acting on those principles. But as far as leading a good life — the life that best suits what is best in us — goes, it is not essential that we agree on the interpretations of those common principles, or that we are committed to them, by some general act of the will. What matters is that they form our habits and institutions, so that we succeed in cooperating practically, to promote the state of affairs that realizes what we each prize. People of different ethical orientations can — and need to — cooperate fruitfully in practical life while having different interpretations and justifications of general moral or procedural principles. Indeed, at least some principles are best left ambiguous, and some crucial moral and ethical conflicts are best understood, and best arbitrated, as failures of practical cooperation rather than as disagreements about the truth of certain general propositions or theories.

This way of construing ethical conflict and cooperation carries political consequences. It appears to make the task of resolving ethical conflicts more modest and, perhaps, easier to accomplish. But it raises formidable problems about how to design the range of educative institutions that bridge public and private life.

* I am grateful to Claude Imbert, Ed Johnson, Steve Gerrard, David Wong, and participants at colloquia at Wesleyan University, Tulane University, and the School of Education at Harvard University, for comments on this paper. I am indebted to the contributors to this volume and to its editors for helpful questions and suggestions.

I

A few terminological remarks and boundary signposts are in order.

The advantages of diversity accrue from cooperation or, at any rate, from the coordination of activities that are central to a person's ethical projects. We can distinguish three layers of ethical worth:

1. Acting in accordance with the minimal *ethics of righteousness* involves attentive care to avoid doing wrong or violating ethical or moral principles (whatever these may turn out to be). To be bound by the (negative) obligations of the ethics of righteousness, a person requires only minimal talents or skills: the capacity to understand what is forbidden, to recognize instances of it, and to resist its lure. Although the ethics of righteousness is egalitarian in assuming that nearly everyone possesses the capacities required to lead an ethical life, it is compatible with an indefinite number of specific substantive views about the criteria for determining what is unrighteous. For instance, the ethics of righteousness can rest on a system of revealed theology, on a theory of human nature, or on one of natural law. Moreover, it does not specify its domain; that is, it does not tell us whether (for instance) what is forbidden includes certain types of thoughts and motives as well as certain actions. It is the ethics of righteousness that gives play to the philosophical postulates of the will, as the faculty of choice and of effort.

2. Acting in accordance with the minimal *ethics of decency* involves making a serious attempt to fulfill positive moral obligations and to do so for morally appropriate reasons. Like the ethics of righteousness, the ethics of decency is compatible with a wide range of substantive theories. Even when its commands are few and general (for example, "Love God and do His Will"), it typically casts a much wider net of obligations than does the ethics of righteousness, and the fulfillment of these obligations requires a wide range of capacities and abilities. Still, for all of that, the ethics of decency is, within a variable range, also typically roughly egalitarian: the assumption is that virtually every human being is bound by these obligations because virtually any human being is capable of fulfilling them.

Although remaining righteous or achieving decency are, particularly in hard times, no mean accomplishments, the point of ethics extends beyond successfully passing the court of righteousness, or having a decent, "good enough" character. After all, a cheap and easy way to be righteous is to remain minimalist, intending little so that one can intend clean. And while the ethics of decency is often admirable, it is rarely generative. It concentrates on being good, rather than on promoting the good. Although they may be appropriately legislative, providing a minimum level of guidance, the ethics of righteousness and of decency cannot, by themselves, be robustly executive. They do not assure the development of the range of abilities and habits of cooperation required for the pursuit of ethical projects.

3. The robust, substantive *ethics of virtue* leaves the world a better place for our activity, going beyond the contribution that might be made by the sheer existence of one more righteous or decent person. To follow the ethics of virtue is to be beneficent, to move inventively towards achieving the end of morality, whatever it may be. The ethics of virtue supplements and fulfills righteousness and decency. Our ethical character—the manner and tone of our presence in what we do—is an essential part of what we do. (Consider a parallel: In principle, the general capacity for avoiding logical errors and fallacies is the minimal qualification for rationality. But however active and acute that capacity may be, possession of it does not assure that a person will be able to generate sound, reasonable inferences. Still less does it assure that he will have the ability to think creatively and fruitfully—which, after all, is the point of being rational.)

From the point of view of the ethics of righteousness and of decency, the beneficent ethics of virtue seems supererogatory, and, indeed, compliance with it is not universally obligatory. The ethics of virtue is not self-imposed as a command or as a duty, but as a guide that must be followed, on pain of loss or shame. Since the capacities, abilities and talents required for following the ethics of virtue are complex and varied, and since the circumstances that promote their development and exercise are contingent, not everyone is equally capable of the ethics of virtue. While the ethics of virtue normally encompasses and fulfills the ethics of righteousness and decency, it can in certain sorts of circumstances come into conflict with them.[1] It might, for instance, sometimes only be possible to achieve some great good by violating an obligation of decency (for example, honesty or loyalty). To deal with such cases, many virtue theories introduce a variant of *phronesis* or practical wisdom as central to ethical character. The role of practical wisdom is to determine when it is ethically appropriate to set aside the dictates of righteousness or decency.

We can distinguish: *ethical character, moral systems, philosophical theories of morality,* and *meta-ethical theories.*[2] Briefly, a person's *ethical character* is a relatively stable configuration of deeply entrenched and widely ramified traits and dispositions of perception, cognition, emotion and motivation, and behavior, as these might systematically vary with circumstance and situation.[3] Patterns of perceptual and emotional attention and sali-

---

[1] Compare Michael Walzer, "Political Action: The Problem of Dirty Hands," *Philosophy and Public Affairs,* vol. 2, no. 2 (Winter 1973).

[2] "Ethics" derives from the Greek *ethos*: habit, accustomed way of doing things. It is a form of the verb *etho*, generally used to indicate that the action designated by a conjoined verb is habitual, frequent, or customary. "Morality" derives from the Latin *mos, moris,* used by Cicero to refer to traditional or ancestral ways of doing things.

[3] I shall stay with an old-fashioned terminology, parasitically relying on others to provide useful analyses of *dispositions, habits,* and *patterns of salience*. Contemporary classifications of personality types are latter-day descendants of classical theories of the humors or temperaments. See Theophrastus, *Characters* (Baltimore: Penguin, 1967); Robert Burton, *The*

ence, patterns and styles of cognitive and motivational organization, habits of social interaction, and typical strategies for coping with conflict often explain—and sometimes are also ingredient in—the structure of a person's beliefs and desires, as they affect choice and action. Traits are individuated by their functional roles; the attribution of character traits is both theory-laden and descriptive. Character traits are layered and often interactive: they include constitutional traits (those, for instance, that might affect perceptual thresholds and emotional lability); socially acquired dispositions; second-order evaluations of first-order traits, including attitudes towards character integration; active principles and ideals of conduct.[4] Many traits—friendliness, persistence, ingenuity, envy, distrust—are themselves clusters of cognitive-and-behavioral dispositions that are magnetizing and sometimes self-activating.[5] They do not depend solely on the chance of circumstance to elicit them: the cognitive dimension of such traits structure a person's interpretations of situations in such a way as to elicit a typical self-sustaining response.[6] There is a good deal of individual variation in the extent to which character traits form an integrated system, and in the capacity to tolerate failures of integration.

The directions of a person's ethical character traits can be articulated as (what has come to be called) her "conception of the good," or as a set of rules and principles that she endorses or affirms, much as she might affirm the truth of some propositions. But even when we are working at our best to do our best, we rarely form our actions by deriving them from general ideals and principles, following a reconstructed model of practical reasoning. When these ideals or principles are constitutive as well as regulative—when they form the cognitive core of a person's habits—they can be described as *values*; but when they are ritualized and rhetorical expressions of the directions that a person might notionally wish to follow, they are more properly considered *ideology*.[7] The difference between the

---

Anatomy of Melancholy (New York: Vintage, 1977); Samuel Butler, *Characters* (Cleveland: Case Western University Press, 1970); Jerome Kagan, *Unstable Ideas, Temperament, Cognition, and the Self* (Cambridge: Harvard University Press, 1989); and Owen Flanagan, *Varieties of Moral Personalities* (Cambridge: Harvard University Press, 1991).

[4] Compare Amélie Rorty and David Wong, "Aspects of Identity and Agency," in *Identity, Character, and Morality*, ed. Owen Flanagan and Amélie Rorty (Cambridge: MIT, 1990).

[5] Compare Amélie Rorty, "Two Faces of Courage" and "Virtues and Their Vicissitudes," in *Mind in Action* (Boston: Beacon Press, 1988), esp. pp. 301–2, 316–17.

[6] For instance, an aggressive person tends to see the behavior of others as oppositional, and to do so in a way that elicits her own confrontational responses. Similarly, someone attentive to issues of power need not want it for herself: she might, for instance, be an egalitarian obsessed with overcoming existing power structures. Still, whatever her principal commitments may be, the realization of her other values will be affected by her sensitivity to issues of power.

[7] To call ideological commitments and avowals "rhetorical" is not to belittle or mock them. It is, after all, *something* for a person to exhort herself to act on a certain principle or ideal, to recognize failures, and to attempt to correct and make some restitution for the harms they bring. Ethical conflict is, after all, sometimes an advance over unconflicted vice: like hypocrisy, ethical conflict can sometimes represent the homage that vice renders to virtue.

two is marked by the extent and the manner in which principles or ethical ideals habitually form action. Unless the rhetoric of self-exhortation moves from programs of self-reform and damage control to developing and exercising appropriate well-integrated habits, it is an ethical principle only by an extension of courtesy to the ideals that might stand behind, and explain, conflicted behavior.

Moral systems are practice-oriented imperative answers to the question "How should we live?": they are normative directives for producing certain types of persons, with specific sorts of mentalities and modes of action, who will attempt to affect the world in certain ways. Most moral systems are multifaceted: they address problems of the compossible realization of ethical projects; they set priorities among aims and provide principles for coordinating a range of primary ideals and values. For some moral systems, what matters is that individual human beings realize an aim or perfection essential to their natures; for others, what matters is that the world — either the social world or, more grandly, the world as whole — achieve a specific aim or form; yet others are focused on characterizing what is right and just. While they presuppose a theory about what is best and worst in human nature, they are focused on the practical problems of how to bypass or transform the worst to develop the best. Moral systems that are primarily focused on norms for social life also present guidelines for promoting cooperation among the various ideals and values of their members. A community's moral system is the configuration of norms and values — often organized in a dynamic system of checks and balances — that are expressed in its institutional structures, and in its practices of praise and blame, rewards and sanctions. Because the directions of a community's moral system profoundly affect, but do not wholly determine, the ethical directions of its members, they often provide sources of moral conflict.[8] And since most communities are historically layered and diverse, archeologically composed of distinct subcommunities, their internal complexity and division set the stage for negotiation (and sometimes the downright opposition) among a range of moral systems, each attempting to define a dominant configuration of ethical projects.

The principles that are implicit in systems of morality can, but need not, be articulated; they can, but need not, be systematized and justified in a *philosophical theory of morality*. Philosophical theories of morality are in a way Janus-faced. As addressed to their contemporaries, they focus on historically and contextually specific problems; they inherit a philosophic idiom and a range of methodological assumptions. But they also typically attempt to abstract from their origins and conditions, to present what they take to be universally valid arguments for a set of norms, principles, or ideals.

---

[8] Compare Rorty and Wong, "Aspects of Identity and Agency."

Not surprisingly, many philosophical theories of morality strive for completeness by developing a *meta-ethical theory* about the ontological status of moral values, the interrelations among primary moral terms, and the criteria for valid moral arguments. But there is no one-to-one correlation between philosophical theories of morality and meta-ethical theories: in principle, distinct moral systems might have the same meta-ethical theory, and vice versa.

It should be clear that neither ethical nor moral differences coincide with cultural differences, with ethnic, religious, racial, or class differences. Even when they promote or privilege a range of ideal types—or, more, likely, stereotypes—cultures are not, at a policy- and action-guiding level, ethically or morally homogeneous. Lacking the kind of variety in focus and in action-guiding priorities that most problem solving requires, a homogeneous culture would have great difficulty managing its practical affairs. Moreover, a community's blend of cultural differences is a matter of the historical accidents of wars, famines, and labor migrations. It would be a matter of remarkable, even freakish historical luck if the events that formed a community's cultural mix happened to coincide with the range of ethical and moral directions that its situation required. Nor do cultural differences necessarily coincide with moral differences. Although cultures tend to moralize their mores when they are confronted or threatened, distinct cultures can have similar moral systems, similar solutions to the problems of coordinating ethical diversity; and similar cultures can, in principle, accept distinct moral systems.

II

With these boundary signposts and terminological strategies in place, let us return to the main lines of our discussion. To convince you of the advantages of ethical diversity, I shall try to remind you of what I think you already believe.

First, despite their nominally having the same general principles and some of the same general virtues, distinct ethical types—distinct character structures—tend, other things being equal, to have at least some significantly different action-guiding agendas, priorities, and values. And, contrariwise, the distinctive agendas of different moral systems are best realized by distinct ethical types.

Second, although there are many circumstances in which they conflict on practical issues, each ethical type depends on the functioning of the others for its own best fulfillment.

Third, the mutually constructive cooperation of distinct ethical types does not depend on their agreeing on unambiguous general moral principles, or on their having the same interpretations of principles of justice. Nor does it depend on their being committed to a set of general attitudes, to mutual respect, *caritas,* or trust. It depends rather on their developing the active detailed habits that are the substance of those general attitudes.

Different character types, different values

Anyone who is capable of substantive, robust morality—a morality that goes beyond that of righteousness or decency—has, at a minimal level, a suitable configuration of the central virtues required for responsible action, the overlapping virtues that typically span those projected by various moral systems.[9] And the ideal ethical person might indeed have the wide range of traits that constitute the virtues, always appropriately balanced as the situation requires. But even if there were a possible world in which we were all capable of being ideal ethical agents, it does not seem to be ours. Somewhere in between the minimal and the ideal ethical agent, there stand the vast majority of us, who are pretty good at some sorts of things and not so good at others. Beyond the minimal level required for standard-issue responsibility, ethical character tends to specialize.[10]

A person is, by character, primarily egalitarian or hierarchical; she follows, coordinates, or claims authority; she is compliant, conciliatory, or oppositional; obsessed with issues of justice and entitlement, with high excellence, or with beneficence and welfare. To be sure, different types of situations tend to elicit distinct traits. An intervener at the office can be an observer at home, suspicious of those she regards as inferiors, yet trustful towards those she considers equals; she is sensitive to issues of justice among strangers and to those of *caritas* among friends. The cluster of traits that constitutes a person's ethical character are subscripted for the sorts of situations in which they typically function. But the traits that form a person's character, appropriately subscripted, tend to cluster in patterns of mutual dependence and exclusion. Their cognitive components stand in logical relations of presupposition, entailment, and contrariety. More commonly, they are psychologically associated in patterns of mutual enhancement, modification, and inhibition. Some traits— friendliness and trust, for instance—reinforce one another. But the actions that are the standard expressions of traits can also typically undermine or

[9] Compare Amélie Rorty, "Solomon and Everyman: A Problem in Conflicting Moral Intuitions," *American Philosophical Quarterly,* vol. 28, no. 3 (1991).

[10] Compare Howard Gardner, *Frames of Mind: The Theory of Multiple Intelligences* (New York: Basic Books, 1983), for distinctions among relatively autonomous strategies and competencies. Jerry Fodor distinguishes general-purpose from modular, context-specific processors and faculties; see his *Modularity of the Mind* (Cambridge: MIT/Bradford, 1983). But there are also studies of patterns of correlation among traits: see Theodore Adorno, *The Authoritarian Personality* (New York: Harper, 1950); and Roger Brown, *Social Psychology* (New York: Free Press, 1965). For critiques of personality theories, see Walter Mischel, *Personality and Assessment* (New York: Wiley, 1968); H. Hartshorne and M. A. May, *Studies in the Nature of Character* (New York: Macmillan, 1928–30); and Owen Flanagan, *Varieties of Moral Personalities,* pp. 301–2, 316–17.

block one another's intended outcomes. Strong patriotic loyalty, for instance, tends to inhibit cross-cultural empathy. The configuration of traits that constitute a markedly just character is rarely significantly magnanimous; a cautious person is rarely trustful; the virtues of innocence are rarely retained in the virtues of experience.[11]

It is, of all people, Plato who introduces the argument that different psychological types have, at an action-guiding level, different ethical values. "The origin of the city," Socrates says in his discussion of the benefits of justice in Book II of *The Republic*, "is to be found in the fact that we do not severally suffice [to fulfill] our own needs" (369B, my translation). Socrates begins with examples from the division of labor that arises from distinct talents. "Our several natures are . . . different. One man is naturally fitted for one task, and another for another" (370B). After distinguishing types of natural abilities that promote the division of labor—the strength of a builder and the manual dexterity of a potter—Socrates moves to the differences between the psychological types central to the discussion in *The Republic*. He distinguishes the mentality, the abilities, and the action-guiding priorities of the merchant-shopkeeper, the military guardian, and the reflective philosopher who is concerned for "the common things" and who thinks holistically, "all-things-considered." Applying the benefits of the division of labor to the division of temperaments seems, on the face of it, an illicit, if not outrageously question-begging, Socratic strategy. But it is also a move which, like so many of those apparently illicit Socratic transitions, is carefully hedged. The division of labor is beneficial only when it is voluntary, and when it coincides with distinctions among psychological types, and vice versa (369B–371E). This neat fit between talent, occupation, preoccupation, and priorities is supposed to assure that each type will engage in activities that best and most happily express its "nature." Maintaining this fit is, as it turns out, one of the tasks, indeed one of the hallmarks, of what Plato considers a "well-ordered city."

However we may want, in the end, to detach ourselves from the political consequences that Plato draws from all this, he seems right about at least this much: whether we like it or not, longstanding occupational activities—particularly those that allow some latitude of choice and are relatively satisfying—form many habitual patterns of attention, focusing, and salience.[12] (In tracing the connections between the division of labor and ethical values, we can generalize to *types* of occupations and professions. For instance, the kinds of traits exercised in the manual crafts—

[11] Compare Stuart Hampshire, *Innocence and Experience* (Cambridge: Harvard University Press, 1989).

[12] For example: whatever their initial inclinations, urban policemen tend to become alertly suspicious of anything that might indicate criminal activity; even indifferent teachers acquire the habit of reading facial expressions of interest or boredom, puzzlement or disagreement; and city-planners become attentive to ways that spaces are defined and used.

making shoes or making pots—are interchangeable. Similarly, the talents and skills of persuasion are fungible: they can be exercised by a rhetorician, an advocate in the courts, or a businessman. To be sure, once specific skills are fully developed, once habits of mind and of action are strongly entrenched, it is not always easy to transfer them. Still, their contributions to common life are similar, and the life that suits one, suits the other.) Besides developing a characteristic range of dispositions and skills, occupations and crafts also tend to develop action-guiding—and sometimes also policy-guiding—preoccupations, interests, and values. Even when they disagree with one another on public policy, even when they did not enter military service through the main directions of their own characters, soldiers typically become focused on those political conditions that affect (what they perceive as) national security. It is their business to represent those interests in the formation of public policy.

Of course this is a gross, absurd, and even disgusting oversimplification. To begin with, there is no strict correlation between a person's occupation and her dispositions and interests. Despite a tendency for stereotypes to realize themselves—for to us become our own caricatures—most occupations and crafts require and promote a range of quite different types of traits, habits, and priorities. There are many different kinds of teachers, and many different ways of being a good teacher. Even more importantly, our abilities and habits—our interests and sense of what is important—are by no means solely formed by our occupations. They are also strongly formed by the patterns of our interactions with our friends and relations, and even by our interactions with our steady adversaries. Indeed, many people identify primarily with the traits that emerge in such interactions rather than with the habits that they acquire through their occupations, particularly since many occupations (especially those we tend to call "jobs") do not express or develop any particular sorts of character traits. Like professionals and artisans, those who work indifferently as store-clerks, bus drivers, short-order cooks, roofers, or temporary office assistants require cross-occupational traits like patience and reliability; but their work does not require, or tend to develop, a set of specific habits or interests. Moreover, as things stand, the contingencies that place a person in an occupation or in a set of social relations and roles—contingencies of socioeconomic class, of education, of opportunity—are by no means always connected to her character traits. Nor is there any reason to suppose that a person always gravitates to, or manages to find, the range of occupations or the roles that suit her temperament and talents. Still, for all of that, steady, occupational activities tend to develop preoccupations and interests, desires and preferences, independently of (and sometimes in conflict with) the rest of a person's traits and values. We need not be Platonists to think that Plato's laborers—the lumpen proletariat of their time—have specific objective interests by virtue of their work, their means of livelihood. It is, in a way, precisely because the habits we develop in our ordinary activities tend to form some of our action-guiding values that we are so keen on the integration of our character traits. It is not only for the sake of greater efficiency, but also to avoid conflicts of interest that we try to integrate, or at least to coordinate, the habits and activities that constitute the daily routines of our occupations with those that emerge from our social roles, from our interactions with our families, friends, and adversaries. When our occupations and our social roles do not suit our temperaments, we suffer the debilities that attend conflicting desires, interests, and values.

Now for the other direction: *different values, different character types.* Differences in moral systems — as articulated in philosophical theories of morality — are most clearly and dramatically represented by differences in the psychology that each would attempt to develop. A moral system focused on the Christian cardinal virtues will, for instance, characterize a set of ideal moral agents who are markedly different from those projected by, and best suited to realize, a moral system directed to maximizing the greatest happiness of the greatest number; both differ from the character best suited to fulfill the projects of Kantian morality, acting from maxims that can be universalized, from a conception of what moral duty requires. If the classical moral philosophers were allowed to become moral educators, they would attempt to develop recognizably different types of character structures. To be sure, many moral philosophers — Plato, Aristotle, Hume — would not project just one ideal type: they would attempt to develop a range of specialized ethical characters. Still the range of ethical characters which Plato would promote is markedly distinguishable from those projected by Aristotle or Hume. Each would attempt to develop a distinctive set of social attitudes and relations — for instance, hierarchical or egalitarian — as well as a distinctive set of dispositions and skills. Even the mode, the stages, and the processes of their education would differ. Other things being equal, the ideal models projected by each moral system would enter situations from different perspectives, with a distinctive set of salient preoccupations. They would focus on different sorts of problems, recommend different kinds of strategies for solving them, and have different criteria for their successful resolution.

To convince you of this, I would like briefly to play at being Theophrastus, sketching a description of the ideal ethical model projected by several familiar traditional moral systems. As is the way of Theophrastean play, characterizations of this kind quickly, imperceptibly, become caricatures. My intention is not so much to present full descriptions of those distinct ethical types, as to suggest that the realization of distinct moral ideals requires distinct types of character structures.

Aristotle was himself his own best Theophrastus: he sketched the character of the *phronimos*, of the person of practical virtue, set to balance — and equipped to achieve — the excellences that are appropriate to each situation. The *phronimos* is the prototype of the Renaissance man: it is not enough that he has a sound, finely atuned capacity of judgment and practical reason, making the right decisions for the right reasons, or that he straightway sees and understands the best that can be made of situations as they present themselves. He must have a wide range of talents, habits, and skills — acquired by imitation and practice — to perform decisively rightly attuned actions. He must be something of a practical psychologist and rhetorician, easily able to persuade cooperation in civic life. Indeed, he must have the skills — the posture, the tone of voice, and the gestures — that are appropriate to each of the virtues. It is no good being courageous in battle if you are not a sound swordsman; it is no good being friendly if you do not have the many skills and graces that go into friendliness: the habits of listening well, with just the right level of attention and respect due to equals or inferiors. The virtues of the *phronimos* include reactive emotional dispositions: he is not only temperate but also indignant or angry in the right way, at the right time, and at the right things. But there are no rules, no maxims, and no algorithms for having the right passions, making the right decisions, or performing the appropriate actions.

Kant, too, was something of his own Theophrastus. In the *Lectures on Ethics* and *The Metaphysics of Virtue*, he describes and prescribes some of the virtues whose development would be commanded by the Good Will, delineating the preoccupations and habits of friendship, prudence, and self-respect. But it turns out that what matters for a person's ethical worth is not solely that he has the habits appropriate to each virtue, but whether, in acting from these habits, the maxims of his actions conform to the conditions set by the Good Will. Where an Aristotelian sees his friend as another self with whom he shares the primary activities of life, Kant sees friendship as involving an uneasy tension between the intimate confidentiality of affection and the reticent reserve that he regards as a mark of respect. Where an Aristotelian *phronimos* suits the rhetoric of persuasion to the character of his interlocutor, a Kantian would consider such forms of persuasion at best amoral, at worst a mark of disrespect for the rationality of an equal. Nothing makes the differences between a *phronimos* and the ethical character of a Kantian clearer than Kant's writing on moral education:

> Moral upbringing must [he says] be based on maxims. . . . The child should learn to act according to maxims, [rather than from] disciplined . . . habits. . . . [T]o form the characters . . . and to cultivate the understanding . . . of children, it is of the greatest importance to point out a certain plan and certain rules in everything, and these must be strictly adhered to. . . . The first step towards the formation of good character is to put our passions to one side. . . .[13]

[13] Immanuel Kant, *Education*, trans. Annette Churton (Ann Arbor: University of Michigan Press, 1960), pp. 83–85, 96–97.

The model Kantian is concentrated on truthfulness, reliability, and steadfastness rather than on the kind of Aristotelian excellence that he would regard as mere virtuosity.

Playing Theophrastus in turn, Hume sketched the character traits of the Skeptic, the Platonist, the Stoic, and the Epicurean. Significantly, each of those essays are written from two perspectives, one expressing the views, preoccupations, and psychology of each position in its own voice, the other describing and analyzing the position and the character from the point of view of a judicious spectator.[14] The judicious spectator has a precise and well-informed sympathetic imagination, one that forms accurate ideas of the conditions, needs, and interests of his fellows. It is these, rather than an abstract faculty of rationality, that enable him to take, and to act from, the general point of view. Coordinating the various perspectives of his fellows, the judicious spectator of civil sensibility is capable of acting from principle-dependent desires. His precise and vivid sympathetic understanding of psychology has been developed by wide reading: novels, drama, and especially history have formed his imagination.

It should by now be easy to carry out the rest of the Theophrastean project of describing the distinctive characteristics of other major moral systems, their typical preoccupations and sensibilities, habits of the imagination, and primary cognitive categories. Each forms typical kinds of social attitudes and relations—egalitarian or hierarchical—is subject to typical kinds of conflicts, and has typical strategies for dealing with them. Each has typical failures and shortcomings, vices and views of vice. We could sketch more sympathetic portraits of utilitarian social planners than Dickens's devastating caricatures of Benthamite calculators. Indeed, Mill himself projected something of the character and the education of an ideal utilitarian, a social planner oriented to promoting public welfare, empirically well-informed and equipped to evaluate public policies by determining their risks, costs, and benefits. Even though Mill himself says that the ideal utilitarian will not only be directly motivated by the principle of utility, but will also act from the virtues of justice and "humanity," those classical virtues acquire a new direction and cast within a utilitarian framework.[15] Ironically, it is even possible to characterize the basic traits of Nietzsche's anti-character, the reliably anti-habitual, self-transcending, self-creating individual.[16]

---

[14] In "A Dialogue," usually appended to the *Enquiries*, Hume ascribes differences in national character to differences in national experience, history, and geopolitical status. See David Hume, *Enquiries Concerning Human Understanding and Concerning the Principles of Morals*, 2nd ed., ed. L. A. Selby-Bigge (Oxford: Clarendon Press, 1902), pp. 334–35. "In a word," Hume says at the end of his essay on the Skeptic, "human life is governed more by fortune than by reason, and is more influenced by a particular humour than by general principles."

[15] John Stuart Mill, "On the Connection between Justice and Utility," in *Utilitarianism*, ed. James Smith and Ernest Sosa (Belmont: Wadsworth, 1969), pp. 82–83.

[16] Compare Alexander Nehamas, *Nietzsche: Life As Literature* (Cambridge: Harvard University Press, 1987).

Theophrastean sketches tend to focus on distinguishing features. In doing so, they run the risk of describing a deeply etched, somewhat grotesque, stubborn version of each type. The best, if less idealized version of each type is more accommodating, ready to promote the civic virtues of mutual respect as well as the minute habits of coordination and cooperation that mutual respect brings. Still, despite their mutual respect and their attempts to incorporate a minimal level of one another's virtues, the ethical characters projected by different moral theories have distinctive habits and action-guiding priorities.

Most moral systems — and certainly most sophisticated philosophical theories of morality — also implicitly acknowledge one another's contributions: a fully fleshed Kantian would, for instance, reintroduce many (modified and reinterpreted) Aristotelian virtues. A sophisticated utilitarian attempts to incorporate the benefits of Humean civility and the duties of Kantian justice. Still, despite the overlap among their respective ideal types — despite their similarities and mutual acknowledgement — the characters projected by hybridized versions of traditional moral theories have distinct preoccupations and directions. For morality, it is not only the conjunction but also the primary configuration of traits that matters. At a fine-grain level, even hybridized versions of moral theories that agree on action-constraining principles, nevertheless also have distinct action-guiding priorities, policies, and habits.

The advantages of diversity

There are several quite different sorts of considerations that argue for the advantages of maintaining and encouraging ethical diversity in its best, most developed forms. Since different considerations will convince different ethical types, it is best to offer a selection of different reasons. Those who are Platonists would be convinced by their own recollections of the arguments of *The Republic*. It is precisely because of the existence of ethical diversity, and because each type depends on the others to do their tasks, that it is necessary to construct institutions to assure the appropriate education of each type and to secure the satisfactory, satisfying coordination of all. While these institutions should promote agreement on certain general common ends, there is no presumption that each ethical type will understand those ends in the same way.

A less Platonic version of ethical diversity follows from the recognition that there are a number of distinct goods and ideals which do (and, we believe, should) direct us. Isaiah Berlin, Stuart Hampshire, and Charles Taylor have argued (each for somewhat different reasons) that a wide and diverse range of incommensurable values and ideals — *caritas*, integrity, justice, artistic creativity, equality, scientific inquiry, the preservation of individual liberty — constitute our historical identities. Because these values are implicit in virtually all our activities, we would have to change virtually all our practices and institutions, if we attempted to abandon any of them.[17]

But the endless minute activities that constitute a life focused on fulfilling the ideals of liberty differ from those that are enjoined by a life devoted to *caritas* or to scientific inquiry. Indeed, the habits and activities required to achieve any one of these goods in a significantly successful way are not easily combined with highly developed forms of the habits and skills required to achieve the others. To be sure, an artist can also be just or, at any rate, can successfully avoid being unjust; and there are scholars capable of *caritas*. Moreover, a person can attempt to lead that sort of life which maintains and balances a wide range of these ideals without attempting to excel at any one of them. But the comprehensively balanced life represents yet another kind of ideal, one that is dependent on more focused and streamlined types.

These sorts of arguments for the benefits of ethical diversity also apply to the diversity of moral systems. It should not be surprising that ethical pluralism should be reflected in moral pluralism. Although most moral systems set themselves a number of distinct aims and tasks,[18] they tend to specialize, analyzing the relation between what is good and what is right, or giving an account of moral psychology, or characterizing a set of ideals. In developing norms for coordinating distinct ethical projects, moral systems typically propose distinct action-guiding principles for morally appropriate social and political coordination. For instance, the perfectionist aim emphasizes the fullest development of what is distinctively best or noblest about us. The utilitarian aim is directed to promoting welfare: the satisfaction of needs and well-grounded preferences. The deontological aim is directed to determining the conditions that define what is right and obligatory. The particularist aim is directed to specifying what is required of us by virtue of special roles, relations, and situations.

The analogy between strata of rationality and strata of morality provides yet another, quite different consideration that argues for the advantages of ethical diversity. The abilities and skills exercised in constructive rationality are quite diverse, and not always strongly correlated.[19] As some cognitive theorists put it, different cognitive strategies and styles make distinct contributions to inquiry. The abilities exercised in seeing the connections between theories are not always correlated with those exer-

---

[17] Isaiah Berlin, *Four Essays on Liberty* (Oxford: Oxford University Press, 1969); Charles Taylor, "The Diversity of Goods," in *Philosophical Papers* (Cambridge: Cambridge University Press, 1985); and Stuart Hampshire, *Innocence and Experience*.

[18] Compare Charles Larmore, *Patterns of Moral Complexity* (Cambridge: Cambridge University Press, 1987).

[19] Compare Alvin Goldman, *Epistemology and Cognition* (Cambridge: Harvard University Press, 1986); Philip Kitcher, "The Division of Cognitive Labor," *Journal of Philosophy*, vol. 87, no. 1 (January 1990), pp. 5–22; and Stephen Stich, *The Fragmentation of Reason* (Cambridge: MIT, 1990).

cised in disambiguating claims; those good at unmasking hidden presuppositions are not always gifted at tracking long-range consequences. As scientific projects benefit from the cooperation of distinct preoccupations, styles, and talents—and as the best results of any one of these depends on their mutual cooperation—so, too, the successes of distinct ethical and moral enterprises depend on their mutual cooperation.

To be sure, criteria for formal validity remain constant through distinct strategies of thought, through distinct criteria for relevance and fruitfulness. But when we go beyond formal validity to generating relevant, robust lines of thought, each moral system offers distinctive guidelines for practical reason; each would attempt to develop different cognitive habits and heuristic cognitive strategies. Because the specific sensibility and mentality of each type is distinctively alert to signs of impending problems that can affect them all, each serves as a specialized early warning trouble-preventive system; each is skilled at producing certain kinds of solutions.

Finally, liberals should already have been convinced of the advantages of the diversity of ethical opinions by Mill's classic defense of liberty. Open discussion of differences of opinion, as they express differences in character and experience, is the best cure for the fallibility of narrow dogmatism; it presses for the refinement of crude and imprecise beliefs. Mill's defense of the advantages of diversity rests, however, on his view that the free expression of diverse opinions is not only the best way to reach a consensus, but also the best way to arrive at the truth. Liberals who no longer believe that inquiry must issue in a consensus on conceptions of the good appear to have retreated from stressing the advantages of ethical diversity to trying to cope with its inevitability. They attempt to define just procedural principles designed to assure political neutrality on issues that might divide those with different conceptions of the good. Amy Gutmann and Dennis Thompson, for instance, have recently argued that it is necessary to ensure that substantive moral disagreements about issues of public policy will be tolerated in open political debate.[20] Recognizing that "consensus on . . . higher order [i.e., procedural] principles . . . is not sufficient to eliminate moral conflict from politics," they argue that "a more robust set of principles is necessary to govern the conflicts that inevitably and *legitimately* [my italics] remain. . . . [T]he higher order principles that constitute the core of consensus [should] permit greater moral disagreement about policy and greater moral agreement on how to disagree about policy."[21]

---

[20] Amy Gutmann and Dennis Thompson, "Moral Conflicts and Political Consensus," *Ethics*, 1990.

[21] *Ibid.*, pp. 64, 76. Gutmann and Thompson leave it for others to investigate the social and political conditions necessary to assure that such respect is substantively realized in the social practices that affect the sense of entitlement, and the skills, necessary to participate

The practical moral of this part of my story is that decision-making bodies need representatives with different types of ethical character. To make the decisions that affect our lives, we need committees composed of Aristotelians, Confucians, Humeans, Kantians, utilitarians, and even Nietzscheans (if there are any who will consent to serve on decision-making bodies).[22] The representatives of traditional moral systems need not be — and probably should not be — philosophers: rather, they should be model psychological representatives of the directions and programs of a range of moral systems. (There is, after all, no guarantee that a card-carrying philosophical Kantian is a psychological Kantian, or that a psychological utilitarian is a philosophical consequentialist). In our practical activities, each type requires the participation of the others to provide the turns of her life that help to fulfill her ideals: here a Humean mother, there a Kantian teacher, now an Aristotelian friend, and then a Nietzschean adversary. Deontologists and consequentialists — as well as those who take long views and those who insist on experiencing the benefits of their actions — help to keep one another in line.

This kind of mutual dependence is, of course, not absolutely *necessary* for the fulfillment of our ethical projects. But you would be wise not to leave home without it. It is safer and easier to be a full-blown consequentialist if you know that there are enough deontologists around to prevent you from doing something awful for the sake of a distant good; similarly, it is safer and easier to insist on rectitude if you know that there are enough utilitarians around to press for the distribution of basic human goods. Morality is not the enterprise of an individual who, as it happens, depends on others for her welfare. It is, rather, the enterprise of a community that is composed of distinct individuals who can and should act independently of one another.

Of course, there are no decisive arguments that can force an Aristotelian to acknowledge, on pain of immorality or irrationality, his moral dependence on a Kantian conception of justice, or to force a Kantian to recognize his dependence on a Humean civil citizen. But there are very few decisive arguments of any kind in this area: at best, we can invite defenders of each position to imagine in detail what it would be like to live in a world populated only by (as it may be) Aristotelians, or Humeans,

---

in public discussions on genuinely equal terms. We shall return to a discussion of whether the liberal program is practically, though not conceptually, circular: the conditions that are necessary to assure fair and just debate in the public sphere appear to presuppose the happy outcome of just those debates.

[22] There are often also *political* and *practical* reasons for introducing special-interest groups — ethnic or racial representatives, the elderly, women, farmers, educators — onto committees whose decision-making charges affect such groups: their experience and expertise is centrally relevant. The advantages of ethical diversity require only that moral diversity *also* be represented: it does not follow that such diversity must be the *only* qualification for membership on decision-making bodies.

or Kantians.[23] In the early stretches of imagining such a world, things might go well enough: there is certainly no incoherence involved. But as the thought experiment becomes more detailed — particularly as defenders of each position attempt to specify their relations to future generations and their patterns for raising and educating children — the thought experiment begins to get more difficult. Important activities and longstanding projects — projects over which considerable moral fervor is expended — have to be classified as morally insignificant, perhaps even morally questionable. More and more activities look akratic or amoral. Of course, any position can entrench itself (as hard-core dogmatic egoism does) and accept the consequences. But if it does, it will have lost some of the force of its original action-guiding substantive directions.

It is at this point, with this sort of realization, that many philosophers attempt to construct hybrid theories that graft the benefits of the insights of competing moral programs onto their own favorite systems.[24] Although the main directions of each theory are initially distinct, defenders of different theories come to recognize the need to accommodate one another's claims. Kantians like Onora O'Neill attempt to incorporate utilitarian welfare programs within a rationalist deontological frame; utilitarians like Peter Railton try to give a consequentialist account of civic and character excellences. I suspect (though, of course, it would have to be shown in considerable detail) that such hybrids have the same sort of benefits and uneasy tensions, the same jockeying for primary position, within their integrative, accommodating moral systems as occur between their unreconstructed forms. From the point of view of practical morality, it makes little difference whether diversity is achieved within one umbrella theory or whether it is achieved by a plurality of theories. The same advantages and problems arise in each case.

---

[23] There is, as Bernard Williams has argued, nothing incoherent about the position of an intractable egoist. The kinds of considerations that might argue against rigid egoism come from thought experiments about what it would be like to live such a life. The ordinary practices of consistent narrow egoism would be so impoverished that no one would sensibly choose it. Or alternatively, the actual practices of such a life, when constructed in such a way that a reasonable person might choose it, are radically different from its theoretical program. Compare Bernard Williams, *Morality* (New York: Harper, 1972).

[24] Neo-Kantians try to show how Kant's deontology can accommodate Aristotelian virtue theory. See Barbara Herman, "Mutual Aid and Respect for Persons," *Ethics*, 1984; J. B. Schneewind, "The Misfortunes of Virtue," *Ethics*, vol. 101 (1990), and "Autonomy, Obligation, and Virtue: An Overview of Kant's Moral Philosophy," forthcoming in *The Cambridge History of Eighteenth Century Philosophy*; Alan Wood, "Unsociable Sociability," *Philosophical Topics*, 1991; and Onora O'Neill, "The Practices of Justice and Virtue," unpublished paper. Neo-utilitarians try to include deontological constraints on the demands of beneficence or to give consequentialist accounts of the development of character traits and virtues. See Peter Railton, "Alienation, Consequentialism and the Demands of Morality," *Philosophy and Public Affairs*, vol. 13, no. 2 (1984); Sam Scheffler, *The Rejection of Consequentialism* (Oxford: Clarendon Press, 1982); Liam Murphy, "The Demands of Beneficence," and Thomas Pogge, "Can Morality Be Productive?" (unpublished papers).

You might be concerned, at this point, that the insistence on the benefits of ethical diversity seems suspiciously upbeat, full of saccharine and light. Don't worry: the movie version is a *film noir*. To begin with, we need not *like* those with whom we cooperate; nor is cooperative activity always enjoyable. Even in its best forms, it can bring the kind of disagreement that escalates to indignation and disruptive conflict. It takes exceptionally benign circumstances to sustain successful cooperation among ethical types who not only promote but also counterbalance and sometimes block each other. When ethical characters differ about matters that are strongly important to them, they often revert to power politics. Raising the covering banner of respect for rational autonomy, they reinterpret their procedural principles in such a way as to suit themselves. In practice, it is often only by myopic hindsight that we can distinguish constructive from destructive opposition, and differentiate persuasive rhetoric from manipulative domination. [25]

We have been riding suspiciously along a vague notion of a cooperative community. But who is the *we* who are benefited by, or have reason to support, cooperation among the variety of ethical character types? Are there an indefinite number of moral positions entitled to sit on decision-making bodies? Should we fear the chaos that attends cacophony? In practice, the range of viable moral positions are limited by historical circumstances. To be understood and effectively realized, a moral position must be grounded in a community's institutions and practices. A community's specific historical and political conditions, the working psychology of its members, and the issues and charges of its decision-making bodies set strong constraints on the serious candidates for the moral systems that are capable of addressing a community's situation. Typically, there would be only a dozen or so chairs around the table of decision-making committees, particularly when decisions remain at a relatively specific action-guiding level.

Another fear is that divided committees tend to form unsatisfactory compromises, deciding on a common denominator that jeopardizes the contribution and integrity of each moral position. As long as there are Nietzscheans on our decision-making body, we need not fear settling down to mediocre compromises. In any case, compromises that merely paper-over seriously troubling practical problems rarely remain in place very long, particularly as they do not use the talents and resources that are most likely to address those problems. For what comfort it may give

---

[25] But despite the fact that there is often disagreement about when constructive opposition has, in a particular case, degenerated to destructive power politics, there are general objective guidelines for distinguishing them. Constructive opposition leaves all the parties better off, within the general terms set by each of their original projects; manipulative bullying closes the options available to one of the parties, in such a way as to frustrate that party's projects.

us, we can count on the recurrence of the unsolved problems that arise from mediocre compromise.

And what about the villains, the Iagos and Hitlers? Should they take an active part in our deliberations? A fear much greater than the threat of cacophony or compromise is the fear of moral imperialism, the domination of a morally suspect position. Presumptively opposed ethical positions are not, after all, always prepared to acknowledge their mutual dependence. Even when they do, they are not always prepared to accord one another the respect due to ethical and moral equals. Some ethical positions might, in what they take to be good conscience, prefer to coerce consent and manipulate cooperation. The most dangerous Hitlers are those who mask their territorial ambitions, those who are prepared to cooperate in civic life only as long as they are in the minority. They are capable of disguising their opposition to arbitration and accommodation, biding their time until they can maneuver themselves into dominant power.

No philosophical argument or moral principle, as such, can prevent ethical cooperation from degenerating into the power politics of ethical combat. Ordinary practice provides a better solution than high-minded morality. In practice, the patterns of alliances and oppositions among the participants tend to shift: Humeans and utilitarians will be allied on some issues, opposed on others; Aristotelians and Kantians will speak with one voice on some matters, divide on others; and so, too, with the interests and preoccupations of those who disguise their moral imperialism. In the best of circumstances, shifts in alliances help avoid chaotic babble, the disruption of discussion and cooperation; they block — though they cannot just in themselves absolutely prevent — the tendency to tyranny that emerges when chaos threatens, the tyranny of the majority or the equally dangerous tyranny of charisma. But when dissent is persistent and profound, there may well be disagreement all the way up: even when they all abide by Robert's Rules of Order, the members of decision-making committees are likely to differ on who should have the floor at any given time. If anything can block the influence of villainy, it is the strategy of segmentation: identifying subdivisions within villainy and placing them in continuously shifting, cross-cutting alliances with their opposition.

Should all those voices and claims have equal weight at all times? I believe, though I certainly cannot show, that there are objective constraints — highly specific, context- and issue-dependent objective constraints — on viable and appropriate solutions. I recommend *fallibilist minimal realism* about the weight that ought to be accorded to any position on any given issues. We should be *realists*: objective factors limit but do not determine the viability and acceptability of some positions on specific issues. The range of acceptable positions on an issue is not wholly open or indeterminate. Many factors enter into the determination of who should *not* be heard on a given issue. Some of these are structural: constraints of systematic compossibility set some closure on the realization of our multiple aims, ideals, and principles. Other constraining factors are procedural: as, for instance, a normative order of precedence that weights matters of life and death over niceties of etiquette, or an order of precedence that weights against a course that would deny or silence the rights or legitimacy of other moral perspectives. Still other constraining and determining factors are substantive. There are general prohibitions, moral taboos whose violation is cross-morally condemned, even when there is little agreement on the grounds for the condemnation. Wanton and pointless cruelty in all its many forms stands as the prime example of a constraining limit on any moral system, even when the criteria for cruelty might be under dispute.

There are further realist constraints that are internal to each moral system, constraints of a largely practical kind that limit the intelligibility and viability of specific policies.[26] It is an open empirical question how much overlap exists (and at what level of generality it exists) among the internal realist constraints on moral systems. Values or principles that seem superficially quite different at an action-guiding level can nevertheless converge at a greater level of generality, where sound ambiguity can flatten differences.

But being clear about when we need to attend to the considerations of a specific set of directions (or, as is more usually the case, knowing when we have heard quite enough from whom) does not by itself provide a royal road to determining what we need to do.[27] There are many particular persistent controversies (for instance, over what sorts of principles should guide the formulation of a policy of taxation) in which we are not in a position to know whether one or both views are mistaken; or whether both are morally permissible in such a way as to leave the choice of policy to be negotiated on political or pragmatic grounds.

---

[26] Compare Sabina Lovibond, *Realism and Imagination in Ethics* (Minneapolis: University of Minnesota Press, 1983); Alasdair MacIntyre, "Relativism, Power and Philosophy," in *Relativism: Interpretation and Confrontation*, ed. Michael Krausz (Notre Dame: Notre Dame Press, 1989); and David Wong, "Coping with Moral Conflict and Ambiguity," *Ethics*, 1992.

[27] It is extremely difficult for fallibilist minimal realists to draw the line between what is objectively determinate and what remains indeterminate, between the constraints set by moral realism and the openness assured by its minimalism. It might seem as if, in talking about the *advantages* of ethical and moral diversity, I am committed to a specific moral system, to a consequentialist (if not actually a utilitarian) moral system. But fallibilist minimal realism does not, I believe, entail any particular moral system. It represents a meta-ethical philosophical position about the interrelations among moral systems. The arguments that can be advanced for the "advantages" of diversity, can be rephrased as showing "reasons for" diversity, or revealing the "virtues" of diversity, or its "justice," or its being grounded in "natural law," or in "the original constitution of our natures." Indeed, I would be more suspicious than I am of the "advantages" of ethical diversity if I did not think that the arguments for them could be rephrased in the terms of most traditional moral systems.

But we should be *minimal* realists in recognizing that there is rarely absolute closure on who should be heard: within the constraints set by moral realism, there are a range of acceptable, morally permissible, and negotiable solutions to the problems of coordinating distinct ethical projects. In practice, we do not have a map laid out by a master surveyor called "Rationality," that shows us how the land objectively lies. Bound together in many shifting patterns of alliances and oppositions for our projects, we are the map-makers. And finally, we should be strongly *fallibilist* in recognizing that ethical and moral convictions are highly unreliable. Formed by all manner of extraneous considerations, neither tradition nor a subjective sense of certainty provide reliable indices of objectivity.

Although fallibilist minimal realism does not entail any specific moral system, it does suggest a good deal of practical advice for decision-making committees: Do not allow alliances and oppositions to become fixed. Avoid globalizing the opposition. Promote numerous intersecting alliances over specific issues. Initiate relatively neutral activities and projects that are likely to elicit successful cross-allegiance cooperation, in the hope of forming mutually beneficial alliances that conduce to habits of mutual accommodation.[28] Since ethical and moral differences also bring differences about criteria for sound practical reasoning, try to formulate issues and justify decisions in terms that address the primary concerns of each participant. Show the utilitarian its advantages, articulate the reasons that favor it in Kantian terms, show the Aristotelian its virtues, and so on. When this cannot be done—when, as is sometimes the case, it is difficult to convince both an Aristotelian and a Kantian of a certain course of action—formulate the considerations in general, ambiguous terms that allow agreement in practice, without forcing intellectual agreement. Save the attempt to persuade unambiguous agreement on the interpretation and defense of general principles for friendly fireside chats or philosophical conferences, when there is nothing in particular at stake.

The practical orientation of moral systems

The point of cooperative discussion in decision-making committees—the point of hearing representatives from diverse moral systems—lies in their finding a way to engage in practical cooperation. Treating moral systems as directives for developing certain sorts of persons allows us to take a practical approach to moral agreement and moral conflict, attempting to find modes of cooperation that might be difficult to secure when moral systems are construed solely as competing theories about the good or about justice.

---

[28] Compare David Wong, "Coping with Moral Conflict and Ambiguity."

It is, to be sure, possible and even useful to formulate and articulate a moral system as a theory about (as it may be) human thriving or the conditions for justice. But although moral systems centrally encompass both conceptual and empirical investigations, they cannot be assimilated to scientific theories, and ethical disagreement and conflict cannot be assimilated to scientific disagreement.[29] Although moral systems attempt, among other things, to explain (what they take to be) the phenomena of morality, they ought not to assume that existing practices are the final or even the most revealing indices of our moral capacities and abilities. Existing practices reflect, and tend to perpetuate, reigning values. Even theories that attempt to derive moral norms from human nature, or from the structure of rationality, address our beliefs for the sake of affecting our practices. Even when they are directed to convincing us of their truth, philosophical theories of morality are also directed to affecting what we do. It is, I believe, disingenuous for them to pretend otherwise.

At the most general level, the question that representatives of different moral systems pose for themselves is: "What should we do?" When we treat this as a practical question, calling for a proposal of the form "Let's now do x," it is convergence in practice, rather than agreement about theory, that matters to us. Although we are practically and morally bound to substantiate our decisions — and to convince our fellows — by advancing all manner of arguments and theories, coming to a sound convergence about what to do does not require that we all have the same (good) reasons for doing so. The conditions for convergence in practice are different from those for agreement about the truth of a theory. The distinction between the two modes of agreement is not that between practical activity on the one hand and science on the other. Practical arrangements involve all manner of straightforwardly verifiable claims and predictions, and scientific investigations involve all manner of shared practices. The distinction between theory and practice is a distinction between activities that are directed to discovering truth (as it might be expressed in unambiguous propositions) and activities that are directed to achieving some other good. To be sure, agreeing to cooperate and coordinate activities presupposes a minimal pidgin mutual understanding of what each party is to do. But this kind of basic agreement does not depend on the participants sharing, or even understanding, one another's interpretations of their activities, the rules or principles that govern them, or their respective reasons for accepting them.

The difference between agreeing to abide *by* certain rules or principles and agreeing *on* them illuminates the distinction between practical agree-

---

[29] Compare Bernard Williams, "Consistency and Realism," in *Problems of the Self* (Cambridge: Cambridge University Press, 1973), esp. pp. 205–6; and *Ethics and the Limits of Philosophy* (Cambridge: Harvard University Press, 1985).

ment and agreement on theories. David Lewis's distinction between *agreeing in desire* and *desiring alike* is helpful: two people agree in their projects just when the same state of affairs suits them both; their projects are alike just when the fulfillment of those projects can be expressed in the same proposition.[30] Adapting his maxim, we might say: "Agreement in projects makes for harmony; having the same projects may well make for strife." Hobbes's description of the state of nature is a description of the strife that arises when people desire alike; Hume's description of the cooperation that gives rise to the idea of justice is a description of the kind of harmony that can arise when people agree in their projects.[31]

What matters in practical cooperation is that the same state of affairs will, over a reasonable period of time, satisfy all parties. Using Lewis's example: to eat to their satisfaction, neither Jack Sprat nor his nameless wife need to understand one another's preferences; nor need they have the same understanding of the rule they use to divide their meat. As Jack understands it, the rule they follow is: "Separate out that white stuff and give me that red stuff." As his wife might understand it, the rule they follow is: "Separate the fat from the protein and give me the fat." They will have agreed to abide by the same rule as long as they agree to promote the same state of affairs, thinly described.

III

Once we realize that ethical diversity is central to substantive morality, as it goes beyond righteousness and decency, it becomes clear that moral education (the formation of habits and preoccupations) is a crucial area of moral concern. Important as it is, agreement on general procedural principles — agreement on rules for public debate — cannot begin to address the need for developing the variety of virtues that a practical polity requires. Respect and tolerance are not merely attitudes of reciprocal positive regard, as they might be developed and expressed in public debate. They must be substantively realized in the institutional and personal practices that affect the sense of entitlement — and the skills — that are nec-

---

[30] David Lewis, "Dispositional Theories of Value," *Proceedings of the Aristotelian Society,* Supplementary Volume 63 (1989), p. 119.

[31] Hume's story suggests a strategy for promoting agreement in practice. First, set the conditions for people to work on projects whose outcome is satisfied by the same state of affairs, however they may be described. With luck — and it takes the luck of the coincidental compatibility of distinct projects — the parties may develop sufficient mutual understanding to formulate certain general rules for the coordination of their activities. They might even develop a set of shared general ends, if only those of maintaining their symbiotically supportive coordination. With even greater luck, they may acquire increasingly overlapping ends, realizing that they would be well served by cooperating as well as coordinating their activities.

essary to participate in such debate on genuinely equal terms. It is no good using the formulas of respect with gestures indicating impatience and contempt.[32] The principles governing the rule of law sound hollow when the courts do not treat like case alike; the principles of democratic civic participation are hollow when public education permits massive illiteracy. In any case, shared civic virtues are by no means sufficient to assure anything like a substantive civic life. The virtues of each ethical type are also essentially required.

But how, where, and by whom are they to be developed? Perhaps cultural and religious diversity can be counted on to reproduce itself. But we cannot assume that ethical diversity will do so. Certainly family life cannot, by itself, assure ethical development, let alone the development of the variety of ethical characters that a polity might need at any given time. The habits and virtues of each ethical type can only be acquired — imitated, practiced, improvised — through the educative institutions that bridge the public and the private spheres. Not only the schools, the mass media, and the high arts, but also virtually every sort of institution and organization — formal or informal — affect appropriate ethical development.

It is in the awful, clear-eyed recognition of the centrality of the role of social institutions in ethical development that Plato wrote *The Republic* and that the Jesuits formed a detailed plan of instruction for the soldiers of Christ. Those of us who are neither Platonists nor Jesuits, and who believe that liberal theories of ethical development are at best radically incomplete, at worst either naive or self-deceived, are faced with an enormous and apparently impossible task. How are we to design educative institutions that promote the development, the best exercise, and the cooperation of Aristotelians, Humeans, Kantians, utilitarians, and Nietzscheans, yet avoid the intolerable forms of Platonic and Jesuitic intervention? How wise are we to leave these matters in the hands of playground organizers, television scriptwriters, and sports commentators?

A final dark note: Whether the varieties of ethically good lives also bring the benefits that are supposed to be essentially connected with them — the respect of those we respect, the ready opportunity to engage in activities we prize, the joys of friendship and family, sharing in the flourishing of what is important to us — is a matter of great and rare good fortune, the fortune of our historical and political conditions. Whether the ethical and moral variety that is essential for fulfilling our own several projects brings practical cooperation rather than the rule of power or irresolvable conflict — whether coordination successfully satisfies the directions of each character type — is, again, a matter of rare good fortune.

---

[32] But traditional moral systems differ about what sorts of actions and demeanor substantively constitute respect.

Even when cooperation and coordination work well—when we devise practical strategies to promote cooperative alliances across distinct ethical and moral directions—the "we" who are benefited by diversity are not always "me and thee" in our own lifetimes. Those of us who suffer from unfortunate historical luck can settle for the benefits of decency; and when things get really bad, the dubious satisfaction of a retreat to righteousness is available, leaving our characters to live as best they can.

Philosophy, Mt. Holyoke College

ON THERE BEING SOME LIMITS TO MORALITY*

By John Kekes

I. Pluralism and Its Values

It is doubtful that our age can lay claim to having formulated a significant moral ideal, but perhaps the most promising candidate is the ideal of pluralism. It involves rejection of the destructive quest for a *summum bonum*, and the growing recognition that the legitimate ends of life are many, that there is a wide variety of good and admirable lives, and that there is no blueprint drawn in heaven which would provide those who gained access to it with the knowledge of how to live well.

The implications of pluralism are many, and some of them are subversive of widely accepted values. The aim of this essay is to discuss one unsettling consequence of pluralism. Pluralism is a thesis about values, and it is part of this thesis that many values are incommensurable and conflicting.[1] It is usual to interpret the plurality of incommensurable values, and the conflicts thereby produced, as obtaining *within* morality. Incommensurability is taken to hold between moral values, and the resulting conflicts are regarded as moral. Much has been written about this,[2] and I do not propose to add to it. My interest is in discussing pluralism as it affects a particular type of conflict *between* moral and nonmoral values.

Since it will be central to the discussion, I must now indicate what I mean by "moral" and "nonmoral" values. All values derive from benefits and harms to sentient beings, but I shall ignore other sentient beings here and concentrate on benefits and harms for human beings. Human benefits and harms may originate from human beings or from some nonhuman source, and they may be beneficial or harmful for the agents who produce them or for others.

* I am indebted to Chong Kim Chong, Felmon Davis, Michael Ferejohn, Jean Y. Kekes, Robert Louden, and Ernest Schlaretzki for their help with this essay. A previous version was presented at Duke University and at a conference on "The Good Life and the Human Good" organized by the Social Philosophy and Policy Center. I am grateful for the comments I received on both of these occasions, as well as for the comments of the editors of this volume.

[1] See, for instance, Isaiah Berlin, *Four Essays on Liberty* (London: Oxford University Press, 1969); Stuart Hampshire, *Morality and Conflict* (Oxford: Blackwell, 1983); Thomas Nagel, "The Fragmentation of Values," in *Mortal Questions* (Cambridge: Cambridge University Press, 1979); Martha Nussbaum, *The Fragility of Goodness* (Cambridge: Cambridge University Press, 1986); and Bernard Williams, "Conflicts of Values," in *Moral Luck* (Cambridge: Cambridge University Press, 1981).

[2] For seminal articles and a good bibliography, see *Moral Dilemmas*, ed. Christopher W. Gowans (New York: Oxford University Press, 1987).

63

The distinction between moral and nonmoral values depends, first, on whether the agents are causing benefits and harms primarily to themselves or primarily to others. Nonmoral values have to do with benefits secured or harms avoided primarily by the agents for themselves, while moral values concern benefits and harms the agents cause others. For instance, peak physical condition is a nonmoral value, while being kind to others is a moral one. Second, moral values originate from human beings, while nonmoral values may have either human or nonhuman sources. Thus, justice is a moral value, but good luck is nonmoral. Third, in the case of moral values, desert plays a central role, while it is irrelevant to nonmoral values. Desert is a difficult notion, and I shall leave it unanalyzed, but the key idea behind it is simple. Benefits and harms are deserved when particular agents are entitled to them in virtue of what the agents are, what position they occupy, or what they have done. We may say that human beings deserve some minimal respect simply because they are human, or that criminals deserve punishment for the crimes they have committed. But desert plays no role in having or lacking a good sense of humor, or in being or not being artistically or scientifically creative.

We can now say what moral and nonmoral good and evil are. Moral good is deserved benefit or harm, and moral evil is undeserved benefit or harm, when they are caused by human beings to other human beings. On the other hand, nonmoral good consists in agents' enjoying benefits or avoiding harms due either to their own efforts or to some nonhuman agency, while nonmoral evil consists in their lacking some benefit or suffering some harm for the same reasons. In the case of nonmoral good and evil, the benefits or harms cannot be reasonably described as either deserved or undeserved.

There are obvious questions about what exactly constitutes benefit and harm, about which benefits and harms (if any) are universal and which are variable, and about how to decide what is deserved and undeserved. I shall not struggle with answering these questions because there are simple cases in which they have straightforward answers, and these will be sufficient for present purposes. I shall simply assume that nonmoral values include beauty, artistic or scientific creativity, a sense of humor, erotic love, adventure, asceticism, charm, peak physical condition, and being witty.

Of course, any value may acquire moral significance in some circumstances, just as any value may come to have aesthetic, religious, or political significance. But there are values (such as kindness, justice, or integrity) whose moral significance is immediate, just as there are other values (such as the multi-party system, regular elections, or the independent judiciary) whose political significance is immediate. I shall concentrate on values whose moral or nonmoral significance is immediate, and, I hope, uncontroversial.

Among the consequences of pluralism are both the fact that there may occur conflicts between moral and nonmoral values and the fact that these conflicts cannot be resolved by simply assuming that moral values should take precedence over the nonmoral values with which they conflict. Anyone tempted to make this assumption owes an analysis of the force of the "should" that establishes the supposed precedence of a particular moral value over a particular nonmoral one. The "should" cannot be moral, because it is question-begging to appeal to the force of morality when the force of morality is at issue. Moreover, if the "should" is taken to be nonmoral, then the case for the precedence of at least one nonmoral value over moral values has already been conceded.

There have been some highly interesting discussions in contemporary moral philosophy about the question of whether morality should necessarily take precedence in conflicts with nonmoral values. The question is usually discussed in terms posed by Philippa Foot: are moral considerations overriding?[3] These discussions follow a pattern. They begin with some statement of the Kantian or consequentialist positions, both of which are committed to the overriding importance of morality. Then they present particular situations in which it becomes implausible, or at least questionable, that morality should override some particular nonmoral claims. These situations, then, are interpreted as counterexamples to the Kantian or consequentialist arguments for morality being overriding.[4]

Responses to these provocative arguments also form a pattern. Defenders of the Kantian or consequentialist claim about morality being overriding charge their critics with failing to recognize the richness and sensitivity of which these conceptions of morality are capable. Given the full resources of Kantian or consequentialist morality, the supposedly nonmoral values with which moral values are taken by critics to conflict can be seen as being themselves moral values. Thus the conflict is said not to be between moral and nonmoral values, but the familiar one between different moral values. This being so, would-be critics of the overriding force of morality are charged with having failed to present any reason for doubting the supremacy of morality.[5]

My own view is that there are genuine conflicts between moral and nonmoral values, that reason does not always require that these conflicts should be resolved in favor of morality, and that the conflicts are not the epiphenomena of an impoverished conception of morality. If this is right,

[3] Philippa Foot, "Are Moral Considerations Overriding?" in *Virtues and Vices* (Berkeley: University of California Press, 1978).

[4] Perhaps the best-known representatives of this approach are Michael Slote, "Admirable Immorality," in *Goods and Virtues* (Oxford: Clarendon Press, 1983); Williams, "Moral Luck," in *Moral Luck*; and Susan Wolf, "Moral Saints," *Journal of Philosophy*, vol. 79 (1982), pp. 419–39.

[5] Two examples of this approach are Marcia Bacon, "On Admirable Immorality," *Ethics*, vol. 96 (1986), pp. 557–66, and Robert B. Louden, "Can We Be Too Moral?" *Ethics*, vol. 98 (1988), pp. 361–78.

we must doubt that morality is as important a guide to life as it has been supposed before pluralism was taken seriously, and we must also doubt the defensibility of the traditional ideal of the coincidence of morality and rationality. Thus pluralism leads to the subversive belief that our commitment to values may legitimately involve immorality.

The strategy I shall follow in arguing for this view is to present two cases in which the agents clearly and unambiguously conduct themselves immorally. Yet they have weighty nonmoral reasons for acting the way they do. The advantage of appealing to incontestable cases of immorality is that, unlike previous arguments against morality being overriding, these cases cannot be reinterpreted as involving conflicting moral requirements. Nor can they be written off as the products of an impoverished conception of morality, since, on any reasonable view of morality, these cases would have to be regarded as involving immorality. Nonetheless, although the conduct is immoral in each case, there are strong nonmoral reasons motivating it. Hence, it follows that, at least in some cases, when moral and nonmoral values conflict the outcome hangs in the balance.

II. REASONABLE IMMORALITY

One of the cases has been suggested by *Utz*, a novel by Bruce Chatwin.[6] In developing this case, however, I depart from the original in the interest of making a philosophical point. The other case is taken from real life, but I have changed it as well, in order to disguise the identity of the subject.

The first case concerns a man whose ruling passion, indeed obsession, in life is a collection of porcelain figurines produced in Bohemia during the eighteenth century. There are straightforward psychological reasons why he has come to be the way he is. He had been a clumsy, insecure, ugly, lonely, and rather stupid child who happened to be given one of these figurines as a birthday present. He began to play with it, fantasize about it, and spin stories involving it. Other children, as well as adults, noticed his growing interest and sensed that there might be something special about the boy, that he was, after all, more than just an unlovable wretch. Thus he was rewarded by the recognition he craved, he was spurred on in the same direction, he learned to make distinctions, he acquired the relevant facts, and he taught himself to be a connoisseur. As he grew in skill and knowledge, his inner life—his dreams, desires, ambitions, hopes, and fears—focused on his growing collection of these rare, delicate, fragile pieces of porcelain. We encounter him as a middle-aged eccentric, a collector and an expert, with his life centered around the treasures whose fame is rapidly spreading among people knowledgeable about such matters. The collection is the focus of his emotional life; his

---

[6] Bruce Chatwin, *Utz* (New York: Viking, 1989).

chief preoccupation is with protecting it and adding to it; and such human contacts as he has all focus in some way or another on the collection.

He lives in Prague, and the events going on around him — the Allied betrayal of his country, the German occupation, the Second World War, the communist takeover, the various waves of terror, the murder of the Jews, the communist purges, the bombings, the show trials, the disappearance and the rare reappearance of people around him — impinge on his life merely as potential threats to the collection, or as opportunities to enlarge it by judicious purchases from those who need money and have the goods. He casually collaborates with whomever happens to be in power, and he is quite willing, indeed eager, to exploit the latest wave of victims. He knows that the Nazis and the communists use him to lend a facade of respectability to their vicious regimes. They exhibit him as testimony to their sensitivity to the finer things in life, to the freedom and support they provide for connoisseurship; they even let him travel abroad to make some purchases. He allows himself to be used because he sees it as a bargain. What he has to provide in terms of collaboration — the occasional false public statements, the infrequent newspaper interviews, the rare propaganda endorsements — seems insignificant to him compared to the protection the collection receives in exchange.

From the moral point of view, the collector is despicable. His obsession has made him violate common decency; he is a spineless accomplice of great crimes, a supporter of vicious regimes, and an exploiter of innocent victims. It is true that he personally has not committed any great crimes, and it is also true that he is not selfishly motivated. He lives in service of art. He cares about himself, as he does about others, only insofar as he is instrumental to perpetuating the collection. He would readily continue to suffer and endure great hardship, as he has in the past, in the interest of the treasures. All the same, he knows what decency calls for, and what he is consenting to; he knows what the regimes whose reputation he is shoring up are guilty of, and he is quite heartless when striking a deal with people who are trying to buy their lives by selling some precious figurine. There is no doubt that the collector is immoral, and the root of his immorality is that he attributes greater importance to the collection than to common decency.

But now let us look at this from a nonmoral point of view. The collector had to weigh the respective importance he attributed to common decency and to the collection. What reason could he have given for thinking that the collection was more important than decency? First, the aesthetic value of the collection was considerable. We may not want to go as far as William Faulkner in proclaiming that "the 'Ode on a Grecian Urn' is worth any number of old ladies,"[7] but we should begin by recognizing that the collector was protecting a unique assemblage of irreplaceable

[7] The Paris Review Interviews, *Writers At Work* (London: Secker & Warburg, 1958), p. 112.

works of art, and not, say, canceled streetcar tickets. If they had been dispersed, lost, broken, or removed from accessibility, there would have been a serious loss. Consider further that, although the collector's hands were by no means clean, he did not commit horrendous crimes. He lied, he was not morally fastidious, he lent his insignificant support to vicious regimes, and he drove heartless bargains. However, there were countless people in Prague, and elsewhere, during those wretched days, who did the same for personal gain, or out of cowardice or mean-spiritedness, and not to protect valuable works of art. But the most important consideration is an appreciation of what the figurines meant to the collector. It is not a cliché to say that they were his life. His identity, the integrity of his personality, his attitude toward the world, the meaning and purpose of his life were inseparably connected to the collection. As some aborigines carry their souls in a box, so the collector's soul was in the figurines. Their destruction would have meant the destruction of the psychological props of his life, and without them he would have been lost. To say to the collector that common decency should take precedence over the collection is to say that he should have opted for an unacceptable life rather than commit the same banal moral transgressions as many people around him were busily engaged in. The cost of decency for the collector would have been too great. It is just not reasonable to expect that much of people. The point is not that agents in his position are unable to do what morality requires of them. They know what it is, and they have the power to act on what they know. But the motivation for exercising their powers—given its cost, their context, and the attractions of the alternative—is simply not there. Thus the collector did have strong nonmoral reasons for acting immorally.

The second case involves a young Englishman in 1940 who felt that he was at the beginning of a promising career. He was from a working-class family, and he had achieved what he had by hard work, talent, and considerable sacrifice. Of course, the times were not kind to his career plans. England stood alone in the Second World War, and the tide was running against her. It was clear to the Englishman that he would soon be conscripted and that the chances of his survival were poor. It seemed to him that even if he were to survive against the odds, and to come out of the war reasonably intact, his future in an England that was likely to lose the war would not give him an acceptable life. He would have an uphill struggle to make a life suited to his talents even in peacetime, since he had the wrong accent and the wrong background, but the prospects of an acceptable life in a defeated country, probably under foreign occupation, he found quite dim. It happened, however, that he was offered passage to America and a promising job. He accepted them, left, and settled in America, where he succeeded in making a distinguished career for himself.

The moral criticism of the Englishman is that he acted disloyally. He took the benefits his country offered, namely, security, health care, education, and a decent standard of living, but when the time for repayment came he left England in the lurch. He put his welfare before the welfare of his country, and he betrayed his fellow citizens who had a right to count on him, especially in those hard times. Being raised in a country confers rights and obligations on citizens, and our Englishman enjoyed the rights without honoring the obligations.

One might reply to this moral criticism by pointing out that it demands too much in exchange for too little. It is true that the Englishman was born into the country and enjoyed the rights and privileges of citizenship, but we all have to be born somewhere, and he did not choose to be born an Englishman. In fact, shortly after he reached the age when people can make responsible decisions about where their allegiances lie, he did make the decision for which he is now being criticized. Moreover, the rights and benefits he received prior to his decision were not all that great, nor were they fairly distributed. His working-class background deprived him of many privileges that more fortunately situated people enjoyed. He had to work much harder for what he got than people higher up on the social scale. Thus, although there certainly was a tacit contract between him and his country, the contract was not indissoluble or particularly fair. However, the most telling point in response to the moral criticism is that it places unreasonably high demands on the Englishman, for it requires him to risk his life, limb, and future, and what he finds in the balance for all this is very meager indeed. Why would a reasonable person risk all that under such circumstances? He has only one life to live, his talents must be employed now, his resources and opportunities are all that he has, and he is required by morality to endanger all that. If he is to have a chance for an acceptable life, certain conditions have to be met, and morality requires him to put those very conditions into jeopardy.

Both the collector and the Englishman can appeal to a nonmoral good as a reason for their immoral conduct. The good is that of having a minimally acceptable life. If the circumstances of one's life produce a conflict between this nonmoral good and any particular moral good, then there is no reason why the moral good should *necessarily* override the nonmoral one, and there is a powerful reason why the nonmoral value may take precedence. The reason is that that particular nonmoral good normally motivates the future functioning of the individual in question as an agent, and, *simpliciter*, as a moral agent. Thus what is involved in the conflict between this nonmoral good and any other moral good may not be the choice between being a morally good and a morally bad agent, but the choice between having or not having the motivation to continue living at all. The reason why for many people the nonmoral good of having a minimally acceptable life may override the moral good of being a good moral agent is that for many people, not being the stuff of which martyrs are made, the first is necessary for the second.

The claim that a nonmoral good may override a moral one may give rise to two different kinds of skeptical questions. First, it may be asked whether any *moral* conclusions follow from the facts of psychological motivation. It may be true that people often opt for a particular nonmoral good when it conflicts with a moral good, but why should it be supposed that what that shows is that it may be reasonable to allow the nonmoral to override the moral good? The alternative is to suppose that the people who opt for the nonmoral good are acting immorally.

But this question overlooks the context in which the conflict between nonmoral and moral values in general is being considered. That they may conflict is clear. The question to which such conflicts give rise is whether reason always requires that the conflicts be resolved in favor of the moral value. To reply by simply asserting the affirmative answer is dogmatism, not argument. Reasons have to be given to support either the affirmative or the negative answer. And surely, one central type of reason that bears on the question of which of the conflicting values it is reasonable to choose is the agents' judgment about the respective importance of the two different values in their lives. This judgment will naturally have a strong influence on their psychological motivation, so it has a clear bearing on the resolution of the conflict. Of course, the judgment may or may not be reasonable, but neither the collector nor the Englishman seems unreasonable in judging that in his own case the importance of having a minimally acceptable life outweighs the importance of acting decently or loyally. At the same time, it must be acknowledged that there are strong and conscientious people who may judge differently in similar situations, and that their judgments may also be reasonable. As we shall shortly see, in these conflicts reason allows more than one answer.

The second skeptical question concerns the reasons for regarding a minimally acceptable life as a nonmoral rather than as a moral good. Why should we not interpret the conflicts of the collector and the Englishman as conflicts between two moral goods, and thus as conflicts *within* morality and not *between* morality and something else? The answer is twofold. First, having a minimally acceptable life carries with it no guarantee regarding the balance of good and evil that the person whose life it is may cause. We need to know a great deal about that balance before we can form any reasonable moral evaluation of the life. It may be Hitler's, Einstein's, or our next-door neighbor's life. So one reason against regarding a minimally acceptable life as a moral good is that, while it certainly benefits the agent who has it, it may turn out to be morally evil because it may involve a preponderance of undeserved harm inflicted on others.

Second, having a minimally acceptable life is one normal, shared, and reasonable goal of all human beings regardless of whether their lives are moral, immoral, or nonmoral, because there are few people who would wish to go on living if they were deprived of a minimally acceptable life. Thus the relationship between an individual having a minimally acceptable life and living a morally good life is like the relationship between a society having institutions and having just institutions. As societies are likely to disintegrate without institutions, so individuals are likely to disintegrate without having a minimally acceptable life.

From a minimally acceptable life being a nonmoral value, it does not, of course, follow that the kind of life we go on to live if the minimal conditions are satisfied is immune to moral criticism. It is indeed a legitimate goal of morality to influence people toward being morally good rather than morally evil agents. The cases I have examined suggest that the way in which morality can go about achieving this legitimate goal has a reasonable limit. The limit is that morality should not oblige people to subject to serious jeopardy that very capacity of theirs which is normally required for the achievement of the goal of morality. This is the reason why at least one nonmoral value *may*, although it need not, override any particular moral value, even if the consequence of doing so is that immoral conduct may be reasonable in the context of a conflict between the two kinds of values.

III. Some Implications of Pluralism

Let us now reflect on the significance of our two cases. What I have said about the nonmoral reasons for the immorality of the collector and the Englishman should not be taken as an attempt to make them appear morally (or otherwise) attractive. The collector has made himself an instrument for the perpetuation of the collection; as a result, he has no life apart from the figurines. He is a boring, empty, unprincipled person whose contact with others is only for the purpose of using them and whose inner life is pervaded by unwholesome fantasies centering on artifacts. The Englishman's career prospers, but he is psychologically damaged. The trouble is not that he lives in a society that is not his own; it is rather that he knows that he is permanently estranged because he is not willing to pay the price of belonging. That is his secret, and he does not want to let on that when the chips were down, he was disloyal and let his country down. As a result, he is hypocritical, ashamed, aggressive, self-deceiving, and defensive. There is, therefore, a considerable cost to living a life in which the nonmoral value attributed to having a minimally acceptable life has overridden whatever moral value competes with it. In both cases, the agents found themselves in situations where it was reasonable to incur that cost, not because it made their lives good, but because they would not have found their lives acceptable if they had chosen otherwise. Thus, in each case, we have an example of a nonmoral value reasonably overriding a moral value.

In describing the cases and attempting to draw out their significance, I have perhaps attributed more articulateness and reflectiveness to the two agents than they are likely to have possessed. So let me stress that I am endeavoring to present a line of thought that fits the agents' conduct, rather than giving a psychological account of what actually went on in their minds. The question is whether a reasonable defense can be offered for their conduct, not whether they themselves could offer such a defense.

In a more or less conscious manner, then, both agents made a choice. The choice was based on imperfect knowledge, but, in each case, it was a reasonable choice to make. The collector calculated well in what he did to protect the collection, and the Englishman was realistic in predicting a dire future for himself in 1940. But the strength of the nonmoral reasons for the agents' immoral conduct does not hinge on the truth of their beliefs, but on their reasonableness. As a matter of fact, the Englishman's belief was partly mistaken, since England's fortune did improve; however, given his circumstances and what he knew, it was reasonable to judge as he did, and that is sufficient for the case I am endeavoring to make.

Furthermore, it would be a misunderstanding to try to assimilate the conflicts I have described to conflicts between morality and selfishness. If by "selfishness" we mean the habitual and exclusive pursuit of one's interest, especially when it conflicts with the interests of others, then only the Englishman is subject to the charge of selfishness. The collector cared greatly about the collection and hardly at all about himself. It is true that the deep reason for the immorality of the collector and the Englishman is that they wanted to assure minimally acceptable lives for themselves, yet what is at the heart of these cases is not selfishness, but the protection of the self. Whether successfully protected selves are or will become selfish depends on the nature of the lives the selves go on to live. Thus the type of conflict these cases are intended to document is between living a minimally acceptable life and living a morally good life. And since, except for some saints and heroes, the first is a condition of the second, there must be possible cases in which the first reasonably overrides the second.

The justification for saying that the nonmoral value of living a minimally acceptable life may override certain moral values with which it conflicts is couched in terms of reasonableness. It is necessary to clarify what the appeal to reasonableness does and does not involve. To say that something is reasonable may mean either that reason requires it or that reason allows it.[8] If something is *required* by reason, then to choose an alternative is unreasonable; only what is required accords with reason. If something is *allowed* by reason, then it is justified, although the choice of some alternatives to it may be equally justified. Thus, alternatives to what reason requires are forbidden by reason, while alternatives to what reason allows may or may not be forbidden. Both being required and being allowed by reason serve to exclude certain alternatives, but being required

[8] See Bernard Gert, *Morality* (New York: Oxford University Press, 1988), ch. 2, and its predecessor, *The Moral Rules* (New York: Harper, 1970).

by reason excludes all alternatives, while being allowed by reason excludes only some of them.

In the light of this distinction, the argument can be interpreted as having a radical and a moderate version. The radical version is that when the nonmoral value of having a minimally acceptable life conflicts with any moral value, reason requires that the nonmoral value should override the moral one. According to this version, it would have been unreasonable for the collector and the Englishman to conduct themselves morally rather than immorally. The moderate version is that when the nonmoral value conflicts with any moral value, reason allows that the nonmoral value may override the moral one, but reason does not require that it do so. Thus, although it was reasonable for the collector and the Englishman to act immorally, there was another reasonable alternative open to them, namely, to act morally by allowing the moral value in question to override the nonmoral one. On this view, both the moral and the immoral courses of action were reasonable in each case.

My argument is intended as a defense of the moderate version. The intention behind it is not to establish that there are situations in which reason requires the violation of the claims of morality, but rather to establish that there are situations in which reason allows overriding the claims of morality and conducting ourselves immorally. Thus my intention is not to replace categorical claims on behalf of moral values with categorical claims on behalf of nonmoral values. Rather, it is to replace categorical claims on behalf of moral values with pluralistic claims which allow that in a certain type of conflict between nonmoral and moral values each may reasonably override the other.

I have been arguing for one half of this claim. It may be thought that, if my arguments are acceptable, then the second half of the claim must be mistaken. It might seem that the more reasonable it is to allow a particular nonmoral value to override a particular moral value, the less reasonable it must be to allow the moral value to override the nonmoral one. But this is not so. The judgment of which should override which may be made by different people, and they may reasonably judge differently. Often, there is no canonical answer to the question of how much risk it is reasonable to take in exposing one's self to disintegration, or just how bad a life would have to be for it not to be even minimally acceptable. In many situations, reasonable people may reasonably disagree in their answers. Such disagreements may occur because there is not always an authoritative weighing of the respective importance of being physically secure over belonging to a community, as in the Englishman's case, or of enslaving oneself to an ideal over having a sense of worthlessness, as was the collector's quandary. The reasonable resolution of these conflicts may not be an all-or-nothing affair; it may involve balancing, trade-offs, trial and error, the capacity to tolerate ambiguity, and the like. There can be reasonable disagreements about these matters even for people who face identical situations. The moderate version of the argument defended here allows for these possibilities, while the radical one, like other nonpluralistic theories, does not.

What, then, is the significance of the moderate version of the argument? First, it follows from it that a moral theory is faulty to the extent to which it is committed to the view that reason requires that in cases of conflict moral values should override nonmoral values. Since such well-known and widely accepted moral theories as those of Plato, Aquinas, Kant, and Mill, among others, are so committed, the argument has considerable critical import. Second, the argument challenges a presupposition that permeates much of moral philosophy from Socrates on, namely, that the requirements of reason and morality coincide. But if reason allows that in cases of some conflicts a particular nonmoral value may override moral values, then the requirements of reason and morality cannot always coincide. Third, it is often supposed that when reasonable agents ask themselves or others why they should act in a particular way, the reply that morality prescribes it is as conclusive as we can get. The argument implies, however, that this supposition is mistaken. For, although morality may prescribe a particular action, nonmoral values may issue in conflicting prescriptions, and the question of which should prevail is open. The fact that morality prescribes an action is *a* reason for performing it, but it is not a *conclusive* reason. The recognition that this is so should have a cooling effect on much of the moral rhetoric to which we are currently treated. Fourth, if we take pluralism seriously, then we must face its implication that incommensurable values may conflict not only within morality but between morality and other important things in life. Part of the purpose of the argument is to begin to explore this implication in some detail.

IV. Against the Overridingness of Morality

Let us now consider the most serious reason for doubting the position I have been defending. This reason has been expressed in a number of ways, not all of which are equally satisfactory. But however convincing the different ways may be, they are all versions of the idea that moral considerations must be overriding because morality just is whatever it is to which we attribute overriding importance. One consequence of this idea is that it can be used to defuse the three best-known counterexamples to the overriding force of morality that figure in recent discussions.

The first counterexample is what Soren Kierkegaard called "the teleological suspension of the ethical." In it, he considers Abraham's willingness to sacrifice Isaac upon being commanded by God to do so.[9] Of

[9] Soren Kierkegaard, *Fear and Trembling*, trans. W. Lowrie (Princeton: Princeton University Press, 1941), pp. 79–101.

course, morality forbids such an action, so it may be supposed that we have here a case where religion overrides morality. The second case is what has come to be known as "dirty hands," from the English translation of the title of one of Jean-Paul Sartre's plays. In Michael Walzer's description of this counterexample, a reasonable and decent statesman is forced by circumstances to do what he regards as morally abhorrent: he is to order the torture of a terrorist to extract information from him necessary for saving innocent lives which would otherwise be lost.[10] In this case, we supposedly have an instance where morality is overridden by political considerations. The third case is constructed by Bernard Williams, who selects some facts from the life of the French painter Paul Gauguin and adds to them a few of his own.[11] Williams's Gauguin abandons his family to dire poverty and departs for the South Sea Islands to paint. By producing his great works of art, Gauguin provides a putative example in which art overrides morality.

Much has been written about these cases, both in support and in criticism. However, Neil Cooper[12] has advanced a simple argument to show that none of these cases succeeds as a genuine counterexample. His argument rests on the distinction between a narrow and a wide sense of morality. The narrow sense is, roughly, conventional morality or the morality of everyday life as it applies to some specific context. The wide sense, on the other hand, counts as moral whatever considerations are claimed to have overriding importance. It is true that Abraham's religious faith, the statesman's political conviction, and Gauguin's passion for art led these three figures to violate conventional morality. However, this does not mean that they permitted nonmoral considerations to override considerations of morality, for Abraham's morality was the command of his God, the statesman's morality was informed by his conception of the common good, and Gauguin's morality was art. We may disagree with these moral commitments and judge the actions based on them immoral, but there is no question here about overriding morality for the sake of something else. Given the wide sense of morality, the requirements of religion, politics, and art can easily be accommodated as forming part of morality. The appearance of conflict is created only when we take the narrow conception of morality more seriously than we should.

However, this argument in defense of the overriding force of morality is too simple. For the identification of the wide sense of morality with whatever particular agents regard as supremely important can lead to the trivialization of morality. People can attribute supreme importance to silly, self-destructive, perverse, or eccentric concerns, and these surely are in-

---

[10] Michael Walzer, "Political Action: The Problem of Dirty Hands," *Philosophy and Public Affairs*, vol. 2 (1973), pp. 160–80.

[11] Williams, "Moral Luck."

[12] For a detailed version of this argument, see Neil Cooper, *The Diversity of Moral Thinking* (Oxford: Clarendon Press, 1981), pp. 97–101.

appropriate as moral concerns.[13] Thus, in order to maintain the identification of the wide sense of morality with what moral agents regard as the most important considerations, it is necessary to explain what makes it reasonable to regard some considerations as having such great importance. The claim that one's conception of morality is intrinsically connected with what one regards as overridingly important cannot be merely formal. The notion of importance must be given some substantive content, so as to rule out reducing morality to absurdity by putting no restrictions on what may legitimately be regarded as important.

Williams's distinction between morality and ethics[14] can be seen as an attempt to supply the missing substantive content of 'importance'. The central concern of ethics is with how one should live. It is this that makes importance inseparable from ethics and, at the same time, gives some content to the notion of importance. All reflective people will recognize that the question of how one should live is of the first importance, and that it has, or should have, what Williams calls "deliberative priority."[15] Since silly, self-destructive, perverse, and eccentric answers to the question of how one should live can be shown to be unacceptable, we have some specific restrictions on what may legitimately be regarded as having deliberative priority and, thus, on what may be part of ethics. By contrast, morality is a particular kind of ethics. Its central concern is with universalizable and impartial obligations. Consequentialism and Kantianism are paradigmatic representatives of it. Champions of morality wish to identify it with ethics, but this is a mistake, because reasonable answers to the question of how one should live must take account of a much more varied set of facts about life than universalizable and impartial obligations.

Employing this distinction, defenders of the overriding claim of morality can show that the putative counterexamples — "the teleological suspension of the ethical" (that is, of the moral), "dirty hands," and Gauguin — miss their mark. While these cases show that what Williams means by "morality" can indeed be overridden by nonmoral considerations, they fail to show that what Williams means by "ethics" can similarly be overridden by nonethical considerations. The cases demonstrate that there are varied answers to the question of how one should live, and pluralists, like Williams, have known and insisted on that all along. The claims of religion, politics, or art may indeed override the claims of universalizable and impartial moral obligations, but they do so because, and only because, they are candidates for answering the overridingly important ethical question of how one should live.

---

[13] See Foot, "Are Moral Considerations Overriding?"

[14] Bernard Williams, *Ethics and the Limits of Philosophy* (London: Fontana, 1985), pp. 174–96. For a recent consequentialist response to Williams's argument, see Robert B. Brandt, "Morality and Its Critics," *American Philosophical Quarterly*, vol. 26 (1989), pp. 89–100.

[15] Williams, *Ethics and the Limits of Philosophy*, p. 183.

Although I think that Williams is right in his criticism of the consequentialist and Kantian views of morality, I do not think that his distinction between morality and ethics can carry the burden placed on it. We may grant that the central question of ethics (in Williams's sense) is how one should live, that it is an important question, and that an answer to it would have deliberative priority and, thus, overriding importance. However, not just any answer will do. Reasonable answers must be action-guiding; otherwise they could not have deliberative priority. But for answers to be action-guiding, they must be capable of deciding between competing and incompatible courses of action. It is well and good to insist that the claims of religion, politics, and art may compete with the claims of morality (in Williams's sense), but we still need an argument that would show how these competing claims could be resolved. This is especially so since Williams himself insists that conflicts are fundamental to (what he calls) ethics.

The consequence of these unresolved competing claims is that no answer to the question of how one should live has been shown to have legitimate deliberative priority, and, hence, we do not know how we ought to act. If the distinction borrowed from Williams is correct, what actually follows from it is that we do not know how we should live. The cost of showing that ethics is richer than morality is to incorporate into ethics the incoherence produced by conflicts between morality and other areas of life. How does it help to defuse the putative counterexamples to the overriding force of morality (in Williams's sense) to relabel them as conflicts between incommensurable values and resituate them in (what Williams calls) ethics? The net result of this use of Williams's distinction is the proposal that instead of having external conflicts between morality and other areas of life, we have them as conflicts internal to ethics. But the change of label contributes nothing to answering the question of how we should live, of which of our conflicting options should be given deliberative priority.

The failure of these two attempts to establish the overriding importance of morality (I return to the accepted usage, and leave Williams's behind) by identifying morality with what we reasonably regard as most important in life makes attractive what I think is the strongest version of the same idea. This is Lawrence Becker's notion of "the all-things-considered point of view."[16] Becker distinguishes between special and general conceptions of morality. Special conceptions interpret morality as one human activity among others. Thus special conceptions of morality may indeed conflict with religion, politics, and art. But the general conception of morality is another matter, for this conception interprets morality as the attempt to answer the question of what reasonable people ought to do from the all-things-considered point of view. That point of view cannot conflict

[16] Lawrence C. Becker, *Reciprocity* (London: Routledge, 1986), ch. 1.

with any other, since any conflict would be a sign that all things have not yet been considered. So the general conception of morality allows conflicts between special conceptions of morality and other areas of life, but the general conception is intended to answer the question of what reasonable people ought to do, given those conflicts and given all relevant considerations.

Thus Becker's approach avoids the difficulty of Cooper's, since the all-things-considered point of view is substantive and not merely formal; it also avoids the impotence of the approach based on Williams's distinction, since it goes beyond acknowledging the possibility of fundamental conflicts and proposes a way of resolving them. Becker's approach can also defuse the putative counterexamples of Kierkegaard, Walzer, and Williams by interpreting them as illustrations of how the prescriptions of special conceptions of morality may indeed be overridden. But Becker can insist that we must still decide how to act, and that the decision, if it is reasonable, will be made from the all-things-considered point of view of the general conception of morality. That conception cannot be reasonably overridden, because any reasonable consideration proposed as possibly overriding it would have to be incorporated into the point of view that that consideration was intended to override.

There remains, however, a fundamental difficulty that Becker's argument for the supremacy of the all-things-considered point of view has not avoided. This is that the consideration of all things may take place from different points of view—such as the agents' own, their lovers', families', political or religious causes', their country's, or humanity's, and so forth—and these may yield incompatible judgments about what the agents who are in the process of considering all things ought to do. Let us take the agents' point of view as one of these possible points of view, and the point of view of what would be best, not for the agents, but for everyone, as an example of another possible point of view. These two points of view may consider exactly the same set of facts, but evaluate them differently. From the point of view of the common good, it would be better for art collectors not to be so obsessed with works of art as to violate common decency, and it would also be better for people not to make their way in the world at the cost of disloyalty. To say that these courses of action would be better from the point of view of the common good is to say that the lives of those affected by the agents' actions would be better if the agents had not acted the way they acted in the examples I have given. But from the agents' own point of view a different conclusion follows. Agents may reasonably judge that when what is at stake is a minimally acceptable life for themselves, then it would be better to safeguard this most important resource of theirs than to subordinate it to the common good. From the point of view of the common good, it would be better if the agents sacrificed themselves; but from the point of view of the agents, it would not be better. Thus the all-things-considered point of view does not remove the possibility of conflicts between points of view which do consider all things, but evaluate the considered things differently.

V. The Conditionality of Values

The basic reason, then, why I think that my counterexamples succeed, while Kierkegaard's, Walzer's, and Williams's fail, is that the nonmoral value to which agents may appeal when they take their own point of view stands to moral values in quite another relation than do the religious, political, or aesthetic values to which Abraham, the statesman, and Gauguin could appeal. It can be said about the latter that if there is a reason for allowing religious, political, or aesthetic values to override moral ones, then, whatever that reason is, it is a reason for assimilating these values to moral ones. For the reason that gives overriding force to these nonmoral values must ultimately be that, from the point of view of the common good, it is better to live according to them than to live according to the moral values with which they conflict. Thus the conflict is defused through the enlargement of our conception of morality by assimilating to it the nonmoral values that conflicted with the moral ones. And the justification for this enlargement is that both the previously nonmoral values and the moral values serve the same purpose, namely, to answer the question of how we can act so as to promote the common good. If morality is understood as providing that answer from the all-things-considered point of view, then some religious, political, and aesthetic considerations may legitimately be regarded as parts of morality.

But it is otherwise with the counterexamples I have offered. For there is no conception of morality that may legitimately incorporate immorality, and violation of common decency and disloyalty are immoral. The reason why the conception of morality centering on the common good cannot be enlarged to include the point of view from which individual agents may resolve conflicts between nonmoral and moral values is that the morality of common good forbids immorality while the point of view of the individual may allow it. And the reason why the point of view of individual agents allows immorality is that when a conflict occurs between having a minimally acceptable life and acting as morally good agents, reason allows that the first should override the second, since the first is normally a precondition of the second. The two cases I have offered are intended to give some flesh and blood to the abstract possibility of such conflicts and to support the contention that it is reasonable in some situations for a nonmoral value to override moral values.

One deep reason for rejecting Becker's argument is the rejection of the optimistic assumptions which underlie it. These assumptions are that if we were indeed to consider all things with sufficient care, then, first, there would emerge a conclusion about what to do, and, second, this conclusion would be one at which all reasonable people would arrive, if they too considered all things with the requisite care. But it is one of the most important consequences of pluralism that these assumptions are mistaken.

Certainly, we can carefully consider all things and decide upon a course of action, but other people can do likewise and decide upon another course. And this is not because some of us operate under some cognitive or moral handicap. Fully informed, reasonable, and morally committed people can reasonably disagree about the same set of considerations because, although some moral conclusions in some contexts are required by reason, there are many other moral conclusions which are allowed by reason and yet may conflict with each other. When these conflicts concern the question of how far we should go in sacrificing our deepest interests for the common good, reason allows more than one answer.

There is yet a deeper consideration that counts against Becker's identification of the moral point of view with the all-things-considered point of view. This consideration is independent of the previous claim that the all-things-considered point of view has not succeeded in eliminating the conflicts it was designed to eliminate. Morality is essentially concerned with human welfare. It is our device for making life have as much good and as little evil in it as is possible in our imperfect world. Reasonable people will be committed to morality, but this commitment must not become so imperialistic as to exclude other commitments. We must leave room for the thought that we may care deeply and reasonably about people we love, beauty, personal projects, intellectual or artistic creativity, traditional ways of life, the challenging of mental or physical limits, and many other nonmoral values. We care about them not because we believe that they are instrumental to the common good, although they may be, but because they are constituents of our individual conceptions of a good life.

These nonmoral values can and often do conflict with moral values. The trouble with the identification of the moral point of view with the all-things-considered point of view is that the latter cannot leave room for this possibility. All-things-considered, agents may put love, beauty, creativity, and so on, ahead of the common good in many contexts. When they do that, they may act immorally, yet they may also act reasonably. If the all-things-considered point of view were the same as the moral one, we could not express this thought and would thus deprive ourselves of an important possibility in life. This would be an impoverishment of such resources as we have. While morality is an important value, there are also other important values. Commitment to these values may limit our commitment to morality, just as commitment to morality may limit our commitment to them. If pluralism is a worthy ideal, all values must be subject to this condition.

Philosophy, State University of New York at Albany

RATIONALITY AND THE HUMAN GOOD

By Warren Quinn

In this essay I want to look at some questions concerning the relation between morality and rationality in the recommendations they make about the best way to live our lives and achieve our good. Specifically, I want to examine ways in which the virtue of practical rationality (conceived in neo-Humean terms as the most authoritative practical excellence) and the various moral virtues might be thought to part company, giving an agent conflicting directives regarding how best to live his (or her) life. In conducting this enquiry, I shall at some crucial points be presupposing something of an Aristotelian perspective, but only in the most general way.[1]

I

In what follows, I shall distinguish *reason*, the faculty or power, from *rationality*, the excellence or virtue (taken in the broadest sense) of that faculty. By *practical reason* I mean that part of reason that tells us what to do and how to live. By *practical rationality* (or, henceforth, *rationality*) I mean the excellence of that part of reason in virtue of which an agent is practically rational as opposed to irrational. By a *neo-Humean* conception of rationality I mean one that makes the goal of practical reason the maximal satisfaction of an agent's desires and preferences, suitably corrected for the effects of misinformation, wishful thinking, and the like. There are various versions of neo-Humean theory, and I shall not here be concerned with their specific differences. Their common essence lies in an appeal (1) to a notion of *basic* desires or preferences, which are not subject to intrinsic criticism as irrational and are subject to extrinsic criticism only by ways in which their joint satisfaction may not be possible, and (2) to a notion of *derived* desires or preferences, which are criticizable only instrumentally. The kind of neo-Humean theory I want to consider allows that basic or derived desires and preferences may be intrinsically criticized as *immoral*. But it does not regard that assessment as automatically relevant to the question of whether it is rational to act on them or aim at their objects.

---

[1] I will also be indebted to Philippa Foot's recent unpublished development of that perspective in *The Princeton Lectures* ("Human Desires," "Miklukho-Maklay and His Servant," and a third, untitled lecture), and also in her later "Virtue and Happiness," and "Happiness II."

Questions of human rationality are conceptually connected in complex ways to questions about human good. Hume himself seemed to be something of a hedonist about both our motivations and our good. But most modern-day Humeans would disagree, casting their net more broadly to include desired items other than pleasure and the avoidance of pain. It would be possible to adopt a neo-Humean view on which the distinctive aim of rationality, the maximization of an agent's desires and preferences, just is his good, however little he desires things that bring him joy and fulfillment or however little he prefers things that make his life richer, more interesting, etc. But it might be more plausible to look for some subset of these desires and preferences that are *self-regarding* in the ways just suggested and to see his good as constructed out of the maximization of these. It would, of course, be no easy task to come up with a suitable sense of the self-regarding, and indeed it might prove impossible. But it might be within the spirit of contemporary Humeanism to try, and in what follows I shall suppose that we have both a neo-Humean conception of rationality and a companion, similarly spirited, neo-Humean conception of an agent's good, with the latter sharing the moral indifference of the former. While basic items that an agent wants *for himself* will be subject to various kinds of serious moral criticism, they will not thereby be excluded from contributing to the intrinsic goodness of his life. Neo-Humean theories of rationality and the good, thus conceived, are not only conceptually linked, they also reinforce each other. In particular, the conception of rationality can be seen as supporting the conception of the good. A possible end, considered in the abstract, is part of my good only because rationality gives it to me as one of my goals; and an end would, in these particular circumstances, be part of the best life available to me only because it could, in these circumstances, be rational for me to pursue it. This means that if the moral indifference of the neo-Humean conception of rationality undermined its credentials as a theory of rational choice, it would also tend to undermine the corresponding neo-Humean conception of the good.[2] Part of my argument will take this route: I will begin by trying to show how hard it is for neo-Humean rationality to maintain its attitude of moral indifference to our choices and ends and still be all the things we want rationality to be.

I spoke earlier of rationality as authoritative. By the *authority* of one excellence over another I mean the ability of the former to prevail over the latter in determining what the agent should, in some unqualified and unrelativized sense, do. Suppose, along with Thrasymachus, that injustice is a form of rationality (if we may thus translate "*sophia*") which can oppose justice in directing an agent toward his good.[3] The question then arises as to which, if either, takes precedence. Thrasymachus thought that

---

[2] Although the latter could perhaps be defended on other grounds.

[3] Plato, *Republic*, 348C–349A.

sophia, the more genuine *arete* (excellence), should trump justice, the mere "noble simplicity and goodness of heart."[4] But it would be possible for someone to counter with the observation that, given Thrasymachus's unpalatable assumptions about rationality, the preference should go the other way. Perhaps on those assumptions, or those of the neo-Humean, we should even wonder whether rationality might not be a minor virtue, or no virtue at all, that is, whether its preoccupation with calculation and maximization might not put the most important human goods out of reach.

What blocks this line of thought is the idea, implicit in almost all philosophical accounts of reason (including neo-Humean ones), that there not only *is* such a thing as practical rationality but that it is very important — indeed, so important that it deserves center stage in normative treatments of action and choice.[5] When David Gauthier, Richard Jeffrey, Leonard J. Savage, and other (partial or complete) neo-Humean instrumentalists write about rationality of preference and choice, we do not take them to be writing about what they consider a minor virtue, like neatness.[6] We take them to be making their own modern, metaphysically minimalist, and elegantly mathematicized contributions to the grand philosophical tradition in which some form of rationality ("*sophia*") is the authoritative perfection of man *qua* agent. The neo-Humean simply takes the perfection to be coherentist and instrumentalist in character. Thus, on all familiar accounts, the pronouncements of perfected practical reason are seen, in one way or another, as having normative authority; and rationality, as that perfection, is seen as *the* excellence of human beings *qua* agents. As

---

[4] *Ibid.*, 348D.

[5] Hume is the maverick here, denying that there is any such thing as practical reason or rationality — any way in which actions or desires can, "except in a figurative and improper way of speaking," be reasonable or unreasonable and, therefore, any way in which reason can pronounce them to be so. See David Hume, *A Treatise of Human Nature*, ed. L. A. Selby-Bigge (Oxford: Clarendon Press, 1888), p. 459. The neo-Humeans I have in mind do *not* follow Hume in this radical conclusion, supposing instead (and rightly, I think) that there is a proper and important way of speaking of actions, and at least derivative preferences, as reasonable or unreasonable.

[6] Different neo-Humeans have different ways of indicating the way in which they take their theories of rationality to be normatively central. The clearest and least technical recent statement of neo-Humean rationality is by David Gauthier in *Morals by Agreement* (Oxford: Clarendon Press, 1986), ch. 2. Gauthier shows the significance he attaches to the theory in his defense of a neo-Humean theory of *value* which, in accordance with his theory of rationality, is subjective, relative, and dependent on preferences that can be criticized only in respect of their mathematical coherence and the extent to which they are well informed. It must be noted that Gauthier is not a complete neo-Humean, since he argues (in ch. 6) that in situations involving the keeping of agreements, instrumental rationality may be constrained. In *The Foundations of Statistics* (New York: John Wiley & Sons, 1954), Leonard J. Savage, after putting "rational" in quotes, as if it were too hot to handle, immediately explains that the suggested criteria and maxims of rationality will have to be judged by the reader according to whether the latter would *try* to behave in accordance with them. Richard Jeffrey, in *The Logic of Decision*, 2nd ed. (Chicago: University of Chicago Press, 1983), presents his theory of rational choice as a theory about *desirabilities* of choice. And what could be more important than the most desirable choice?

already indicated, I shall rely on this assumption in arguing that there is something in the moral indifference of neo-Humean rationality that keeps it from shining forth in this role.

Another of my major assumptions concerns morality. I shall assume that judgments about what is good and bad, or more precisely, judgments about what is shameful, contemptible, petty, unworthy, etc. can sometimes be objectively true.[7] The conflict I am interested in examining is not between neo-Humeanism and morality conceived as a mere projection of feelings and attitudes. I am interested, instead, in the more resounding clash between neo-Humeanism and morality conceived as a system of evaluative truths about our actions and lives. That is, I am assuming that sometimes we are ashamed *because* we correctly see that we have done something shameful, and that sometimes we have contempt for someone *because* we see that he has acted contemptibly.

II

Neo-Humean rationality and morality can seem irreconcilable in a variety of situations that raise different problems and demand different solutions. In one kind of case, discussed by Philippa Foot in her recent work, someone takes great pleasure, and may even (in some sense) find great "fulfillment," in some intrinsically evil end such as killing innocent people in the name of "purifying mankind."[8] Other, less ideological examples come to mind: the intense pleasures of arsonists and rapists, for example, or the pleasure some may find in the very act of taking dishonest "shortcuts."[9]

These objects of desire cause trouble because, as we have seen, a neo-Humean rationality, in its indifference to the moral, tolerates, or even recommends, aiming at them. (Remember Hume's claim that "'tis not contrary to reason to prefer the destruction of the whole world to the scratching of my finger.")[10] And while an agent who does aim at them may face dangers from neighbors or police, he may also find that the expected satisfaction to be gained from braving the dangers outweighs the risks.

---

[7] That is, I assume that someone who denies a judgment of this sort could simply be mistaken, in the way that someone who denied that Hume was intelligent would simply be mistaken.

[8] Foot's example in "Virtue and Happiness" is Gustav Wagner, a Nazi deputy commander of one of Hitler's death camps. According to Foot (p. 2), Wagner "said when he was finally apprehended at the age of 68, that whatever happened next he would not be 'the real loser'." He is reported to have added: "I thoroughly enjoyed Brazil, and I didn't think about the past."

[9] Naturally, I am assuming in all these cases that the pleasures are objects of basic desire and preference.

[10] Hume, *Treatise of Human Nature*, Book II, part III, section III, p. 416.

Suppose, for example, that someone enjoys, and therefore basically desires, forms of quite *nasty* interaction with his fellow human beings (for instance, spreading lies that put his "friends" at odds with each other). Let us also suppose that he has good reason to think that he can safely have this pleasure—that his nasty machinations will not be finally exposed, as in a Molière farce. What are we to say of rationality if it gives him a green light, recommending the activity as a fit object of pursuit?

Before answering this question it is important to step back and raise another. What *kind* of thing is the excellence of practical rationality, whether we adopt a moralized or amoralized version of it? I think it is first and foremost a quality of character, taken in a broad but recognizable sense (as in: "What was the character of the woman . . . what was she like?" "She was an aesthete," or "She was devoted to religion," or "She was a meticulous planner of her career," or "She was a coward," etc.). Rationality, no less than aestheticism or bravery, is a quality whose actualization gives shape to the personal character of our choices and lives. The prudent woman is a woman of a certain character, no less than her opposite, the reckless woman. So, too, is the man who conceives his good as the maximal satisfaction of his self-regarding desires even though they are nasty. He is a man whose ideas and choices have a certain spin, quite different from that of others, even if the spin is sanctioned by the supreme practical virtue.

If it is right to treat rationality as a quality of character, then what can we say of the character of this man's rationality? The moralist might be tempted to conclude straight away that such a rationality is nasty. But this inference would be too swift. For the agent must have many other desires for himself, including desires for things that he likes, that are in perfect moral order—desires that his rationality also counsels him to maximally satisfy. Moreover, it is not the nastiness of what he wants for himself that makes his rationality speak in its behalf. It is simply that his rationality is *indifferent* to the nastiness.

But what can we say of this indifference, which seems so essential to the rational life constructed on neo-Humean lines? Suppose the end in question were a perverted one. Would not a quality that was indifferent to that fact, show the same fault? I am inclined to think so. And something similar seems to follow in the case of the nasty, odious, offensive, disgusting, etc. Personification may be a helpful exercise here. Suppose you aim at something nasty, and I, seeing that you do, advise you to go ahead. Surely my indifference to the nastiness of your goal implicates me in that nastiness—makes me, to that extent, a nasty person. I cannot see why the same should not be true of the qualities of our own character that advise and direct us. To the extent that such qualities do not turn us away from the negative moral features of our ends, they are subject to the corresponding negative charges. A rationality that is indifferent to the nastiness of our pleasures is to that extent a nasty form of rationality.

We can conclude from this, I think, that neo-Humean rationality, in its indifference to the shameful character of our ends, is shameless. Its shameless side will not, of course, be manifest in someone without shameful desires, but it will be latent. This latency must now be placed against the idea that neo-Humean rationality can be the most perfect expression of our practical reason — the *summa virtus* of our practical selves.

III

Of course, I have been presupposing in all this that the neo-Humean agent *sees* as nasty, and hence shameful, the proposed pleasures and activities that he basically desires. But what if, as is often true, he does not? Does practical reason then fail to be implicated in the opprobrium attaching to the activities? I do not think it is thereby off the hook. Indifference to what is in fact clearly nasty, but is not recognized to be so, seems just as nasty.[11] If practical rationality is authoritative, it must be sensitive to all knowable aspects of its agent's ends, which if known, would bear on its status as a real virtue. It must, therefore, be sensitive on pain of a negative moral charge to the various modes in which its ends might be shameful.

Suppose, seeing that you delight in spreading lies that put people at odds with each other, I advise you, without noticing the nastiness of that desire, to go ahead and spread the lies. This makes me, I would have thought, a pretty nasty person. For my very ignorance of the moral fact is, as Aristotle would have pointed out, culpable.[12] Similarly, a practical reason, cast in its essential role as our internal advisor, that was ignorant of the nastiness of our ends would be, to that extent, nasty. Moral ignorance does not, therefore, seem to provide an escape from the *modus tollens* argument that I am trying to construct.

IV

But now we must face a new problem. There is no getting around the nastiness of an intrinsically nasty end. But what about situations in which morality blocks a choice not because the end is bad considered in itself but because the morally unobjectionable end can be obtained only by a shameful means? Here there is something that morality and neo-Humean rationality must agree upon as good to be put in the balance against the immoral choice needed to bring it about. The desire, for example, is not for sadistic pleasure, but for a lovely fling. The trouble is that having such a fling would mean cheating on someone who deserves better.

---

[11] Of course, I am thinking of sane adults here.
[12] Aristotle, *Nicomachean Ethics*, 1110b27–32.

One strategy for dealing with these cases is to argue—although it would take some sophisticated and speculative psychologizing to do so—that the willingness to gain the good by the wrongful means makes it impossible to get what is *really* wanted in the end. Foot has suggested in unpublished material that a deeply dedicated Nazi cannot really have, in his personal life, what he seems to want, for example, the love of family and friends.[13] There is a great deal of plausibility in this. How could I really cherish a friend, or love my children, if I would wish them dead were I to come to believe them Jewish, or Gypsy, or gay?

It is perhaps surprising how far this strategy can be extended. The point underlying it is that many of the good things that we want, essentially (if obscurely) involve friendly or respectful relations to human beings as such. The love of art, it might be argued, is the love of something whose essential function is to widen and deepen our appreciation of the feelings that bind us together as human. To sacrifice others in the name of art may therefore be to reveal in oneself an incapacity to appreciate those feelings and, therefore, to get the good that lies concealed at the center of art. Similarly, the love of fame, a powerful motive in human affairs, is something one could reasonably make a central aim only on condition of having some considerable respect for those in whose eyes one hopes to seem important. Thus, a contemptuous readiness to step on others in the pursuit of fame might seem to put the true object out of reach.

How far this line could be pushed is unclear to me. It is certainly a very important part of the proper response to the idea that rationality might recommend immoral means, but I am inclined to think that it cannot be the whole story. Perhaps what I want is scientific knowledge of something important—say, the basic physical structure of the universe. What I need is money for instruction and research. I can get the money only by cheating or stealing—or by violating some fair principles of distribution for educational funding. It might be possible to argue that the proper object of scientific research is the intellectual and material betterment of mankind, and thus that someone with little regard for the rights of others cannot enter into the proper spirit of the scientific enterprise. But even if this is partly true, there is surely an important solipsistic residue to the love of knowledge—a simple desire to understand, for oneself alone, how things are. It seems hard to deny that someone might strongly desire such knowledge even though it could, in the circumstances, be gotten only by shameful means.

V

A neo-Humean who agrees with me that there is a conceptual tension in the very idea that our first excellence as agents might be shameless

---

[13] Foot, "Virtue and Happiness" and "Happiness II."

could perhaps make the following argument: There are certainly some, and perhaps many, situations in which one basically desires a morally acceptable end that can be obtained only by shameful means. In such cases, the shamefulness of the action must, if it is given negative weight, be balanced against the strength of the desire for the end. If that desire is strong enough, then rationality may declare the end to be *worth* the cost of the shameful action and so recommend its pursuit. It could be argued that in so recommending, rationality would not be subject to the charge of shamelessness that it sustained in the case where it was indifferent to shameless ends.

Such an argument might be modeled on other familiar cases in which negative features of action do not rub off on an agent or his qualities. Someone might have to make an *aesthetically awkward* reach for some badly needed medicine perched high up on a shelf. It would be ludicrous to conclude that his decision to reach for it showed any aesthetic fault. It would be equally absurd to conclude that he showed any *trait* of physical awkwardness in making the movement. Here we see that the person and his aesthetic qualities are insulated from the aesthetically negative character of his physical movement. In another case, poised between the aesthetic and the moral, one might have to destroy something good — for example, a finely wrought door — to escape from a fire. The act, considered narrowly, is destructive. But because the escape is *worth* the damage, one does not show oneself in making it to be in any degree an aesthetic or moral barbarian.

It might seem that the situation with morality is like these. Something immoral must be done to get something that reason says to be nevertheless worth it. Because it is worth it, the agent shows no shamelessness in going ahead. Thus, there need be nothing shameless in his rationality insofar as it gives him this advice.

But surely there is something wrong in assimilating this case to the others. If a generally shameful action remains so *in the situation,* it is because the good at which the action aims cannot cancel or outweigh the negative moral charge. I do not mean to be considering cases in which an act that is generally shameful (for example, stealing) is not shameful here and now because it is done for such and such an obligatory end (for example, to feed one's family). These cases do not present a conflict between neo-Humean rationality and the moral virtues. I mean to be speaking instead about readily recognizable cases in which it remains shameful to do something even though such and such desired good will come of it (for example, the case of falsifying experimental results in order to get more funding for one's otherwise legitimate and important research).

The difference between the shameful act and the aesthetically awkward or physically destructive act is that the shamefulness, unlike the awkwardness or destructiveness, is already something internal to the agent. One expresses a shameless side to one's character in performing a shameful act, and, similarly, a shameless side in recommending one. This is how the concept of the shameful works. Even if reason judged an end to be *worth* a shameful act, then, reason would show itself as shameless in recommending the act. The concepts of the aesthetically awkward and the physically destructive are quite different. One need not express an awkward or destructive side to one's character in performing an awkward or physically destructive act. It would first need to be established that the act was incompatible with the relevant virtue (for example, of physical grace, or of a due regard for aesthetically valuable property). In the cases we considered, there was no such incompatibility.

In the case of the shameful choice, however, nothing insulates the shamefulness of the action from the shamelessness of the agent in doing it or — and this is the important point — the shamelessness of his reason in recommending it. The same holds true, I believe, of all moral qualities that specify the shameful. A rationality that would recommend a nasty choice is to that extent a nasty quality; a rationality that would recommend a cowardly choice is therefore a cowardly quality; and so on. This ought to give a neo-Humean pause. For whatever else we may be prepared to say of human reason at its most excellent, it seems that we must shrink from saying that it could be nasty or cowardly.

VI

Before proceeding with some of the implications of this argument, I would like to consider two objections. First, one might reply that there is no single, supremely authoritative virtue of reason: there is moral rationality (the moral perfection of reason), preference-governed rationality (the instrumentalist perfection of reason), prudential rationality (the prudential perfection of reason), and possibly other forms. The most my argument shows is that moral rationality could not be shameless. It leaves open the possibility that other forms of rationality might be.

Part of my reply to this is *ad hominem*. Such an objection will not appeal to a neo-Humean, who wants to co-opt rationality for his own instrumentalist view. Nor, to my knowledge, has it had much appeal in other theoretical quarters. Some philosophers (for example, Plato, Aristotle, and Kant) think that rationality is essentially moral in its incapacity to deliver any immoral advice. Others (for example, such neo-Humeans as Frank Plumpton Ramsey) think that rationality is essentially amoral in its exclusive attachment to the agent's mathematically coherent preference orderings. [14] But while many wonder what perfected reason would in the end demand when morality and advantage seem to conflict, few would suppose that there are two or more rationalities in the sense of two or more

---

[14] Frank Plumpton Ramsey, "Truth and Probability," in *The Foundations of Mathematics* (London: Routledge & Kegan Paul, 1931), p. 174.

equally authoritative and supreme excellences of practical reason that can give conflicting advice.

The other objection is this: One may say that in the situations I am imagining the conflicts are merely between the rational and the *morally* shameless. It should not bother us that rationality is wanting when assessed from some external viewpoint. What matters is whether rationality is all right in its own terms — whether it is stupid, unimaginative, uninformed, etc. In the cases we have been considering, it was not accused of any of these faults.

I have two replies. First, we must reject any suggestion that there is some specific, moral use of terms such as "shameful" to be contrasted with other uses. It might seem at first that something might be intellectually or aesthetically shameful without being morally so, and that defenders of neo-Humean rationality need only be worried about cases in which rationality would be cognitively shameful. But on closer examination we will find that all uses of the range of terms I have in mind are moral. Something can be called intellectually shameful only when it is the product of something like laziness or fraud. Simple failures of intelligence, for example, are not shameful.

Second, and more important, accusations of shamelessness or its specific varieties do not get their force because morality is assigned some antecedent importance. On the contrary, morality commands our attention precisely because these accusations are so gripping. They constitute rather than draw upon the force of morality. This gives them their clout in the present argument. No neo-Humean who wants to preserve the supremely authoritative status of rationality as our chief excellence as agents should be entirely undisturbed if his rationality turns out in whole or part to be a proper object of shame. Therefore, no neo-Humean can draw upon such a rationality to support the claim that an agent's good might sometimes consist in taking shameful means to otherwise acceptable ends.

VII

It might be asked at this point why I have not conducted the argument in terms of the wrongful or unjust, rather than the shameful. I might have argued in the the following way: Suppose some intrinsically good end can be reached only by performing an act that is, even considering the end, morally wrong. Could rationality as the supreme virtue recommend such a choice and still retain its luster? It might seem that it could do so *if* we place emphasis on the fact that the act is *morally* wrong. For "wrong" has other, perhaps more pertinent, uses. An answer can be wrong without being immoral (whatever that would mean), and even a practical choice can be wrong aesthetically, or from the point of view of etiquette, without being morally wrong.

The proper understanding of these various uses of "wrong" is, of course, very complicated. As I see it, "X-ly wrong" has at least three different senses. On the reading just suggested, there is *no* absolute sense of "wrong." Different senses are created by the various points of view which we may, without being right or wrong in any more basic sense, adopt or reject in evaluating things. "Wrong from the X point of view" is often used in modern moral philosophy to express this deeply relativistic conception.

Against this, we may see "wrong" as having an absolute sense such that different factors may weigh for and against the ultimate wrongness of a choice. Some of these factors may be moral, but others may not. Something might have nothing against it morally speaking but be a bad tactic in bringing something about, for example, getting an appointment approved by the dean. Or, again, it might be wrong to dress in a certain way for the opera, but, unless one were trying to give offense, not morally wrong. On this reading, the various considerations feed together to determine the basic character of the choice as right or wrong in the circumstances. Many who accept such a core sense will suppose that moral factors typically override, for example, tactical or sartorial factors (but perhaps not when the moral considerations are very weak and the others very strong).

"Morally wrong," in this sense, might have two sub-readings. First, it might mean "wrong, considering moral factors alone," which would allow something to be morally wrong but not wrong overall. Second, it might mean "wrong for moral reasons," a reading on which its moral defects are claimed to be decisive. Thus, everything depends on which use of "morally wrong" we have in mind when we imagine reason knowingly advising in favor of morally wrong actions. If we mean it in the last sense, then the neo-Humean is faced with the paradoxical possibility of perfected practical reason knowingly telling us to make the wrong choice, which seems just as absurdly unacceptable as perfected theoretical reason knowingly telling us to make the wrong inference. The neo-Humean is also faced with the equally paradoxical idea that an agent's life might be better by virtue of her going wrong in the way she lives it.

I have not made the argument in terms of "wrong" because to do so would have required me to argue that morality feeds into (and indeed can dominate) an absolute sense of "wrong" that transcends the moral. While I believe both these things, I could not defend them here. I have conducted the argument in terms of the shameful and its specific varieties, first, because it is so much less plausible to see these terms as relativized to "different points of view," and second, because, unlike "wrong" taken even in an absolute core sense, these terms do not appear to admit of nonmoral grounds. Something shameful cannot, I think, be shown otherwise by reference to nonmoral reasons that point the other way, for example, reasons of tactics or etiquette. This is in large part why it is so difficult to slide out from under a charge of shamefulness.

VIII

The argument of Sections IV and V tried to convict a neo-Humean rationality that is prepared to advocate shameful means to morally unobjectionable ends as to that extent shameless, and therefore unworthy of its status as the supremely authoritative practical virtue. But what if one goes ahead with the shameful deed and is successful, getting the end that one desires for oneself? Has one then gotten something good? Well, by hypothesis, one has gotten what one wanted and judged worth the cost. For we have put to one side the interesting cases in which a readiness to do the shameful act betrays an incapacity to enjoy or profit from the desired end.

But there is a problem that we have not yet touched upon. In choosing means to an end, one is choosing a larger object that includes both: living in such a way as to obtain the end by way of the means. A question must therefore arise about that larger whole. Is it something that someone who accepts the argument so far can see as part of the agent's good?

Someone who accepts that argument shrinks from the idea that rationality might be shameless, and must therefore count the fact that the means in such a case is shameful as showing that it could not be recommended. In that case, the whole comprised of getting the end by that means could not be recommended either, since recommending the means as a way of getting the end and recommending getting the end by way of the means seem to be equivalent. But in the cases we are considering, the attractions of such a whole are for the agent, and therefore would have to belong, if they fitted into the neo-Humean conception of welfare sketched earlier, to the agent's good. Thus, to the extent that we were right in supposing that the neo-Humean identifies something as good only because he thinks that rationality could *recommend* it in the circumstances, he could not see the whole as part of the agent's good.

But could he hold it to be such on other grounds? Let me try, tentatively, to construct an argument that he could not. First let us raise the question of whether the whole is something the agent ought to be *ashamed* of, containing as it does a shameful act. Remember that we have set aside cases in which what would ordinarily be shameful is not in the special moral circumstances. In the cases before us, the general shamefulness of the act is not canceled or outweighed by any morally redeeming feature. Its shamefulness stands.

Is there anything to be ashamed of in these cases other than the action under a description that gives nothing more than its generally shameful feature, for example, that it is lying, stealing, betraying, etc.? It seems to me that there is this in addition: that one is trying to get a certain end by such an action, an end that does not, *ex hypothesi*, cancel its shamefulness. But if an agent should be ashamed of trying to get the end at such a cost, then surely he should also be ashamed, after the fact, of having gotten it at that cost. And having gotten it at the cost is precisely the means-end whole that we are evaluating.

The next step is a variation of my earlier argument. If the interconnected means-end whole is something that the agent ought to be ashamed of, then there must be a problem for someone who accepts my line of argument in seeing it as the best the agent could have brought about for himself. For while most of us would deny that the relevant sense of "best" is straightforwardly moral, it does go with the idea of that which, given our available options, makes our lives most worth living. However much pleasure, love, or friendship a life contained, it would be hard to see it as worth living if the totality of those items in connection with the acts that brought them about did not add up to something worthwhile or meaningful. But these notions import a certain kind of *dignity* that properly belongs to the prudential. The dignity that our lives can achieve as goods for us, no less than the dignity of our perfected faculties, is something serious — something that sets us far above the other animals. Thus, it is uninviting to suppose that something could be part of our good, that is, could dignify our lives by making them more worth living, and yet be something of which we ought to be thoroughly ashamed.[15]

IX

The neo-Humean, who wants to allow for the victory of rationality over morality in the kinds of cases we are considering, might try to disarm my argument by simply accepting the idea that our perfected reasons and lives might, after all, be shameless. Perhaps, in accordance with some Nietzschean conception of the soul, we are at our most vigorous and unfettered, and in closest contact with our deepest and most ineliminable drives, when we are prepared to be shameless in the way we live. Per-

---

[15] Some — including most notably James Griffin, who has written with uncommon insight and good sense about human good in *Well-Being: Its Meaning, Measurement, and Moral Importance* (Oxford: Oxford University Press, 1986) — find this line of argument particularly implausible in cases where the shameful deed is done to preserve one's life, which then goes on to contain many prudentially good things (see *ibid.*, ch. 4, esp. p. 69). Perhaps many will agree that a life-segment composed of, say, stealing a car and then enjoying its use cannot, because of its shamefulness, make the life to which it belongs more worth living. Perhaps the same is true of the life of the wrongful usurper, despite its prizes of power and control. It is often possible to restore the worthwhile status of such lives by simply giving up the illicit gain, but this may not be a morally acceptable option where life itself was wrongly purchased. And this may make our thinking about these cases special. For in all cases where we have brought shame upon ourselves, including these, we want there to be some way of restoring our lives (or some particular element of them) as worth having. Where the ill-gotten gain is life itself, most of us think that this restoration can be brought about by a combination of sincere regret (which seems, by the way, compatible with the disturbing thought that we would again succumb to the temptation), good works expressive of that regret, and, finally, the simple passage of time prudentially well spent.

haps there is honesty and truth (and even a kind of nobility) in shame-lessness, so long as it knows itself.

There are some species of the shameful which might make this re-sponse barely plausible. But let me close by pointing to other species that could scarcely be seen in this light. Consider first the *petty*, taken in the pejorative sense it almost always now has. We are used to thinking of the adoption of certain ends as petty (for example, setting too much store by small honors), but there are also petty means to certain small, but per-fectly sensible and therefore in no way pejoratively petty, ends. Everyone needs pencils and stamps, but it would be petty to save oneself incon-venience and expense by stealing them from the office. Suppose, how-ever, one could easily conceal the theft and enjoy its benefits. If rationality would therefore recommend the pilferage it would, in accordance with our earlier assumptions, show itself to be a petty excellence. If our life would thereby be more worth living, its betterness would be a petty per-fection.

The tension is even clearer in the case of the contemptible. Suppose the only way in the circumstances to achieve the support of influential peo-ple is to join in their cruel criticisms of a good friend. To go ahead with this kind of opportunistic infidelity would be contemptible in the extreme. To recommend it to others as an acceptable strategy of personal advance-ment would be just as bad. Thus, again, rationality would, in giving it the nod, be exerting a contemptible influence on the will. Similarly, the worthwhileness of the part of the agent's life in which the advancement was achieved by the betrayal of friendship would show itself to be a con-temptible worthwhileness. But surely it is doubtful whether either the ex-cellent or the worthwhile *can* be contemptible. The ideas do not seem to cohabit comfortably in the same logical space.

X

There is more than one possible moral to be gathered from this argu-ment. First, of course, there is the moral I prefer: that a neo-Humean con-ception of rationality and the good should be given up in the face of the objectivity of the moral and a proper respect for human life and practi-cal reason. But other responses are possible. One is to retain the neo-Humean accounts but give up the idea that the powerful moral terms we have been deploying can be used objectively. If some things that we most want as ends or need as means can be shameful, nasty, petty, contempt-ible, etc. then perhaps we should say that the use of such epithets is just so much emotive name-calling.

This might not be Hume's own response. While morality for him is rooted in the passions, it is also considerably objectified: by being universal, [16] by attaching itself to objective distinctions of character and action, [17] and by having the means to correct various biases of private connection. [18] Hume's response would surely be more radical, falling back on his rejection of the idea that there really is such a thing as *practical* reason or rationality — a rejection most sharply epitomized in his famous claim that reason (by which he clearly means theoretical reason in both its *a priori* and *a posteriori* forms) "is, and ought only to be, the slave of the passions." [19]

In any case, it is good to see what pressures the argument has placed upon us. If we are, as most of us seem to be, inclined to accept the objectivity of the shameful and the concepts that fall under it, and if we are also inclined to embrace a neo-Humean conception of practical rationality and the good life, then it will be hard for us to retain a certain form of self-respect as it applies to our reasons and lives. I think many of us will want to have it both ways. But perhaps we cannot.

Philosophy, University of California, Los Angeles

[16] Hume, *Treatise of Human Nature*, Book III, part I, section II, p. 474.

[17] See, for example, Hume, *An Enquiry Concerning the Principles of Morals*, section IX, in *Hume's Ethical Writings*, ed. Alasdair MacIntyre (London: Collier-Macmillan Ltd.), p. 109.

[18] Hume, *Treatise of Human Nature*, Book III, part I, section II, p. 472.

[19] *Ibid.*, Book II, part III, section III, p. 415.

ON SOME WAYS IN WHICH A THING CAN BE GOOD*

By Judith Jarvis Thomson

I

There are a great many ways in which a thing can be good.[1] What counts as a way of being good? I leave it to intuition. Let us allow that being a good dancer is being good in a way, and that so also is being a good carpenter. We might group these and similar ways of being good under the name *activity goodness*, since a good dancer is good at dancing and a good carpenter is good at carpentry. Everything good at doing something D is good in a way, and for each activity D, being good at D-ing falls into the class of ways of being good which I call activity goodness.

Again, let us allow that being a good hammer is being good in a way, and that so also is being a good butter knife. We might group these ways of being good under the name *equipment goodness*, since a good hammer is good for use in hammering nails and a good butter knife is good for use in buttering bread. Everything good for use in achieving a purpose P is good in a way, and for each purpose P, being good for use in achieving P falls into the class of ways of being good which I call equipment goodness.

Again, let us allow that tasting good is being good in a way, and so also are looking good, sounding good, and so on. The class here is *aesthetic goodness*.

Is all goodness goodness-in-a-way? Intuitively, the answer is yes: it seems right to think that everything is good only insofar as it is good in one or more ways. (Isn't it always legitimate to ask about a thing said to be good: in what way is it good? Not just what makes it good, but in what way it is?) But this too I must leave to intuition, for there is no answering this question in the absence of an analysis of what counts as a way of being good. The question will reappear in Section IV, however.

A class of ways of being good that will be of particular interest to us is what I will call *goodness-for*: its members include goodness for you, good-

* I am grateful to the other contributors to this volume — and to its editors — for their helpful comments on an earlier version of this essay. Many others made helpful comments on a later version; I am particularly indebted to Jonathan Bennett and David Gauthier.

[1] I take the very good idea that we should be attending to the ways in which a thing can be good from Georg Henrik von Wright, *The Varieties of Goodness* (London: Routledge & Kegan Paul, 1963), ch. 1. He divides the territory into what he calls forms of goodness. My division into ways of being good is finer-grained: he aims at a list of forms such that no one form is reducible to any other, whereas the ways I will mention include some that are reducible to others.

ness for your cat, and goodness for the birch tree in my back yard. We attribute goodness for Alfred when we say of Alfred, who has a cold, "Lemonade is good for him."

If "Lemonade is good for Alfred" is true then that is presumably because "Alfred's drinking lemonade is[2] good for Alfred" is true. (It is drinking that is normally the point, not, for example, bathing in.) More generally, it seems true, and I will assume it to be true, that goodness-for is always ultimately possessed by events and states of affairs, and only derivatively possessed by other things. Indeed, I will henceforth ignore the differences between events and states of affairs and suppose it true that goodness-for is always ultimately possessed by states of affairs.

Alfred might have a cold and yet drinking lemonade not be good for him. For example, it might be that Alfred's constitution is peculiar: his drinking lemonade would make his cold worse. Or second, it might be that although Alfred's drinking lemonade would alleviate his cold, his execution is being postponed only until his cold is alleviated. When one says that such and such is good for so and so, what one means is that the such and such is on balance in the so and so's interest — or so anyway I will suppose. And Alfred's drinking lemonade is not on balance in Alfred's interest if either of those two possibilities is true of him.

In short, I will assume that goodness-for is always ultimately possessed by states of affairs, and that what is good for a thing is what is on balance in the thing's interest.

I think it pays to distinguish the class I am calling goodness-for from the class I will call *goodness-from-a-point-of-view*, whose members include goodness from your point of view and goodness from my point of view. Philosophers who write of "agent-relative goodness" typically have both goodness-for and goodness-from-a-point-of-view in mind, perhaps not noticing the differences between them, perhaps not thinking the differences between them worth marking. But the differences do seem to me to be worth marking.

What I mean by goodness-from-a-point-of-view is (roughly) prizing, or, as I will put it, valuing: a thing is good from a person's point of view just in case the person values it.

It is clear that a thing can be good for a person without being good from that person's point of view. Suppose that Bert's drinking lemonade would be good for him: he has a cold, his drinking lemonade would alleviate it, and since the alleviation of his cold would on balance be in his interest, his drinking lemonade would on balance be in his interest. But

---

[2] We might well prefer the subjunctive here, thus: "Alfred's drinking lemonade *would be* good for Alfred." (And similarly: "Lemonade *would be* good for Alfred.") The subjunctive is preferable where the relevant event (Alfred's drinking lemonade) or state of affairs is not currently occurring or obtaining; the indicative is preferable where it is. There will be many cases to come in which the subjunctive would be preferable to the indicative, but I will for brevity and simplicity often use the indicative.

he might not know that his drinking lemonade would alleviate his cold, and therefore not value his drinking lemonade. If so, then while his drinking lemonade would be good for him, it is not good from his point of view.

It is also clear that a thing can be good from a person's point of view without being good for that person. Bert might think that his drinking furniture polish would alleviate his cold, and therefore value his drinking furniture polish. That is compatible with its being the case that his drinking furniture polish would not be good for him.

There may well be a more complex linkage between goodness-for and goodness-from-a-point-of-view. Thus it might be argued that a thing is good for A only if the thing itself, or something it is appropriately related to (causally, for example?), is good from A's point of view. It might be argued, more generally, that what is good for A is ultimately a function of what A values. Or perhaps that what is good for A is ultimately a function of what A values 'for its own sake'. Or, to bypass a familiar kind of objection, that what is good for A is ultimately a function of what A would value — or would value for its own sake — if A were fully informed, free of neuroses, and assessing the matter in a cool hour. On such theories, goodness-for is reducible to goodness-from-a-point-of-view.

According to a different kind of theory, goodness-from-a-point-of-view is reducible to goodness-for. Thus it might be asked why A would value doing such and such if A did not think that doing the such and such was, in some way, in his or her interest.

These (and their cousins) are substantive theories, and have to be argued for. I suggest we bypass them. It is clear, anyway, that a thing can be good for A without being good from A's point of view, and can be good from A's point of view without being good for A.

Now I left the question of what counts as a way of being good to intuition. I am sure that intuition yields that goodness-for is a class of ways of being good, but we might ask: does intuition yield that goodness-from-a-point-of-view is a class of ways of being good? I think not. Suppose that Bert's drinking lemonade would be good for him. Then his drinking lemonade is plausibly viewed as good in a way, for what makes it good for him is that it is, really and objectively is, on balance in his interest. But a person's valuing something is an entirely subjective fact about that person and the thing he or she values, a subjective fact whose existence does not itself seem to imply that the thing valued is itself in *any* way good. If Bert values his drinking furniture polish, then it follows (by definition) that his drinking it is good from his point of view. But on the assumption that Bert is physically constituted as the rest of us are, there is no way at all in which his drinking furniture polish is good. Being good from Bert's point of view, then, does not seem to be a way of being good, and goodness-from-a-point-of-view generally does not seem to be a class of ways of being good. I will not lean any weight on this point, however.

II

Let us now turn to a distinction that cuts across ways of being good, namely that between what I will call *derivative goodness* and *nonderivative goodness*. Very roughly, the derivatively good inherits its goodness, and the nonderivatively good does not.

In fact there are two distinctions in the offing here. In the first place, there is derivativeness and nonderivativeness *within a way of being good*. Nothing can be good in way W because it itself is good in way W; so let us say that a thing's goodness in way W is derivative within way W just in case the thing is good in way W because something else is good in way W. For example, let S be the state of affairs that consists in A's drinking lemonade, and suppose that S is good for A. Suppose also that S is good for A because a state of affairs that S will cause is good for A. It follows that S's goodness for A is derivative within goodness for A.

We really should make room for the possibility that a thing's goodness in way W is partly derivative and partly nonderivative within way W. For example, let T be the state of affairs that consists in the alleviation of A's cold, and suppose that T is good for A. Perhaps T is good for A partly because some state affairs that T will cause is good for A. (Perhaps it will cause A's feeling renewed enthusiasm for running next week's race.) Mightn't it be the case also that T is good for A partly just because of what T itself *is*? (T is an improvement in A's health, after all.) If so, then we should say that T's goodness for A is partly derivative within goodness for A and partly nonderivative within goodness for A. But for simplicity, I will for the most part ignore this more complicated possibility.

Consider the states of affairs that are good for A. Which of them are such that their goodness for A is nonderivative within goodness for A? What should we think of the alleviation of A's cold, which I called T in the preceding paragraph? I asked: mightn't it be the case that T is good for A (partly) because of what T *is*? We may think, intuitively, that the answer is yes. But here substantive theory may clash with intuition, for it might be held on theoretical grounds that there are drastic constraints on the range of things whose goodness for a person is nonderivative within goodness for that person, and on some such views, the alleviation of A's cold does not satisfy them. (Thus, for example, you might think that only states of affairs that consist in a person's feeling pleased are states of affairs whose goodness for a person is nonderivative within goodness for that person. The alleviation of A's cold might cause, but is not itself, A's feeling pleased.) I will throughout leave open what is the correct theory here.

But it might pay to mention that there surely are some ways of being good such that the goodness of anything at all that is good in that way is nonderivative within that way. I happen to own a good hammer. Is it a good hammer because something else is a good hammer? I should think not. I should think that nothing is a good hammer because something else is a good hammer. If so, then goodness in the way 'being a good hammer' is everywhere nonderivative within the way 'being a good hammer'.

In my first example of a thing derivatively good within a way W, the relation between the derivatively good thing, and the thing from which it inherits its goodness, was 'causes'. Thus I invited you to suppose that S, which is A's drinking lemonade, is good for A because a state of affairs that S will cause is good for A, and it followed that S's goodness for A is derivative within goodness for A.

The relation 'causes' is the most salient of the relations that can generate derivative goodness, but it is by no means the only one. Suppose that I have a cold, and that my drinking lemonade would be good for me. Then my making lemonade would be good for me. Indeed, my making lemonade would be good for me precisely because my drinking lemonade would be good for me. Thus the goodness for me of my making lemonade is derivative within goodness for me. But the relevant relation in this case is not 'causes': my making lemonade is not good for me because it is going to cause my drinking lemonade—it certainly is not going to cause my drinking lemonade. Presumably the relevant relation here is 'makes possible': my making lemonade is good for me because it makes my drinking lemonade possible.

Consider Charles's winning the state lottery, or being given a large sum of money. That might not be good for him. But if it is good for him, we can suppose that it is so, not because it will cause things that are good for him, but rather because it will make things that are good for him possible. If so, its goodness for him is derivative within goodness for him, though the relevant relation is 'makes possible', and not 'causes'.

Still other relations that can generate derivative goodness will come out shortly.

We have now met the distinction between derivativeness and non-derivativeness within a way of being good. A second distinction is between derivativeness and nonderivativeness *across ways of being good*: a thing's goodness in way W is derivative across a way of being good if the thing is good in way W because it itself, or something else, is good in some other way W'. For example, it might be that a certain thing is good for me because it itself, or something else, is good for you. If so, the thing's goodness for me is derivative across a way of being good.

Again, there are views according to which all ways of being good are reducible to just one fundamental way W. If some such view is correct, then a thing's goodness, for each other way W' in which it is good, is derivative across a way of being good.

Another example is the goodness of a good sign.[3] In what way is a good sign good? A good sign is presumably good in being a sign of some-

[3] I take this example from Fred Feldman, *Doing the Best We Can* (Dordrecht: D. Reidel Co., 1986), p. 26.

thing good, and perhaps we can say that being a good sign is itself a way of being good—we might call this way of being good *sign goodness*. (Good evidence is not good in this way. Everything that is evidence is a sign of something, but a thing can be good evidence without being a sign of something good.) What about the goodness of the good thing which a good sign is a sign *of*? Presumably that will vary from case to case. A thing might possess sign goodness in virtue of being a sign of something good for you, or good for me, or good in some other way of being good. In any case, the sign goodness of every good sign is derivative across a way of being good.

This example is of interest for yet another reason, since the relation between a good sign, and the good thing it inherits its goodness from, need not be, and in fact typically is not, 'causes' (or 'makes possible', for that matter). Suppose you have just developed a purple splotch on your knee. Your doctor may say, with pleasure, "That's a good sign!" Here what is in question is not the relation 'causes' itself, but the probability of a causal connection. Moreover, the connection between a good sign and what it inherits goodness from need not be entirely forward-looking. Thus while I suppose there could be cases in which your developing a purple splotch on your knee is a good sign in virtue of what it will itself (probably) cause, that is surely rare. Far more common are cases like this: you have a certain ailment, and the doctor has injected you with a drug which often cures it, but whose starting to work has as a side-effect the appearance of a purple splotch on the knee. Here your developing the splotch inherits sign goodness from its having (probably) been caused by something which will (probably) cause something good for you.

It is an interesting question whether the following kind of example supplies us with yet another relation that can generate derivativeness. Let S be the state of affairs that consists in A's admiring, or feeling pleased at or by, some entity X. Some philosophers would say that S is good if X is good, and that S is not good, or anyway not as good, if X is not good. Suppose they are right. Suppose also that X is in fact good. Then S is good and inherits at least some of its goodness from X.[4] But the relation between S and X in virtue of which S inherits goodness from X is not among those we have canvassed so far, for S neither causes X, nor makes X possible, nor is a sign of X. What is the relation? I leave it dark.[5]

---

[4] The kind of example I have in mind here is discussed by G. E. Moore in *Principia Ethica* (Cambridge: Cambridge University Press, 1903), ch. 6. An interesting recent discussion is Thomas Hurka's "Virtue as Loving the Good," in the present volume.

[5] Could it be said that the relation in this case is 'being caused by', and thus that S is good because it is caused by X? Among the difficulties for that idea is the following. A thing can plainly inherit goodness from what it causes; *can* a thing inherit goodness from what causes it? I should think not. It is worth noting, however, that my belief is correct only if goodness-from-a-point-of-view is not a class of ways of being good, for it is entirely possible to value a thing because of valuing what caused it. (For example, I might value a dent in my fender because, and only because, it was caused by my car's being driven into by my favorite movie actor.) This possibility issues from the very subjectivity in goodness from this

The prior question, however, is whether those philosophers *are* right. Suppose that X is the alleviation of your cold; S, then, is my feeling pleased at the alleviation of your cold. Suppose that X is good for you, and thus is good in a way. Is S therefore good? Well, in what way could S itself be thought good? It certainly needn't be good for you—or for me, or for anyone else.

Should we say that *moral goodness* is a way of being good, and that *that* is the way (or one way) in which my feeling pleased at the alleviation of your cold is good?

It is common enough in the literature for people to object to the idea that moral goodness is a way of being good. What exactly is wrong with that idea? "The notion of *moral goodness* . . . craves for a definition," says G. H. von Wright.[6] But why does it crave for a definition? One answer is perhaps plain enough: the fact that things of so many different onto-logical categories are said to be morally good. Some states of affairs (such as my feeling pleased at the alleviation of your cold) are said to be mor-ally good, but so also are some people, lives, character traits, acts, inten-tions, institutions, and so on and on. What can moral goodness *be* that it should be possessed by things in this wide array of categories?

But the discomfort von Wright expresses surely has a deeper source than merely the wide array of categories across which the term applies. Where a term T applies to things falling into a wide array of categories, one response is to look for the common essence: a property that the things all have in common, in virtue of which they are all T. If we respond in this way in the case of the term 'morally good', it would be no won-der if we felt discomfort, for what could morally good states of affairs, morally good people, morally good lives, and so on and on, be thought to have in common in virtue of which they are all morally good? But as we well know, this is not the only possible response, and in the case of some terms it is plainly the wrong response. (I hazard a guess that it is the wrong response in the case of any term that has cross-categorial ap-plication.) We do not ask what healthy people and healthy food have in common, in virtue of which they are healthy; we take the healthiness of certain foods to be derivative from the fact that a person's eating them makes the person healthy. Why should it not be the same for moral good-ness? And if it were clear enough (i) what it is for entities of one partic-ular ontological category C to be morally good, and (ii) that the moral goodness of entities in C is fundamental, then the notion of moral good-ness would trouble us less than it in fact does. Of course, the array would still generate discomfort—that is, we would still feel a need for an account for how entities in categories other than C inherit moral goodness from

---

or that point of view, which yields, intuitively, that goodness-from-a-point-of-view is not a class of ways of being good.

[6] Von Wright, *Varieties of Goodness*, p. 18.

morally good entities in category C. Nevertheless, I am sure that the notion of moral goodness does trouble people to the degree it does precisely because they think there is no category C of which both (i) and (ii) are clear enough. Indeed, they think there is no category C of which even (i) is clear enough.

That is not true of everyone, of course. What I have in mind by way of exceptions are those according to whom (i′) for an entity in the category of states of affairs to be morally good is for it to be either *intrinsically good* or appropriately related to an intrinsically good state of affairs, and (ii′) the moral goodness of states of affairs is fundamental. There are a variety of possible theories in the offing here. Most usually, I think, such a theory says that only things in the category of states of affairs are intrinsically good, but it might say that things in other categories are also intrinsically good, while saying that the intrinsic goodness of those other things is reducible to the intrinsic goodness of states of affairs.[7] Again, such a theory might be more or less ambitious: it might reduce not merely moral goodness, but also all (or only some) of the other ways of being good, to the intrinsic goodness of states of affairs. Another way in which such a theory might be more or less ambitious: it might reduce the moral goodness of *all* morally good things, of whatever category, to the intrinsic goodness of states of affairs, or it might reduce only the moral goodness of morally good acts to the intrinsic goodness of states of affairs, while offering an I.O.U. for the case of other morally good things, such as morally good people and governments. What will interest us from here on is, not the exact form such a theory might take, but rather the notion of intrinsic goodness itself.

Before turning to that notion, however, it pays to stop to stress that derivative goodness is not itself a way of being good. A derivatively good thing is a thing that inherits goodness from something, and what it inherits is not derivative goodness, but rather goodness in way W, for the appropriate W. What it inherits might be goodness for this or that person, or goodness from this or that person's point of view (if goodness-from-a-point-of-view is a way of being good), or sign goodness. And so on and on. Being told that a thing is derivatively good is not being told in what way the thing is good, but only that it inherited its goodness, either within or across a way of being good.

Since derivative goodness is not a way of being good, neither is non-derivative goodness.

---

[7] It is of interest how often one finds it said in the literature that *people* are intrinsically good. Mostly, I think, the philosopher who says this thinks that the intrinsic goodness of a person is reducible to the intrinsic goodness of the state of affairs that consists in the person's surviving, or to the intrinsic goodness of some other intrinsically good state or states of affairs involving the person. (Sometimes one simply cannot tell what such a philosopher means.) I suppose it possible to believe that people are not merely intrinsically good but irreducibly intrinsically good, but I find it hard to see what one who held this belief could have in mind by it.

My reason for thinking these points worth stressing will come out in Section IV below.

III

What is intrinsic goodness? The literature on the nature of intrinsic goodness is murky, but three classes of suggestive locutions turn up very often. Authors who define intrinsic goodness in terms of what "is good in itself" and what "is good in virtue of its intrinsic nature" are making use of members of the first class. Those who define it in terms of what "is valued for its own sake" and what "is good as an end" are making use of members of the second. Those who define it in terms of what people "ought" to do, or are under a "duty" to do, are making use of members of the third.[8]

Christine Korsgaard brings out that the ideas that seem to be pointed to by the first two classes of locutions are different.[9] She says that the claim that something "is good in itself" seems to be a claim about the source of its goodness, whereas the claim that something "is valued for its own sake" seems to be a claim, not about the source of the thing's goodness, but rather about how people feel about it.

Moreover, those two ideas differ from the idea that is pointed to by the third class of locutions. Claiming either that a thing's goodness has a certain source, or that people feel about it in a certain way, is surely different from claiming that people ought to behave in this or that way in respect of it.

What is to be made of this clutter?

IV

Those who opt for the first class of locutions say that S is intrinsically good just in case S "is good in itself" or "is good in virtue of its intrinsic nature."

---

[8] A rewriting of "has intrinsic value" in terms of the word "ought" turns up in the preface of Moore's *Principia Ethica*. He says: "I have tried to shew exactly what it is that we ask about a thing, when we ask whether it ought to exist for its own sake, is good in itself or has intrinsic value" (p. viii). But he here implies that "ought to exist for its own sake" and "is good in itself" are trivial rewritings of each other. Thus, his "ought to exist for its own sake" is not a member of the third class of locutions: it is rather a member of the first.

Elsewhere, Moore produces a sentence-form containing the word "duty" which he thinks is equivalent to (though not a definition of) a certain sentence-form containing the expression "intrinsically good," but it ascribes no duty to people. Rather, it tells us what would have been or was the duty of a creator, if there had been or was such a thing. What he has in mind by his sentence-form containing the word "duty" is therefore probably best understood as an explication of goodness in itself; it falls, not into the third class of locutions, but into the first. See G. E. Moore, "A Reply to My Critics," in *The Philosophy of G. E. Moore*, ed. P. A. Schilpp (New York: Tudor Publishing Co., 1942), pp. 608–9.

[9] See Christine Korsgaard, "Two Distinctions in Goodness," *The Philosophical Review*, vol. XCII, no. 2 (April 1983).

What is plainly in the minds of those who define intrinsic goodness in this way is the notion of nonderivative goodness, which we discussed in Section II. But it cannot be said that intrinsic goodness just is nonderivative goodness if intrinsic goodness is to be a way of being good, for nonderivative goodness is not itself a way of being good. *Is* intrinsic goodness supposed to be a way of being good? I said earlier that it seems right to think that everything is good only insofar as it is good in one or more ways. In particular, then, every intrinsically good thing is good only insofar as it is good in one or more ways. Is intrinsic goodness supposed to be a way of being good such that all intrinsically good things are good in at least that way?

Suppose it is. Then presumably it is *the* way of being good such that a thing's goodness in that way is not inherited. More precisely, intrinsic goodness is *the* way of being good such that S is good in that way just in case S is good and the following three conditions are met: (i) S is not good only because something else is good in that way, (ii) S is not good only because something else is good in some other way, and (iii) S is not good only because it itself is good in some other way. S's meeting condition (i) secures that its goodness is nonderivative within intrinsic goodness; S's meeting conditions (ii) and (iii) secures that its goodness is nonderivative across ways of being good.[10]

But is there such a way of being good? What fixes that there is a unique way of being good such that all good things S that meet the three conditions are good in that way? Mightn't there be no one way such that all of them are good in that way? We have not here been told anything positive about what this (putative) way of being good is; what we have been told is wholly negative. I said at the outset that I would leave to intuition what counts as a way of being good, and I therefore have no argument to the effect that what we have reached does not itself count as a way of being good. But I can see no good reason to think it does.

An interesting further question emerges as follows. Suppose that a state of affairs S is good, and does meet the three conditions, and that we therefore say that it is good in the way 'intrinsic goodness'. Suppose, further, that a state of affairs R causes S. I am sure that friends of intrinsic goodness would conclude that R is good: R, they would say, inherits goodness from S. (Strictly speaking, they would conclude only that R is in a measure good, since R might cause bad things too, and the bad outweigh the good. Let us ignore this possible complication.) In what way is R good? *What* did R inherit from S?

Again, suppose that a state of affairs Q makes S possible. I am sure that friends of intrinsic goodness would conclude that Q is good: Q, they would say, inherits goodness from S. In what way is Q good?

---

[10] Those who say that my feeling pleased at the alleviation of your cold is intrinsically good, *and* that it possesses more intrinsic goodness if the alleviation of your cold is good than if the alleviation of your cold is not good, will have to modify this construal of intrinsic goodness. A number of possible revisions are available; I will not canvass them.

Again, suppose that a state of affairs T consists in a person's feeling pleased at S. Many friends of intrinsic goodness would conclude that T is good: T, they would say, inherits goodness from S. In what way is T good?

Is there supposed to be a unique way of being good such that R, Q, and T are all good in that way? We cannot of course say that they are all good in the way 'intrinsic goodness', since by definition, intrinsic goodness cannot be inherited. And we cannot say that they are all good in the way 'derivative goodness', since derivative goodness is not a way of being good.

We seem to be in need of another concept. Suppose we were to say that there is a way of being good — borrowing a term from Moore, I will call it *absolute goodness*[11] — such that S is nonderivatively good in that way, whereas R, Q, and T are derivatively good in that way. We could say that S's absolute goodness is nonderivative within absolute goodness, that being what marks S as intrinsically good; and we could say that what R, Q, and T inherit from S is absolute goodness, though their absolute goodness is derivative within absolute goodness.

We now have on our hands the question what absolute goodness is. We have been told that intrinsically good things possess it nonderivatively, and that things that inherit goodness from intrinsically good things possess it only derivatively, but we have not been told what it comes to for a thing to be good in that way.

One thing that will not do is to define absolute goodness as *the* way in which states of affairs can be good, and thus say that an absolutely good state of affairs just is one that is good of the kind 'state of affairs'. For states of affairs can be good in many different ways. Some are good for me, some good for you. Some are good signs.

Perhaps we feel an urge to say: absolute goodness is just pure, straight, neat, bare goodness, some inherited and some not. That cannot on any view be a *way* of being good.

Alternatively, we may feel an urge to say: absolute goodness is not a way of being good at all. And perhaps we feel an urge to say that intrinsic goodness is also not a way of being good. So perhaps we went off the track at the outset.

Let us go back. I said that it seems right to think that everything is good only insofar as it is good in one or more ways. If so, then every intrinsically good thing must be good in one or more ways. But we need not say that intrinsic goodness is a way in which they are all good; we can allow that intrinsically good things may be good in a variety of different ways, and that there may possibly be no way in which they are all good. We can say that intrinsic goodness just is nonderivative goodness, and not be at

---

[11] We will get to Moore's own use of this term in the following section.

all troubled by the fact that it is therefore not a way of being good. Similarly for the broader notion of absolute goodness.

But I doubt that this would really satisfy those who think that the notion of intrinsic goodness has an important role to play in moral theory. For one thing, if intrinsic goodness is interpreted in this way, it is not clear what intrinsic betterness could consist in; yet friends of intrinsic goodness do make heavy use of the comparative. For another, interpreting intrinsic goodness in this way deprives it of content. For example, I mentioned in the preceding section that some people take the view—I called it (i′)—that for an entity in the category of state of affairs to be morally good is for it to be either intrinsically good or appropriately related to an intrinsically good state of affairs. If intrinsic goodness just is nonderivative goodness, then what (i′) tells us is that for a state of affairs to be morally good is for it to be either nonderivatively or derivatively good. In short, for a state of affairs to be morally good is for it to be good. If "morally good" has for you a sense narrower than the sense of "good" itself, you will think this plainly false.

Let us turn to a second way of defining intrinsic goodness, one which does not deprive it of content.

V

Those who opt for the second of the three classes of locutions I mentioned in Section III say that S is intrinsically good just in case S "is valued for its own sake" and "is good as an end."

What are we to make of "is good as an end"? It is typically contrasted with "is good as a means," and perhaps some who so use it mean merely "is good in itself." Under that interpretation, it belongs in the class of locutions discussed in the preceding section.

Under a second possible interpretation, it means the same as "is valued for its own sake." And what are we to make of that idea? Valued for its own sake *by whom*? Anyone? It is altogether too familiar a fact that what some people value for its own sake is a pretty nasty affair.

I drew attention in Section I to a similar objection to the idea of reducing goodness-for to goodness-from-a-point-of-view. A familiar way of dealing with that objection is to impose a constraint: we should ask, not what people do in fact value, but rather what they would value if they were fully informed, free of neuroses, and assessing the matter in a cool hour. Perhaps imposing that constraint would allow us to reduce goodness-for to goodness-from-a-point-of-view; that is, there really is room for the idea that what is in a person's interest is what is, or contributes to, what he or she would value under this constraint. Thus if a person would love the nasty even under this constraint, then perhaps we should say so be it: it *is* in his or her interest.

Would imposing that same constraint do the trick here? Is it plausible to think that what has intrinsic goodness just is what a person (all people?) would value for its own sake if he or she were fully informed, free of neuroses, and assessing the matter in a cool hour? No, unless we can show that people really would not love the nasty under this constraint. Can we show this?

On the other side of this coin is the fact that many people do not value for their own sakes many things which surely must be intrinsically good if anything is. Consider the newborn infant, put out with the trash. Can we show that those who put the infant out would have valued its survival had they been fully informed, free of neuroses, and assessing the matter in a cool hour?

I will not dwell on these difficulties. In light of them, it would presumably be better to say that for a thing to be intrinsically good is not for it to be *valued* for its own sake, but rather for it to be valu*able* for its own sake. Another way of expressing this idea is to say that intrinsic goodness is a function of what is *worth* valuing for its own sake, or of what *deserves* to be valued for its own sake. That, intuitively, seems a closer approximation to what is really at work in those who define intrinsic goodness in terms of locutions in this second class.

What is it for a state of affairs to be valuable for its own sake, or to be worth valuing for its own sake, or to deserve being valued for its own sake? One possible answer is this: for a state of affairs to be valuable for its own sake, and so on, is for it to be "good in itself." This merely sends us back to the first class of locutions.

An interesting second possible answer is suggested by some remarks made by G. E. Moore in the course of discussing egoism in *Principia Ethica*.[12] Moore says:

> The only reason I can have for aiming at 'my own good,' is that it is *good absolutely* that what I so call should belong to me . . . (p. 99)

and

> if [a thing] is not good at all, what reason can [a man] have for aiming at it? how can it be a rational end for him? (p. 100).

These remarks are premises in an argument to the conclusion:

> When, therefore, I talk of anything I get as 'my own good,' I must mean either that the thing I get is good, or that my possessing it is good (p. 98)

---

[12] Moore, *Principia Ethica*, ch. 3, pp. 98–102.

—good absolutely, as he later says. Thus for a thing to be 'my own good' is for it or my possessing it to be good absolutely. There are a number of ways in which this conclusion can be interpreted, according to whether we interpret 'my own good' as goodness for me, or as goodness from my point of view. Is Moore concluding here that goodness-for is reducible to absolute goodness? Is he concluding here that goodness-from-a-point-of-view is reducible to absolute goodness?[13] No matter for our purposes; what is important for us here is not Moore's conclusion but his premises.

His thought seems to be this: I have reason to aim at my getting a thing if and only if my getting it is good absolutely. I have reason to aim at my doing a thing if and only if my doing it is good absolutely. More generally, I have reason to aim at a state of affairs if and only if it is good absolutely. A fortiori, if a state of affairs is good absolutely, I have reason to aim at it.

Moore then goes on to say:

> But if it is *good absolutely* that I should have [a thing], then everyone else has as much reason for aiming at *my* having it, as I have myself. (p. 99)

Thus if a state of affairs is good absolutely, then not merely do I have reason to aim at it: everyone has reason to aim at it, and indeed, has as much reason to aim at it as I do. In short:

(1) If a state of affairs is good absolutely, then everyone has equal reason to aim at it.

---

[13] A third possibility is that it is goodness-for-its-own-sake-from-a-point-of-view that Moore concludes is reducible to absolute goodness. (After all, the man who says "Money is my good" presumably does not mean merely that he values money: he presumably means that he values money for its own sake.)

A fourth possibility is that Moore's conclusion is a denial that there is any such thing as goodness-for, or goodness-from-a-point-of-view: under this interpretation, he is saying that the only goodness is absolute goodness. I *think* this is how Eric Mack interprets the conclusion in "Moral Individualism: Agent-Relativity and Deontic Restraints," *Social Philosophy & Policy*, vol. 7, no. 1 (Autumn 1989), p. 85. But I find it hard to believe that Moore would deny that a state of affairs might be in a person's interest, or that a person might value this or that. If one or other of those concepts is his target here, then surely his point is derivativeness and not denial.

But perhaps Moore has nothing like this in mind at all. Under a fifth interpretation, his target is neither goodness-for nor goodness-from-a-point-of-view, but rather a first cousin of what students have in mind when they say "Ah, that proposition may be true-for-you, but perhaps it isn't true-for-others," and reject the following gloss on their words: "Ah, you may think that proposition true, but perhaps others don't." Among its first cousins is: "Ah, that state of affairs may be good-in-way-W-for-you, but perhaps it isn't good-in-way-W-for others." I think there is much to be said for the idea that this is what concerns Moore here, and that he does not mean that goodness-in-way-W-for-a-person is derivative, but that there is no such thing. For he thinks it relevant to say: "The *good* [of a thing] can in no possible sense be 'private' or belong to me; any more than a thing can *exist* privately or *for* one person only." He might as well have said: "any more than a proposition can be true privately or for one person only."

Moore does not in these pages explicitly say, but seems plainly to believe also

> (2) If everyone has equal reason to aim at a state of affairs, then it is good absolutely,

and thus

> (3) A state of affairs is good absolutely if and only if everyone has equal reason to aim at it.

But what are we to take "good absolutely" to mean in (3)? Not intrinsic goodness, I should think. A friend of intrinsic goodness might well accept

> (1′) If a state of affairs is intrinsically good, then everyone has equal reason to aim at it,

but is sure to reject

> (2′) If everyone has equal reason to aim at a state of affairs, then it is intrinsically good.

For suppose that a state of affairs S is intrinsically good. It seems plausible to many people to conclude that everyone has equal reason to aim at S. Suppose that a state of affairs R causes S. It seems plausible to those people to conclude that everyone has equal reason to aim at R—for after all, if one brings about R, one by hypothesis thereby brings about S. But no one would conclude that R is intrinsically good. R might well not be intrinsically good: R might merely inherit goodness from S. I am inclined to think it is for this very reason that Moore speaks (in the pages I refer to) of absolute goodness rather than of intrinsic goodness. And it suggests itself that what he had in mind by his term "absolute goodness" is what I used it to refer to in the preceding section.

Now while it seems plain that Moore would have accepted (3), he plainly would not have accepted it as a definition of absolute goodness. (As we know, he thinks that good cannot be defined at all.) But others would accept it,[14] and they might then go on to define intrinsic goodness in this way: a thing's intrinsic goodness is that part of its absolute goodness which is nonderivative within absolute goodness. And it may

---

[14] The underlying idea here is widespread in current ethical writing. Here, for example, is Shelly Kagan:

> To say that from the moral standpoint one outcome is objectively better than another, is to say that *everyone* has a reason to choose the better outcome.

See Kagan, *The Limits of Morality* (Oxford: Clarendon Press, 1989), p. 61.

seem satisfactory to define intrinsic goodness in this manner, since doing so may really seem to capture what it is for a state of affairs to be intrinsically good in the sense of being valuable for its own sake, or being worth valuing for its own sake, or deserving to be valued for its own sake.

Notice, moreover, that this definition tells us nothing about the relation between intrinsic or absolute goodness and other ways of being good. People who define intrinsic goodness in this manner may be expected to have views about such things, but their views about them are substantive, to be argued on their merits, and not to be accepted as analytically true. This is itself an attractive feature of the definition, since it gives content to those arguments—it gives them something to be *about*.

On the other hand, we are entitled to ask for examples. What exactly can be thought intrinsically good in the sense just given this term? Indeed, what exactly can be thought absolutely good in the sense of (3)? Which things does everyone have equal reason to aim at? Consider the alleviation of your cold. Other things being equal, *you* have reason to aim at it. So do I, if you matter to me. But what if you do not matter to me? Does Queen Elizabeth have reason to aim at it? Consider your becoming happier than you currently are. Do Queen Elizabeth and I have reason— in fact, as much reason as you have—for aiming at it? I cannot bring myself to believe that we do.

Of course, it could be granted that we do not all have equal reason to aim at the alleviation of your cold or at your becoming happier, and the conclusion could be drawn that neither of these states of affairs is absolutely good. A fortiori, neither is intrinsically good. But this is not a happy conclusion for friends of intrinsic goodness to be forced to. Many (all?) of them would insist that a person's becoming happier *is* intrinsically good, or at least that a person's becoming happier is, other things being equal, intrinsically good. (I add the qualification in light of the fact that some people would say that a person's becoming happier is intrinsically good only if the person deserves to become happier—and thus, for example, that a villain's becoming happier is not at all a good thing.)

The word "reason" slithers in current moral philosophy, and I fancy that those who define intrinsic goodness in terms of what everyone has reason to aim at are really doing so because of the existence of a quite different use of the word. Whether

(4) A has reason to aim at X

is true surely turns on what A values, or on what is in A's interest, or on both; and the range of things that we all value equally, or that are equally in our interests, or both, is surely drastically limited. But there are other uses of "reason." Consider:

(4′) There is reason to believe A ought to aim at X.

Whether that is true does not turn on what A values, or on what is in A's interest, or on both. For most (all?) people A, there surely are things X such that there is reason to believe A ought to aim at X, though A does not value X, and X is not in A's interest.

But it is not a slither from the use of "reason" in (4') to its use in (4) that explains the inclination to define intrinsic goodness in terms of what everyone has reason to aim at. Schema (4') is purely epistemic. Suppose some wise commentator on the passing scene—Dora, let us say—arrives at the conclusion that A ought to aim at X. Dora being wise, the very fact that she arrives at this conclusion is reason to believe that A ought to aim at X; therefore, there is reason to believe that A ought to aim at X. Thus, (4') is true in this case. But a philosopher who defines intrinsic goodness in terms of what everyone has reason to aim at does not have something purely epistemic in mind.

Something of interest to moral philosophy is missing in the story about Dora. No doubt Dora's arriving at her conclusion is reason to believe that A ought to do X, but, as many philosophers would say, Dora's arriving at her conclusion is not itself *reason for A to do X*. Given Dora arrives at her conclusion, (4') is true. But that leaves open whether

(4") There is reason for A to aim at X

is true.

I think (4") a piece of technical terminology, invented by philosophers to fill a gap in English; I think that the layman does not say the likes of (4"), or at least that the layman who says such words does not mean by them what philosophers do. No matter. We are familiar enough with what is being got at by a philosopher who says the likes of (4"), just as we are familiar with other locutions, such as

Prima facie A ought to aim at X,

and

Other things being equal, A ought to aim at X,

which such a philosopher would accept as equivalents of (4").

Now I fancy that it is a slither from the use of "reason" in (4") to its use in (4) that explains the inclination to define intrinsic goodness in terms of what everyone has reason to aim at. What philosophers who so define intrinsic goodness have in mind is not what everyone does in fact have reason to aim at, or what there is reason to believe everyone ought to aim at. They have in mind, rather, what—*prima facie*, or other things being equal—everyone ought to aim at. Thus philosophers who accept

(3) A state of affairs is good absolutely if and only if everyone has
    equal reason to aim at it

as a definition of absolute goodness really have in mind something that
can be expressed in a number of ways, including:

(3*) A state of affairs is good absolutely if and only if for all A, other
    things being equal, A ought to aim at it.

The appearance here of the word "ought" brings us to the third of the
three classes of locutions that turn up in definitions of intrinsic goodness,
so we should turn to it.

I drew attention earlier to the fact that saying that people feel about a
thing in a certain way — that they value it for its own sake — is surely different from saying that people ought to behave in this way or that. Yet
it really is no wonder if a person who begins by trying to define intrinsic goodness in terms of what people value, ends by defining it in terms
of what people ought to do. What people in fact value is a mixed business, and in some cases thoroughly unappetizing. Hadn't we better exclude those cases by shifting from what people in fact value to what is
worth valuing? And (we may very naturally go on to ask) what could it
come to for something to be worth valuing if not that people ought to do
their appropriate share of seeing to its production and preservation?

VI

No one, I think, supposes that for a thing to be intrinsically good is for
it to be the case, simply, that everyone ought to aim at it. Friends of intrinsic goodness make quite clear that one thing's being intrinsically good
is compatible with another thing's being intrinsically better, and they allow for the possibility that one ought to aim at the better rather than at
the good. And I say only "the possibility," for they tell us that the question whether we ought to aim at one state of affairs rather than another
turns on other things besides the relative degree of intrinsic goodness of
the two states of affairs. There is, in particular, the question what would
be the consequences of aiming at the one rather than the other, and what
are *their* degrees of intrinsic goodness. On some views there is also the
further question whether aiming at the one rather than the other would
constitute violating a right. (Perhaps most philosophers who make use of
the notion of intrinsic goodness are consequentialists, but their making
use of the notion does not itself fix that they must be.) Thus if you wish
to define intrinsic goodness in terms of what people ought to aim at, you
need to incorporate a qualifier. One way to do that is by defining intrin-

sic goodness as absolute goodness that is nonderivative within absolute goodness, and then defining absolute goodness as follows:

(3*) A state of affairs is good absolutely if and only if for all A, other things being equal, A ought to aim at it.

This leaves open for further discussion what might or might not make other things be unequal. As it also leaves open what might make it harder or easier for other things to be unequal—we need an account of that too, the absolutely better presumably being that in respect of which it is harder for other things to be unequal.

First cousins of two questions we asked in the preceding section arise here too. What exactly can be thought intrinsically good in the sense just given that term? Indeed, what exactly can be thought absolutely good in the sense of (3*)? Consider the alleviation of your cold. Is it true that, other things being equal, I ought to aim at it? Is it true that Queen Elizabeth ought to? Consider your becoming happier than you currently are. It is true of Queen Elizabeth and me that, other things being equal, we ought to aim at it? But perhaps we should bypass these questions, since they cannot be answered in the absence of an account of what might or might not make other things be unequal.

A more serious problem is this: defining intrinsic goodness in terms of the word "ought" gets things backwards for the purposes of the contemporary philosopher who makes use of that notion. The concept 'intrinsic goodness' does not figure in contemporary moral philosophy because it is thought to be, itself, of interest; what really interests contemporary moral philosophers who attend to intrinsic goodness is what a person ought to do. Philosophers who make use of the concept 'intrinsic goodness' begin with it, inviting us to agree that we already have it. Well, perhaps they recognize that their readers need a bit of nudging. ("See, it's not just goodness, it's goodness *in itself*, valuableness *for its own sake*.") But then they turn straightway to the main enterprise of working out what we ought to do. The theory they then arrive at tells us what more or less complex function of intrinsic goodness determines what a person ought to do. Now it is plain that if their theory is to tell them this, they cannot also define intrinsic goodness in terms of what a person ought to do, on pain of turning their theory into a triviality. They must have an independent source of understanding of intrinsic goodness in order for their theory to have content.

No one owns the expression "intrinsic goodness," of course, and philosophers are free to define it as they wish, and free to go on to make such theoretical use as they wish of the concept thereby singled out. In particular, they are free to define it in terms of what people ought to do. There might well be some interesting theoretical use to be made of a concept so defined, but I have no idea what it would be.

VII

A number of moral philosophers have objected to the concept 'intrinsic goodness' in recent years.[15] As is plain, I think it is, at best, a concept in dire need of clarification.

And what would happen to moral philosophy if we simply washed our hands of intrinsic goodness? Philippa Foot suggests that then consequentialism could be laid finally to rest. Many philosophers, Foot among them, reject consequentialism since they think it yields counter-intuitive consequences about what people ought to do. But she says it continues to "haunt" us. "What," she asks, "is so compelling about consequentialism? It is, I think, the rather simple thought that it can never be right to prefer a worse state of affairs to a better."[16] We are inclined to think that must be true. But when we come to see that there is no such thing as one state of affairs' being worse or better than another, we no longer have that thought, and are therefore free of the spell.

Let us take this more slowly. The consequentialist begins at stage (i) by introducing us to intrinsic goodness, and then tells us at stage (ii) that what people ought to do is a simple function of it — what we ought to do is maximize it. We let the consequentialist get through stage (i), although as I said, we may need a bit of nudging before we are able to absorb the idea of intrinsic goodness; we object only at stage (ii). Our objection consists in our drawing attention to consequentialism's counter-intuitive consequences. But we continue to feel a lurking discomfort, for we have granted the consequentialist the concept 'intrinsic goodness' at stage (i), and how can it ever be right to prefer a worse state of affairs to a better? Foot says that we should not have allowed the consequentialist to get to stage (ii): we should have objected right at the outset, at stage (i).

Now consequentialism is standardly defined as the thesis that one ought to maximize intrinsic goodness, and if there is no such thing as intrinsic goodness, then consequentialism so defined certainly should not haunt us: it is mere confusion.

But what philosophers find tempting about consequentialism is not, I think, the concept 'intrinsic goodness' itself — or, rather, not *only* that concept. Consider a theory which, in light of standard usage, probably should not be called consequentialism, and which I will therefore call interest consequentialism: one ought to maximize goodness-for. (I call it interest consequentialism since what is good for a thing is what is on balance in the thing's interest.) Some might impose a constraint to the effect

---

[15] See, for example, John M. Taurek, "Should the Numbers Count?" *Philosophy and Public Affairs*, vol. 6, no. 4 (Summer 1977). But I am not absolutely clear whether Taurek thinks that there is no such concept at all, or merely that the survival of more people is not to be considered intrinsically better just by virtue of being the survival of more people.

See also Philippa Foot, "Utilitarianism and the Virtues," *Mind*, vol. XCIV, no. 374 (April 1985); her target is plainly the concept 'intrinsic goodness' itself.

[16] Foot, "Utilitarianism and the Virtues," p. 198.

that it is only goodness for people that counts; others might allow goodness for all sentient creatures to count; still others might allow goodness for all living things to count (including the birch tree in my back yard). No matter. I am inclined to think that those who are tempted by consequentialism, as standardly defined in terms of intrinsic goodness, are tempted, in part, because they are tempted by the idea expressed in interest consequentialism.

Interest consequentialism, however, is a theory that says nothing whatever about intrinsic goodness, and therefore is safe against any assault on intrinsic goodness.

Now interest consequentialism (in all of the possible versions I mentioned) has consequences that are fully as counter-intuitive as does consequentialism standardly defined. Indeed, the most familiar of the putative counter-cases to consequentialism as standardly defined are equally counter-cases to interest consequentialism. (Consider, for example, the transplant surgeon who can save five people by extracting organs from a sixth.) And I think that Foot would ask: why would you be attracted by interest consequentialism if you did not think that maximizing goodness-for *is* maximizing intrinsic goodness? I think there is something right here. Insofar as we think the world will be intrinsically better if we do a thing than if we do not, we find it hard to resist the step to the conclusion that we ought to do the thing. (How can it ever be right to prefer a worse state of affairs to a better?) Suppose we merely think that the world will be better for more people if we do the thing than if we do not; the step from there to the conclusion that we ought to do the thing is a longer one.

In short, interest consequentialism is a more clearly *substantive* moral thesis than is consequentialism as standardly defined. Consequentialism as standardly defined feels close to analytic;[17] interest consequentialism does not. And like any other substantive moral thesis, interest consequentialism stands or falls with the acceptability of its substantive moral consequences. Putative counter-cases to it cannot be brushed aside as mere intuition; they are no more mere intuition than is interest consequentialism itself.

On the other hand, there isn't nothing lying behind interest consequentialism. How can it ever be right to prefer a state of affairs that is in the interest of fewer people to a state of affairs that is in the interest of more? We do, I think, feel some pressure to say it cannot, and to the extent to which we do, the temptations of accepting *some* version of consequentialism remain. But so also does the problem of making clear exactly what sets limits to it.

---

[17] This fact has an obvious connection with the temptation to define intrinsic goodness in terms of what people ought to do.

VIII

The question to be asked about intrinsic goodness seems to me really to be this: does it have any role to play? Is there any moral phenomenon that cannot adequately be accounted for or understood without making appeal to *some* such concept? Perhaps the answer is yes. Certainly no assault on the existing definitions of intrinsic goodness — such as mine in sections IV through VI — shows by itself that the answer is no. I said I think that the concept 'intrinsic goodness' is, at best, in dire need of clarification. The clarification it really needs is the description of something in moral life that we have to call on it for an explanation of.

Philosophy, Massachusetts Institute of Technology

THE HUMAN GOOD AND THE AMBITIONS
OF CONSEQUENTIALISM

By James Griffin

I want to look at one aspect of the human good: how it serves as the basis for judgments about the moral right. One important view is that the right is always derived from the good. I want to suggest that the more one understands the nature of the human good, the more reservations one has about that view.

I. One Route to Consequentialism

Many of us think that different things make a life good, with no one deep value underlying them all. My own list includes: enjoyment, accomplishing something with one's life, deep personal relations, certain sorts of understanding, and the elements of a characteristically human existence (autonomy, liberty).[1]

Most of us also think that moral right and wrong are based, in some way or other, in how well individual lives go, and that the moral point of view is, in some sense or other, impartial between lives. Utilitarianism is a prominent, but not the only, way of spelling out this intuition. There is no reason why an account of the human good needs to be confined, in the classical utilitarian way, to happiness or to fulfillment of desire (on the usual understanding of that notion). Nor is there any reason why impartiality has to be confined to maximizing the good, counting everybody for one and nobody for more than one. We may generalize.

Let us broaden the notion of the good. We might say, for instance, that though happiness is a good, so are the other items on my list. But though broadened, this notion of the good stays within the confines of individual goods; it still has to do with human well-being, with what promotes the quality of one person's life.

But it may be that further features of consequences — say, that individual goods are distributed equally or that no human rights are violated — also help to determine right and wrong. Let us broaden the notion of the good further: we add to individual goods such moral goods as equality and respect for human rights. When we look at consequences, we now

---

[1] I start where other discussions finish. See, for example, my book *Well-Being* (Oxford: Clarendon Press, 1986), pt. I, and a more recent article, "Against the Taste Model," in *Interpersonal Comparisons of Well-Being*, ed. Jon Elster and John Roemer (Cambridge: Cambridge University Press, 1991).

look not just at the quantity of individual goods but also, say, at their pattern of distribution.

Now, an intuitive feature of the word 'consequences' is that the consequences of an act flow from, and thus follow, the act. But that restriction excludes goods that make essential reference to what precedes the act — for instance, the fact that a certain act would keep a (past) promise, or that it would bring a just distribution seen over life as a whole (past, present, or future), or that it is what persons deserve given what they have done (in the past). Therefore, let us now broaden the word 'consequences' to include any state of affairs that makes up a history (past, present, or future), and thereby broaden the word 'good' to include desert, promise-keeping, historical conceptions of justice, and so on.[2]

We have said nothing so far about another feature of classical utilitarianism: that it uses the maximization of good as the standard of right and wrong. But the 'maximum' is the greatest quantity, and once the notion of the good grows to include, say, promise-keeping, there is no obvious quantity to be maximized. But there is a more general notion than the maximum, namely the 'optimum'. The optimum could be, but need not be, the greatest in size. We could say, then, that consequentialism is the view that it is wrong to produce less than the optimum. But why confine the consequentialist standard to the optimum? One might regard as morally right the first available action whose consequences score above a certain level of aspiration.[3] Therefore, let us broaden the standard of the right by linking it not to the optimum but to the 'satisfactory' or 'good enough', interpreted in such a way that one option is that only the optimum is good enough.[4]

Where does this leave us? It leaves us at what we now call 'consequentialism'.[5] Consequentialists, on this wide and commonly accepted defi-

[2] Derek Parfit, for instance, takes this step in his definition of 'consequentialism' in *Reasons and Persons* (Oxford: Clarendon Press, 1984), p. 26.

[3] Michael Slote does this in his book *Common-Sense Morality and Consequentialism* (London: Routledge, 1985), ch. 3. He there develops Herbert Simon's 'satisficing' model of rational strategy. On this model, one should: (1) fix an aspiration level, (2) enumerate one's options, (3) evaluate them as one proceeds, and (4) accept the first option to meet one's aspiration level. See, for example, Herbert Simon, "A Behavioral Model of Rationality" in his *Models of Bounded Rationality* (Cambridge: MIT Press, 1982).

[4] This step takes us beyond what a lot of our contemporaries *say* about 'consequentialism': it is common to make optimizing part of the word's definition. See, for example, Samuel Scheffler, *The Rejection of Consequentialism* (Oxford: Clarendon Press, 1982), p. 1; and Parfit, *Reasons and Persons*, p. 24. However, Michael Slote argues for including the 'satisficing' standard within the bounds of consequentialism. See his *Common-Sense Morality and Consequentialism*, pp. 36–37. But these authors are unlikely to resist my broadening of the standard of the right; it contradicts nothing important in what they say.

[5] See, for example, Parfit, *Reasons and Persons*, section 10; Scheffler, *The Rejection of Consequentialism*, pp. 1–2; Shelly Kagan, *The Limits of Morality* (Oxford: Clarendon Press, 1989), pp. xi, 7; and Philip Pettit, "Consequentialism," in *A Companion to Ethics*, ed. P. Singer (Oxford: Blackwell, 1991). This is a big change from what Elizabeth Anscombe meant when she coined the term in 1958 in "Modern Moral Philosophy," *Philosophy*, vol. 33 (1958). On her

nition, are those who derive the right from the good in this sense: moral prohibitions on, or permissions to, an individual agent — the *do's, don't's,* and *may do's* that are addressed to a particular person — are derived from judgments about the amount of good (in this broadened sense of 'good') in the consequences (in this broadened sense of 'consequences') of his possible actions. In contrast, nonconsequentialists are those who hold that some *do's, don't's,* and *may do's* are not derived from the good, even in this broadened sense. In short, consequentialists hold that all goods are to be promoted, while nonconsequentialists hold that some goods are to be honored.[6] An innocent person's right not to be killed is one of the goods (in the broadened sense). Consequentialists respond to this good by bringing about its respect by agents generally — that is, by promoting it. Nonconsequentialists respond simply by respecting it themselves in their own actions as individuals — that is, by honoring it.[7]

II. BACKING UP: A THREAT OF EMPTINESS

I think that there is something deeply puzzling about consequentialism, on this wide definition of it. The puzzle, for me, centers on how one is supposed to move from the expanded notion of the good to the right. It is not especially puzzling how a utilitarian makes the move. A utilitarian starts with a more or less comprehensible account of the good, which is supposed to be independent of the right, and then adds rules for deriving the right from the good. But once we expand the good in the way that we have just seen, many of the goods that are added do not lend themselves easily to this derivation. It is hard even to understand what it is to 'promote' them.

---

account, nonconsequentialists hold that certain acts are ruled out morally whatever the results; on the current use, they hold merely that some acts are ruled out morally on grounds other than their results.

[6] I borrow Philip Pettit's handy way of summarizing the distinction. See his "Consequentialism."

[7] I prefer summarizing the distinction between consequentialism and nonconsequentialism in terms of 'promoting' and 'honoring' values, rather than in the more widespread terms of 'agent-neutral' and 'agent-relative' obligations. Derek Parfit suggests that consequentialism gives to all agents common moral aims and is, thus, agent-neutral, while nonconsequentialism gives different agents different aims and is, thus, agent-relative (see his *Reasons and Persons,* p. 27). But some nonconsequentialist *do's* and *don't's,* such as "Do no murder," are also given to all agents. What Parfit means, of course, is that for me that prohibition is statable as "Griffin, do no murder," and for him it is statable as "Parfit, do no murder." This merely brings out a feature of *do's* and *don't's.* The feature in question, however, does not go morally very deep. Consequentialists, too, may hold that agents must be given *do's* and *don't's;* they may even hold that our decision procedures will be largely constituted by *do's* and *don't's.* The important difference is that for a consequentialist these *do's* and *don't's* derive from the promotion of the good, while for a nonconsequentialist some of them do not. A nonconsequentialist says that some *do's* and *don't's* are not the creatures of the promotion of the good and, thus, are not challengeable merely by its more efficient promotion, even though they may be overrideable by it when a sufficient amount of it turns out to be at stake.

Take what I suppose is a limiting case. On the wide interpretation of consequentialism, morality itself could be regarded as a good and, therefore, could be given either the consequentialist or nonconsequentialist treatment. Consequentialists would act so as to bring about the most, or a satisfactory degree of, moral behavior in the world at large. Nonconsequentialists would, so far as possible, act morally themselves.

Look more closely at consequentialists. They have a good before them — acting morally — which they put into their formula for the derivation of the right: the morally right act is the one that most (or, at least, satisfactorily) promotes morally right acts. But this formula is empty. The good that consequentialists start with is supposed to give content to the right, but since the good that they start with in this case *is* the right, no content enters. This problem does not face utilitarians, who are supposed to form one species of consequentialist. It is true that utilitarians start with a good, namely the quality of life, and that they, too, can put content into the notion of the right only if they put content into the (far from crystalline or substantial) notion of the quality of life. One might ask: Then why are consequentialists any different? They too, one might say, need to put content into their notion of acting morally, but, once they do, the problem disappears. After all, utilitarians go outside the immediate bounds of the derivation of the right from the good to find content for their notion of the quality of life. But the two cases are not analogous in the way needed. Consequentialists are supposed to derive a contentful standard of the right from a substantive good, but some of these added goods that appear in the course of the expansion we have just traced, cannot play this role, while the notion of the quality of life can.

I do not offer this as a fatal objection to consequentialism; it is not. It is only the first of a series of puzzling features. In any case, one cannot rest too much weight on such a marginal example of a good as acting morally. The extended good that consequentialists themselves usually cite includes such things as keeping promises, not lying, acting justly, and respecting rights. The threat of emptiness is not necessarily avoided, though, just by shifting to more specific goods such as acting justly and respecting rights. The notions of justice and rights both have great elasticity: they are sometimes used to cover the whole of morality and sometimes only a part of it. The more broadly they are interpreted, the more emptiness threatens.

True, there are other goods that fall under the expanded notion of the good, such as keeping promises and not lying, that have content of their own. Let us turn to them now.

III. Backing Up Further: An Odd Picture of Agency

In turning to these other goods, the puzzles do not disappear, but merely change.

There is an unclarity in act descriptions. Do I keep my promise only if I act to some extent voluntarily, or do I also keep it if, kicking and screaming, I am forced to do what I said I would do? Consequentialists aim at producing optimum (or, at least, satisfactory) promise-keeping overall. But do they have in mind a voluntary act or mere conformity of action? Either answer is puzzling. If they mean a voluntary act, then they are adopting an odd conception of agency. If they mean mere conformity, then it is hard to see why they regard such actions as moral goods in the first place. Let me take up the alternatives in turn.

It is within the realm of possibility for one person to break a promise in a way that gets many others autonomously to keep theirs. George, let us say, a prominent politician, is fed up with his colleagues' regularly welching on their word and finds himself in a position to welch on them so spectacularly that they would decide that the rules of the game had to be changed. He might be able to work a kind of conversion. But how often are such conversions within one's power? It would probably be a unique chance for George, so it would be unreasonable of him to elevate his response to this one case to a policy for his whole moral life. I doubt that I have ever been in such a position; nor, I suspect, have most people. Normal agents are not. If I, situated as I am, were to break a promise in order to bring about more cases of autonomous promise-keeping, then, unlike George, I should merely be dropping my act into a causal stream in which so many other eddies and currents and undertows are at work that I could have, at best, only the faintest hope of producing the desired effect. Thus, though such conversions are not psychologically impossible, they are so rare, so unlikely ever to present themselves in the course of a life, so much a fluke of fate, as, for all practical purposes, not to figure in the formation of goals in life. In a certain loose sense, 'ought' implies 'can'. All moral theories work implicitly with a picture of what lies within human capacity. The limits of human capacity help to define the limits of moral obligation. But acts like maximizing the universal observance of promise-keeping or of fairness are simply not in our repertoire. Our moral life is not so much a matter of what we do as of what we choose to do. What I choose to do has to be, roughly speaking, within my power. I do not have to be 100 percent sure of bringing it off; I can, for instance, choose to go to London first thing tomorrow morning, although British Rail might let me down. But if the chances are only one in several million of my carrying something off, then I cannot be said to choose to do it. I can choose to have a flutter on the Irish Sweepstake, but not to win. Winning may enter my hopes and plans but not my intentions. The chances of my promise-breaking making others (plural) autonomously keep their promises approach Irish Sweepstake proportions. There is, therefore, something quite unreal in consequentialists' choosing as one of their goals in life, "Promote promise-keeping impartially." It is not the sort of action-guiding goal that one would ever give to, or adopt as, an agent.

Still, breaking one's own promise is not the only means at one's disposal for promoting promise-keeping. One can persuade or indoctrinate. But this addition to our causal resources does not much change our prospects of success. Few of us are in a position effectively to persuade or indoctrinate. I was when my children were young, but a person's moral character is pretty much fixed in childhood and little, certainly not sermons or lectures, is likely to change it afterward. George's making a speech in favor of probity in public life would have little chance of success. My making a similar speech would have even less. The strangeness of the goal remains.

What is strange is, precisely, consequentialists' choosing as goals in life the promotion of acts of promise-keeping, acts of justice, and the like. It is not strange that opportunities for conversions are rare. After all, opportunities for saving babies who fall face down into puddles are rare, too: normal agents will probably never have such an opportunity in their lives. One can choose as a goal helping others in distress when the cost to oneself is small. Saving a baby in a puddle fits under this heading. Although that particular case is rare, cases of that kind certainly are not, and acts of compliance with the principle are within our powers. What makes a moral principle strange, however, is not the rarity of one particular instantiation of the kind of situation it regulates (there is nothing strange in that) but the unlikelihood of being able to comply with it at all. Why choose a standard for moral action so remotely connected to what one can do? Of course, 'strange' does not imply 'wrong'. But 'ought' implies 'can'. Action-guiding principles must fit human capacities, or they become strange in a damaging way: pointless.

Perhaps the promotion of promise-keeping is not meant as an action-guiding principle. There is a familiar distinction between a decision procedure (what we appeal to in deciding how to act) and a criterion (what makes an act right or wrong). Perhaps a doctor is best advised to follow certain procedures in diagnosing and treating patients — best advised because those procedures have the best results overall, though not necessarily in each case. But the criterion for successful medical practice is clear and independent of any diagnostic procedures: namely, health. Perhaps, similarly, the promotion of promise-keeping should be regarded, not as the immediate goal that we use in our thought and action, but as the criterion of moral practice.

It is not clear whether, or how much, this reply solves the earlier puzzles. Although criterion and decision procedure can diverge, they should not, I think, get too far apart from one another. Our decision procedures must take account of our capacities, but any criterion for a human practice cannot become too remote from our capacities without losing its point even as a criterion. Health is a reasonable criterion for medical practice because doctors can, directly or indirectly, act to bring it about. In contrast with that, a very demanding moral criterion (say, Jesus's "Be ye therefore perfect") may go too far even to be a moral criterion. Take perfection to be counting one person's interests as much as any other's. Some philosophers think that, as long as we can try to be perfect, although we are bound to fail, the principle is not pointless. But I am inclined to think that if such perfection is (as I believe) well outside our reach, it loses interest even as a criterion. In certain respects, the promotion of promise-keeping is more remote from human capacities than is perfection. In seeking perfection, the problem is making one's own reluctant will conform. In promoting promise-keeping, the problem is making an altogether more independent world conform. If it is strained to say that one "intends" to promote promise-keeping, it is also strained to say that one will "try" to promote it. Unless one can afford to buy a great number of tickets, one cannot "try" to win the Irish Sweepstake either.

Suppose, then, that consequentialists adopt the other reading of "keeping my promise" — not voluntary promise-keeping, but mere conformity. Here, too, there clearly are cases in which one can break one's promise and consequently force others, in some sense or other, to keep theirs. I have promised my two children, let us say, not to interfere any more in their lives, but then they each promise their mother to stay at home one evening and, just as they are about to sneak out, I lock them in. I have broken my (one) promise, but they, kicking, screaming, and trying to get out, are keeping their (two) promises. Or are they? It is misleading to say that they "keep their promise," even misleading to say that they are "staying in," when they are being kept in. And why should we classify mere conformity as a moral good? What is the intuitive justification for considering a world with more cases of mere conformity as being morally better than a world with fewer? We might sometimes be able to explain why the first world is better than the second by appealing to the narrower sort of consequentialism that I shall shortly recommend, a form of consequentialism that uses the term 'good' to refer only to individual goods and couples this conception of the good with some conception or other of equal respect. If one falls back on this narrower form of consequentialism, though, one abandons the aim of promoting acts of promise-keeping (or of fairness, or of respect for rights) that is characteristic of the wider form. The narrower form of consequentialism explains why the world with more cases of mere conformity is better than the world with fewer, by appealing to the pattern and extent of the satisfaction of interests (which has some intuitive force), rather than, as the wider form would, by appealing to the number of merely conforming actions (which, to my mind, does not have intuitive appeal).

This leads to a further puzzle. Does one promote promise-keeping just by acting to maximize the number of promises kept, or to minimize the number of promises broken, regardless of whether what is at stake is trivial or important? That would be a very odd goal. But if not that, then what? Can we rank cases of broken promises, except perhaps by ranking the interests at stake in the various cases? Can we rank the interests at stake without undermining the status of promise-keeping as one of the goods added to produce the expanded notion of the good? Do I really minimize promise-breaking by bringing it about that there are only n breakings rather than the $n + 10$ that there would otherwise have been, although the n violations seriously damage the lives of the persons affected, whereas the $n + 10$ are not especially damaging? Could I maximize promise-keeping by setting up the following sort of promising teams? Your team makes and keeps several trivial promises to the members of mine, whereupon we turn around and do the same to the members of your team, and so on. As this example shows, it is puzzling to regard promise-keeping as the sort of thing to be promoted. The same is true of justice, honesty, and respect for rights. It is odd to seek to promote acts of fairness; it is more natural to seek to promote one's own or other persons' interests fairly (or unfairly).

There is a bad fit between the idea of *general promotion of the good* and these *moral* goods that were added in the expansion of the notion of the good that we traced at the start. That bad fit is at the center of the wide definition of 'consequentialism' now commonly accepted, and is a good enough reason, I think, to abandon the definition for a different one. It is not that no taxonomy of moral positions should allow any position to be odd or incorrect, but that it is better if all positions are plausible enough to be interesting.

IV. Where Does This Leave Us?

How might we amend consequentialism? It has to retain the derivation of the right from the good; otherwise it would not be consequentialism. Its live option is to reverse the expansion of the notion of the good that we traced at the start. But how far? I think that we have to bring the notion of the good back to such notions as well-being, the quality of life, human interests—back to what I have been calling 'individual goods'. Whether this is to bring it all the way back to the notion of utility depends upon what we think 'utility' means.[8]

[8] Amartya Sen thinks that there are two "traditional meanings of utility," namely "happiness" and "desire-fulfillment," and he gives narrow interpretations to both. See his *On Ethics and Economics* (Oxford: Blackwell, 1987), p. 3. I do not think that it does violence to the term 'utilitarian' to let it cover pluralist and objective value theories. But for our present purposes, my suggestion is that we let the class of the good contract to individual goods, on any account of what they are. We may leave open whether that means that the notion of the good will be reduced to the notion of utility.

Whether or not this move to limit the notion of the good is a retreat to utility, it is clearly not a retreat all the way back to utilitarianism. For there are many derivations of the right from the good besides utilitarian ones. The right could be what maximizes the good, or achieves a satisfactory level of good, or distributes the good equally except when inequalities are to the advantage of the worst off, or brings everyone up to some minimum level of good above which obligations cease, and so on. Though it is not clear exactly where to draw the line between utilitarian and nonutilitarian positions, some of the ones I have just listed are nonutilitarian. There are two characteristic features of all these positions: they assess outcomes in terms of individual goods and they derive the right through a function representing equal respect. Certain elements of justice enter into the derivation with the function representing equal respect: for example, counting everybody for one, nobody for more than one; or being governed by the difference principle; or maintaining a minimum acceptable level of welfare.[9] But these conceptions of justice enter into the process of derivation and not into the list of goods. Agents are directed to distribute according to one of those standards, not to promote the universal observance of the standard.

If, in this way, we shrink the class of goods used in the wide account of consequentialism, we shall get, to my mind, a more interesting distinction between consequentialism and nonconsequentialism.

V. The Failure of Pure Consequentialism

However, that does not end the troubles. I wonder whether we do not have to give up the distinction between consequentialism and nonconsequentialism altogether.

No one could plausibly claim that the right is derivable solely from the good. One would have to claim, instead, that it is derivable from the good through some function interpreting the requirement of equal respect: maximizing, achieving a satisfactory level, equalizing, and so on. No form of consequentialism yields any judgments of moral right without the aid of some conception of equal respect. But a conception of equal respect is, on the face of it, an abstract moral view, a high-level principle of right.

---

[9] Should 'consequentialism' encompass even an interpretation of equal respect that allows partiality—for example, the view that equal respect requires only that agents render to others what is 'due' them (my children, say, are due more from me than strangers, and so on)? There is a problem with this interpretation: does 'due' mean something other than 'right,' in which case it is not, after all, a function for deriving the right from the good? Still, the doubts about consequentialism that I am in the process of raising apply as well to nontrivial versions of this view; this view regards what is 'due' as an expression of the moral notion of equal respect, and I shall argue that what is 'due' others is often determined by a partly arbitrary picture of human agency. I shall, however, concentrate on interpretations of equal respect that require some sort of impartial promotion of the good: maximizing, equalizing, and so on.

It would seem, therefore, that no form of consequentialism can derive the right except from the good plus at least one key element of the right.

There are pure consequentialists, I think, who would resist this conclusion. They would allow that some of those functions do indeed express moral requirements (for instance, equalizing, or equalizing except when inequalities help the worst off), but others represent irresistible nonmoral requirements of rationality (for instance, maximizing or achieving a satisfactory level — there is dispute as to which of these two does represent the requirement of rationality[10]). Thus, pure consequentialists can claim to derive the right from the good plus a morally neutral standard of rationality.

But I think that pure consequentialism is untenable. I have argued elsewhere that, at least in morality, maximization is not a requirement of a thin, irresistible form of rationality.[11] If it is a rational requirement at all, it is a requirement of a fairly thick conception of rationality that already incorporates certain judgments about what are good moral reasons — for instance, whether one has more reason to maximize than to equalize. Maximization can look as if it were only a thin requirement because it can be taken to hold merely that, as enjoyment (say) is good, more is better. On that weak interpretation, though, maximization is a standard for ranking outcomes; it has not yet left the domain of the good for that of the moral right. To enter the domain of the right, one has to take a fateful decision as to when benefiting one person justifies harming another. One can adopt a maximizing standard there, too, but it is hardly any longer thin and irresistible. Consequentialism is a moral view. The only tenable form of consequentialism is an impure one in which lower level judgments about the right are derivable from the good plus at least one high-level principle of the right. The right and the good cannot be kept on opposite sides of a line of inference.

VI. Human Good and Human Agents

There is a further way in which the human good and human agency raise trouble for consequentialism. There are many forces at work shaping moral norms. One force is the human good itself. Recall the list: deep personal relations, accomplishment, understanding, and so on. Most of these goods involve commitment to particular persons or causes. Commitment reduces freedom: one cannot take up and put aside this sort of life at will.[12]

A second force is the limits of the will. Our biological nature ties us to certain individuals. Our conception of a good life strengthens those ties

---

[10] See note 3.

[11] See my *Well-Being*, ch. 9.

[12] See *ibid.*, ch. 10, section 2; see also my paper "On the Winding Road from Good to Right," in *Value, Welfare, and Morality*, ed. R. G. Frey and C. Morris, forthcoming, section 1a.

and leads us to make many more. How much freedom is left to us? 'Ought' implies 'can'. Where are the limits of the will—and, especially, where are the limits of our capacity for impartiality? These are crucial, complicated, and neglected empirical questions. We know that these limits shift. One can do more for strangers if their plight becomes vivid to one. One can make greater sacrifices if one is stirred enough by the cause. But in the end, I think, there are important limits to the will: one cannot be completely impartial[13]—at least, not if one is living the kind of life that realizes the human good.

A third force shaping moral norms is the demands of social life. Our social life requires us to hit upon, or at least to take part in, stable patterns of cooperation. Sometimes we explicitly strike a bargain, but many key social institutions emerge without conscious calculation and choice. Institutions of property, for instance, are shaped by deep forces. They may be a human correlate of animal territoriality. They are probably influenced by not fully conscious beliefs about the limits of the will—about, for instance, the strength of one's commitments to one's family. Moreover, many social institutions generate rights and obligations: if it is your property, I must keep hands off. The rights and obligations generated are important; the institutions that generate them produce most of the major goods of our lives.[14]

A fourth force is the limits of knowledge. Some information is beyond our intellectual capacity, not just for now but forever. What set of norms would, if they were dominant in our society, maximize utility impartially? What set of dispositions would, if they were ours, lead us to behave in a utility-maximizing way over the course of our lives?[15] The answers are beyond me. There are, of course, degrees of ignorance. Sometimes we know enough to be able to estimate probabilities: for instance, such-and-such is as likely to maximize utility as so-and-so. But at other times we know too little even for that. The daunting questions that I just asked are no doubt answerable, at least in probabilistic terms, when we must judge between two sets of norms-*cum*-dispositions that are far apart in quality. But there will be a wide range in which they are closer in quality and in which our ignorance defeats even judgments of likelihood. We are often as ignorant about an individual social institution as we are about institutions collectively. How far can we assess an institution of property? We can assess egregiously bad forms of it. We can assess this or that part of decent forms of it. But institutions of property in advanced societies are

---

[13] Shelly Kagan denies this in his book *The Limits of Morality*. See my review of the book in *Mind*, vol. 99 (1990); the views expressed there are developed further in my "On the Winding Road from Good to Right," section 1c.

[14] See my *Well-Being*, ch. 10, sections 1 and 2; see also my "On the Winding Road from Good to Right," section 1d.

[15] One finds this question asked, for example, by R. B. Brandt, *A Theory of the Good and the Right* (Oxford: Clarendon Press, 1979), chs. 9–10.

so complex that there will be a wide range of acceptable forms that no doubt differ in quality among themselves, but that we have no hope of ranking. If our institution falls within this range, what is behind the claim that we ought to do this or that is not (that is, not entirely) the promotion of interests but also the fact that this is the institution that we happen to have. Another piece of information permanently beyond us is where the limits of the will are. We can rule out some implausible views on the subject, but here, too, there is a wide range of views that we cannot rank even probabilistically. Since there will be no morality at all until we take a view on the subject, we simply adopt one. The view we adopt is bound to be arbitrary to some degree, and our moral norms will share in this arbitrariness. For instance, we adopt (fairly arbitrarily) a view about how much a typical moral agent can deprive his own children to help distant strangers; having done so, we can work out a policy (which will inherit the arbitrariness) on giving to charity. When our knowledge runs out, contingency and arbitrariness enter to fix what we morally ought to do.[16]

Consequentialism, I have proposed, is the view that the right is derived from the good through a function interpreting equal respect. The four forces I have discussed (and others) push any such consequentialist principle well into the background of moral life. In the foreground, in our everyday moral thinking, are principles such as "Hands off the property of others," "Look after your own children," and so on. Most consequentialists nowadays accept that their principle, "Promote the good impartially," belongs in the background, but that it still plays an enormously important role there, justifying and systematizing all the norms in the foreground. Consequentialists often appeal to the distinction we considered earlier between a decision procedure and a criterion. Although these four forces, they say, make the moral decision procedure (largely) nonconsequentialist, the forces leave the criterion fully consequentialist. The impartial promotion of the good, the consequentialists claim, remains the sole criterion or right-making feature of morality. But these four forces seem to me more powerful than that.

One familiar reason for resisting the consequentialist claim that promotion of the good is the sole right-making feature of morality, is that there are further, deontological right-making features. I want to leave that matter aside. I want to suggest that, quite apart from any possible deontological features, the correct conception of the human good and of human agency lead us to resist this consequentialist claim.

There are interpretations of the claim on which it may well be right. If, for instance, some feature of our institution of property were known to promote the good less well than an available alternative, then, without special reasons, it may not produce a morally authoritative norm. It is

---

[16] See my "On the Winding Road from Good to Right," section 1e.

plausible that an issue is *moral* only if the promotion of individual good is at stake. It is also plausible to think of the whole apparatus of morality as having an object, namely, to make our lives go better than they otherwise would. Still, although the promotion of the good may be the sole right-making feature in some senses of that phrase, it is not in another: that is, it is not the only consideration that ultimately determines a moral reason for action. In this last sense, there are further right-making features: for instance, the limits of the will and the institutions that happen to have emerged in our society. These further right-making features give us such moral reasons for action as "It's her property" and "He's my son."

The promotion of the good cannot play the strong justifying and systematizing role that consequentialists assign it. It plays the role with some norms but not with all. The fact that certain money is yours, say, has moral weight in my life. It does so partly because our institution of property helps promote the good, but also because that is the institution of property in my society and I respect it. The respect I give it does not rest on a case-by-case calculation of its promotion of good, so I will not normally resort to a case-by-case calculation of interests to decide when to put the institution's norms aside. The institution generates a norm of a rough-and-ready nature—"Hands off the property of others." Since the norm is not justified by case-by-case estimates, it can be set aside only in extreme cases. The norms of property lose authority when following them conflicts with the whole object of morality: for instance, a government may seize property for national defense. The norms lose authority when following them is beyond human capacity: for instance, I may seize property to save my child's life. It is not that a norm of property does not get authority from its promoting the good; it is just that it does not get all of its authority in that way. A norm of property also gets authority from the fact that it is part of *our* institution, and from the fact that adherence to it (except in extreme cases) is the best that limited agents like us can do.

Consequentialists think that we can do better, that we can extend the rationality of promoting the good into the selection of norms, policies, and dispositions. For instance, rule utilitarians say that we should act in accordance with the nicely elaborated rules (or in accordance with simpler first-order rules for everyday life, and probably fairly complex second-order rules to resolve conflicts) that would best promote the good impartially and in the long run. Motive utilitarians say that we should follow the finely tuned dispositions that would have the same result. But I doubt that we could perform the large-scale calculations of what is best that they require, or even determine reasonable approximations of what is best. I have acknowledged that we can make these judgments when faced with extreme alternatives—say, when a set of rules or dispositions is quite bad—and that we can make judgments about this or that feature of a nonextreme set. But there will be a wide range in which we cannot make judgments, and there will have to be something else at work in those cases to carry us to a determinate norm. Moral norms must be tailored to fit the human moral torso. They are nothing but what such tailoring produces. There are no moral norms outside the boundary set by our capacities. There are not some second-best norms — norms made for everyday use by agents limited in intelligence and will — and then, behind them, true or ideal norms — norms without compromises to human frailty. Moral norms regulate human action; a norm that ignores the limited nature of human agents is not an "ideal" norm, but no norm at all.

But have I really taken the distinction between a decision procedure and a criterion seriously enough? The distinction seems to be at times useful: for instance, as I said earlier, in medical practice. In medicine, though, the criterion (health) is not so remote that it cannot actually be applied: in time, doctors learn whether their treatments work. In parts of moral life, we can also learn how the major interests at stake have been affected, but, in many other parts, we never do. What most promotes interests is often permanently beyond our reach. Then a "criterion" like that can play no role, not even that of criterion.

Consequentialists say that moral norms are justified, perhaps indirectly, by their impartially promoting the good. My suggestion is that moral norms arise from various sources: for example, from solutions to cooperation problems and from commitments to family. They also arise from important values, such as life itself: "Do not deliberately kill the innocent." These norms are not, and could not be, justified by long-term effects on the promotion of the good. Even the norm "Do not deliberately kill the innocent" derives directly from the importance of life, not from the unmanageable calculation of the effects of our adopting this norm rather than any other possible one. Consequentialism assumes that morality is more thoroughly determined by the promotion of the good — and less determined by convention, arbitrariness, and the needs of very limited agents — than it is. In this way, consequentialism is too ambitious: it tries to derive all moral norms from the promotion of the good plus equal respect. Wide though that base may be, it is not wide enough. Consequentialism tries to rationalize morality more than it can be rationalized. Norms are not always fully rationalizable.[17] That does not create problems: we are not bereft of norms. Many norms are present in our lives independently of our deliberation and choice. We treat certain norms as authoritative even though they are not backed by the rationality of individual good. Such reasons can be used to criticize and change those norms, but they do not create or authorize them.

---

[17] We should have found further support for this conclusion if we found irresolvable conflict between moral norms. In another paper, I work out the consequences for moral conflicts of the four forces I have been talking about here; see "Mixing Values," *Proceedings of the Aristotelian Society*, Supplementary Volume 65 (1991), section 4.

VII. Consequentialism and Nonconsequentialism

Many of us start by thinking that any account of the good can be incorporated into consequentialism, but that seems not to be true. Once we understand the nature of human goods, once we see the good life that they describe, once we recognize the sort of agent who can live that life, we find it hard to accept certain claims of consequentialism. It is not, I think, that we have to abandon much of what is intuitively appealing about consequentialism (for instance, the belief that in some, perhaps indirect way the moral right rests on the individual good, that nothing can be right or wrong independently of effects on interests), but perhaps we have to abandon enough to want also to give up the name. Nevertheless, I do not think that distancing oneself from consequentialism takes one toward deontology. The firm ground, I think, lies in neither position.

Philosophy, University of Oxford

THE GOOD LIFE AND THE GOOD LIVES OF OTHERS*

By Julia Annas

It is well-known that in recent years, alongside the familiar forms of modern ethical theory, such as consequentialism, deontology, and rights theory, there has been a resurgence of interest in what goes by the name of "virtue ethics"—forms of ethical theory which give a prominent status to the virtues, and to the idea that an agent has a "final end" which the virtues enable her to achieve. With this has come an increase of theoretical (as opposed to antiquarian) interest in ancient ethical theories, particularly Aristotle's, an interest which has made a marked difference in the way ethics is pursued in the Anglo-Saxon[1] and European[2] intellectual worlds.

In this essay, I shall not be discussing modern virtue ethics, which is notably protean in form and difficult to pin down.[3] I shall be focusing on ancient eudaimonistic ethical theories, for in their case we can achieve a clearer discussion of the problem I wish to discuss (a problem which arises also for modern versions of virtue ethics which hark back to the ancient theories in their form).

* I am grateful for helpful discussion of this essay from this volume's editors and contributors, especially from Judith Jarvis Thomson, Shelly Kagan, John Kekes, Wayne Sumner, Warren Quinn, and Fred D. Miller, Jr.

[1] Apart from the influence of books such as Alasdair MacIntyre, *After Virtue* (London: Duckworth, 1981) and *Whose Justice? Which Rationality?* (Notre Dame: Notre Dame Press, 1988), the following have been influential: Philippa Foot, *Virtues and Vices* (Oxford: Blackwell, 1978); James Wallace, *Virtues and Vices* (Ithaca: Cornell University Press, 1978); N. J. H. Dent, *The Moral Psychology of the Virtues* (Cambridge: Cambridge University Press, 1984); Robert B. Kruschwitz and Robert C. Roberts, eds., *The Virtues* (Belmont: Wadsworth, 1987); P. French, T. Uehling, and H. Wettstein, eds., *Midwest Studies in Philosophy*, vol. XIII: *Ethical Theory: Character and Virtue* (Notre Dame: Notre Dame Press, 1988); and *Philosophia*, vol. 20, nos. 1 and 2, (1990).

[2] Interest in "neo-Aristotelian" theories of ethics and practical reasoning has been particularly strong in Germany and Italy. See Herbert Schnädelbach, "Was ist Neoaristotelismus?" in *Moralität und Sittlichkeit*, ed. W. Kuhlmann (Frankfurt am Main: Suhrkamp, 1986), pp. 38–63; and Enrico Berti, "La philosophie pratique d'Aristote et sa 'réhabilitation' récente," *Revue de Métaphysique et de Morale*, vol. 95 (1990), pp. 244–66.

[3] There is little agreement as to what *kind* of theory virtue ethics is. Sometimes it is taken to be a theory in which independently established premises about virtue are used to derive conclusions about action (unsurprisingly, this produces absurdities). Sometimes virtue ethics is held to bring with it a radical stance about ethical theory as such, one which rejects, as silly or unfeasible, most of the tasks which modern ethical theories set themselves, or even the very idea of ethical *theory*. See Robert Louden, "Virtue Ethics and Anti-Theory," *Philosophia*, vol. 20 (1990), pp. 93–114; and S. Clarke and E. Simpson, eds., *Anti-theory in Ethics and Moral Conservatism* (Albany: SUNY Press, 1989). Comparatively little attention has been paid to the formal possibilities of virtue ethics as a kind of theory.

Ancient theories are called eudaimonistic because of their characteristic structure. The entry-point for ethical reflection is not, as for many modern theories, bafflement at moral disagreements or hard cases; rather, ethical reflection arises from the agent's reflection on her life as a whole and the way in which her values and projects do (or do not) fit together into an overall structure which gives her life coherence and direction. Such a structure is formed by one's projects being pursued for the sake of a further, ultimate goal, one's "final end"; and while there is consensus that all but the wildly disorganized have a final end — and that it is *eudaimonia* or happiness[4] — this is merely a thin and indeterminate specification. Ethical theory enters in, not as a mechanism for resolving ethical problems (a role it often plays today), but as a means of achieving clarity about our final end, and specifying it determinately, in a way which will enable us to set properly the priorities involved in our various projects, and, hence, to act in a way which expresses those priorities. For all ancient theories, this process involves more or less *revising* our priorities; our initial intuitions about happiness have to be modified or rejected to some degree.[5] And for ancient theories a crucial part of the clarification and revision of our priorities is acquiring an understanding of virtue and the extent of its demands in the way we set our priorities and, hence, in the way we live. I have argued at length elsewhere[6] that in ancient theories virtue is moral virtue, not some undifferentiated excellence, and that the ancient debates about the place of virtue in happiness are analogous to modern debates about morality, its place in our life, and the extent of its demands.

Modern interpreters of ancient eudaimonism, even if they are otherwise sympathetic, are often impressed unfavorably by one feature of the structure of these theories. And an analogous problem is often felt with modern versions of virtue ethics, quite apart from their historical antecedents. For in this kind of theory, the agent's concern is with his own life: the initial trigger to ethical reflection comes from dissatisfaction with the way one's life is going, and ethical theory is a guide to revising and improving one's own priorities. One has reason to acquire the virtues because they turn out to be, in the light of ethical theory if not intuitively, required if one is to achieve *eudaimonia* as that is clarified and made de-

[4] Recently there have been some attempts to avoid "happiness" as a translation for *eudaimonia*, and to use instead "human flourishing" or the like. However, "happiness" remains the best and most convenient translation, provided we make an effort to distance ourselves from inappropriate associations of pleasant feeling and satisfaction imported into modern discussions of happiness by utilitarianism.

[5] Stoic and Epicurean theories are notably more revisionary here than Aristotle's; when it is assumed that ancient theories are conservative rather than revisionary, this usually comes from over-concentration on Aristotle. The major debate in ancient ethics, as we can see from a work like Cicero's *de Finibus*, was over the question of *how much* ethical theory should revise one's priorities, *how far* in one's life the demands of morality should reach.

[6] In my book *The Morality of Happiness*, forthcoming from Oxford University Press.

terminate by ethical theory. Are not theories of this form doomed to be egoistic? And if they are egoistic, then they cannot be of serious concern to us if we are looking for a viable *ethical* theory.[7]

There is an obvious answer to this. Eudaimonistic theories are formally self-centered, because they develop from the agent's reasonings about her own life. But this need not make them self-centered in *content*. Whether they are, depends entirely on what the theory's candidate is for the specific determinate content of the agent's final end. Hedonist theories, for example, do *prima facie* face a problem in giving the interests of others intrinsic value in the agent's life; if the final goal of my life, which sets all my other priorities, is pleasure, then how can I care about the good of others unless it contributes to my pleasure?[8] Ancient hedonists did struggle with this problem. The Cyrenaics just accept the conclusion that their theory is egoistic, whereas Epicurus goes to considerable, if not ultimately successful, lengths to show that his is not.

A modern move which would avert egoism at this point is not available to ancient theories, and it is worth discussing why. *Eudaimonia* is my final good, and as such is *teleios* or "complete": that is, I aim at other things for its sake, but do not aim at it for the sake of anything further. Thus, I regard it as being, as we now say, good in itself or intrinsically good. However, to regard something as intrinsically good is to regard it precisely as being *good*, not just good for me; therefore, to the extent that I have reason to bring it about, I seem to have reason to bring it about for others as well as myself. (In some theories I have reason to maximize it, regardless of who gets it.) However, the ancients never regarded *eudaimonia* as something that I can bring about for others, still less maximize. Why not, if they regard it as being intrinsically good?

For ancient theories, with the conscious exception of the Cyrenaics, *eudaimonia* is not an experience or state of affairs that someone else could bring about for me. Rather, my happiness consists in my own activity, and this is not something that anyone but myself could bring about. Trying to make someone else happy is as futile as trying to live someone else's life.[9] Hence it was a standing complaint against hedonist theo-

---

[7] I do not have the scope in this essay to defend the assumption that egoist theories cannot fulfill the role of ethical theories. I take it that this is a widely shared assumption; it is at any rate widely enough shared to form the basis of frequent criticisms of eudaimonist theories, and in this essay I am meeting this criticism, leaving for others the task of discussing whether eudaimonist theories would be defensible even if they were egoistic.

[8] Ancient forms of hedonism all work from the assumption that what is sought is the agent's pleasure; it does not occur to anyone in the ancient world that one might reasonably seek pleasure, regardless of whose it is. This is because of a more general assumption which is examined in the next paragraph.

[9] "Bodily and external goods are called productive of happiness by contributing towards it when present; but those who think that they fulfill (i.e., make up) happiness do not know that happiness is life, and life is the fulfillment of action. No bodily or external good is in itself an action or in general an activity." Arius Didymus, ap Stobaeus, *Eclogae*, II 126.20–127.2. See *Stobaeus*, ed. C. Wachsmuth (Berlin: Weidmann, 1884).

ries—one which Epicurus's theory tries to meet—that pleasure is unsuitable as a final good, because pleasure is too passive; if thought of as an experience, pleasure cannot fill the role of living a certain kind of life, which is something we *do*.[10] Hence, although in modern terms my *eudaimonia*, is an intrinsic good, there are structural reasons, deriving from the basic conception of *eudaimonia*, why I cannot try to maximize this, or to bring it about for other people.[11]

Nonhedonistic theories all accept that an agent needs the virtues to achieve her final goal. And the virtues are the moral virtues; they are, minimally, dispositions to do the morally right thing for the right reason, and for one's feelings and emotions to be in harmony with this. But the issue of what is the morally right thing to do is established in ways that are independent of what is in the agent's interests. Moral virtues, such as courage and justice, commit the agent to respecting the good of others: sometimes to furthering it, sometimes (as with justice) to relinquishing goods when others have a just claim on them. Thus, the content of eudaimonistic ethics (other than the hedonistic ethical systems, which I shall not consider further) is not egoistic.[12]

Further, it is a fact of experience that we do care about the good of others for their own sake, even where this is not directly a requirement of virtue; we love our family and friends, for example. The good of these people figures directly as part of our good when we are considering our own lives;[13] we do not feel concern for them in a way which is merely instrumental to our own good, but rather our own good is expanded to include the good of these others. Ancient ethics pays quite a lot of atten-

[10] See *ibid.*, 46.13–22, where Epicurus is criticized on these grounds, although he in fact tries hard to argue that the pleasure which is our final end is not just an experience.

[11] But couldn't I try to make you happy in an *indirect* way, namely by bringing about conditions in which it is more rather than less likely that you can act in the appropriate way? In ancient theories, this kind of consideration comes in under political or social philosophy, usually in the form of theories about the ideal form of social organization.

[12] In the case of theories which make virtue sufficient for or a prominent part of happiness, there is the further point, analogous to one stressed by Kant: nobody else can make me moral—only I can make myself moral. Thus, there is a specific as well as a general reason why nobody else can bring about my *eudaimonia* for me if my *eudaimonia* consists of my virtuous activity.

[13] For the sake of simplicity I shall use the expression (intuitive in both ancient and modern theories) of "parts" of one's own good or happiness. The reader should be warned, however, that in ancient theories this mode of expression is only acceptable at the intuitive level, and that certain theoretical implications of it are denied. One's own good does not contain others' good, or indeed anything, in a way which allows of quantitative measurement of the different goods' contributions. This is basically because (on the ancients' view) our final good is not a state of affairs but activity, as indicated above. Further, items which one's overall good intuitively "contains" or which are intuitively "parts" of it cannot be added, since most theories recognize fundamental differences of kind between different sorts of good. As the Stoics most uncompromisingly hold, we cannot add health or wealth to virtue to make a better life, since goods like health and wealth have value in a life only insofar as virtue makes proper use of them. Generally, the kind of value that a good may have in a life cannot be simplistically assessed without regard for the place it has in that life and the agent's scheme of priorities.

tion to this phenomenon, which is called *philia*. This is usually translated "friendship," although our concept applies only to chosen relationships involving some degree of intimacy, whereas *philia* also covers one's relationships to one's family, as well as relationships which involve acquaintanceship but not intimacy. Perhaps what covers all these disparate cases best for us is the idea of *commitment*. You are committed to certain people having first claim on your energy and concern — your family, your friends, your colleagues. *Philia* is another way, besides justice, in which the agent in a eudaimonistic theory finds himself giving noninstrumental weight to the interests of others. Aristotle argues that *philia* is required for the agent to achieve a satisfactory specification of his final end; to achieve my own good, I must include the good of others in my final end, and give it intrinsic value.[14]

Virtue and commitment do not always deflect the charge of egoism. For, critics urge, the good of others should matter to the agent just because it is the good of others, and not because it is viewed as part of the agent's own overall good. If my friends matter to me, it should be because they are my friends, not because having friends improves my life. Eudaimonistic ethical theories, however, locate the good of others in the wrong place — as something which contributes to my own final good.

But the response to this is obvious. Eudaimonism does not imply that its forming part of my good is the *reason why* I should care about the good of others. I care about others for their own sake. Their good is part of my own final good. The second thought does not undermine the first. If this objection had any force, it would apply equally to the place of virtue in eudaimonistic ethics. The objection would be that the agent would be brave and just in order to achieve her final good, which undermines the status of virtue. But the response to this objection is equally obvious: in a eudaimonistic ethics, while virtue is required in order to achieve happiness, the fact that it is required is not a reason for the agent to be virtuous; rather, the virtuous agent is the person who does the morally right thing for the right reason (that is, without keeping one eye on happiness).

This reply is decisive; yet doubt tends to remain about the adequacy of eudaimonistic theories as theories of ethics where the good of others is concerned. This doubt centers on two issues, and these will be the focus of this essay. One is the issue of *scope*. *Philia* is an attractive concept, and in recent years much work has been done on the importance of attachment and friendship in the development of an ethical outlook. But it has often been felt that these points are not really relevant to the *moral* problem of concern for others: should a moral theory not demand that one have noninstrumental concern for others whether or not one has a commitment of a personal kind towards them? The scope of *philia* does not

[14] See John Cooper, "Aristotle on Friendship," in *Essays on Aristotle*, ed. A. Rorty (Berkeley: University of California Press, 1980), pp. 301–40.

seem to be the ethically required scope of other-concern. One might even go further, and argue that concentration on *philia* may even tend to *weaken* the other-concern that morality requires: the more emphasis one puts on the benefits of *philia*, the less one will be interested in those others to whom one has no personal commitment. If a theory sanctions this, can it be a *moral* theory?

The second issue is that of *status*. Even when we accept the point that an agent's own good is not what gives him a reason to care about others, we may still feel that eudaimonistic ethics does not give the interests of others the status which they demand in a moral theory. For in a eudaimonistic theory, the agent's own view of his own life is not only the entry-point but the perspective of ethics. Should a moral theory not demand that the interests of others have a nonderivative status which, right from the start, has a status in the theory as important as that of the agent's own concerns?

Both these worries are, I think, reasonable, and do not depend on shallow confusion about eudaimonism, as some charges of egoism do. Nonetheless, they depend on a defective understanding of eudaimonism, and I shall try in this essay to show that eudaimonism does not really face problems over scope or status, once we fully take account of the kind of theory it is.

I deal first with the question of scope. This worry arises, often, because of over-concentration on Aristotle's theory. In his ethical works, Aristotle does indeed take surprisingly little notice of concern for others which does not fall under the head of *philia*. At the beginning of his discussion in the *Nicomachean Ethics*, when gathering common beliefs which show why friendship is ethically important, he includes the following:

> There seems to be a natural friendship of parent for offspring and offspring for parent, not only among humans but among birds and most animals, and among members of the same species for one another, and especially among humans, whence we praise lovers of humanity. One might see in one's travels how every human is familiar to and a friend to another human.[15]

But Aristotle's own theoretical account of friendship turns out to require a degree of acquaintance with and personal concern for the other person which is such as to exclude this kind of case; these are not proper cases of *philia*, for Aristotle, and he gives no other account of them. Indeed, some of the ideas developed in the *Politics* would suggest that these cases are actually faulty; love of humanity would seem to be severely limited by due recognition of the naturalness of slavery, the defects of

---

[15] Aristotle, *Nicomachean Ethics*, 1155a16–22. Translations are all mine. The word translated "familiar" is *oikeios*, which also means "akin to"; Aristotle uses words from this root frequently when talking about kin relationships. It is the root from which comes *oikeiōsis*, the word for the basic concept in Stoic theory on this subject (which I come to shortly).

barbarians, and the importance of the contexts of family and city for developing ethical habits and ties.[16] It is fairly easy to see why Aristotle limits the scope of other-concern. Familiarly, he thinks of the moral agent not as an isolated individual relating morally to other isolated individuals, but as the product of moral education and development in particular contexts, especially the family and the city-state. He also thinks of moral character as being displayed in the same contexts as develop it. If our final end requires us to act morally, and moral activity is the exercise of moral character which has been developed in certain specific contexts, then how can the achievement of our final end demand moral activity outside those contexts? Take a person in a different society from ours, whom we do not and never will know personally; the ancient tag for this is "the remotest Mysian."[17] We have not developed morally in any context which includes the remotest Mysian; how can the remotest Mysian make any moral demand on us? According to Aristotle's theory, it does not appear that he does. This does not imply that Aristotle's theory sanctions attitudes of immorality or indifference towards the remotest Mysian, but it does imply that Aristotle ignores the problem of the kind of moral demand, if any, which the remotest Mysian makes. Aristotle's theory is in this respect seriously incomplete.

That theory is, however, only one of the options available in ancient ethics. Another option is represented by Stoic ethics.[18] The Stoics hold that moral development in humans is the culmination of a process of natural development which they call *oikeiōsis* or "familiarization."[19] This has two aspects, for according to the Stoics we have two basic instincts: self-concern and other-concern. We begin by being concerned for ourselves in a primitive way, seeking the things which our nature requires us to need—food, warmth, security, and so on. But since we are rational, it is natural for us to develop as creatures which recognize and act on reasons, and to develop an increasing respect for the force of long-term and connected reasoning, as opposed to short-term impulses. Finally, the Stoics claim, we develop to the point where we come to appreciate (if our reason develops properly) that the value of acting on certain kinds of reasons

[16] Aristotle also has difficulty fitting other intuitive examples of *philia* into his own account—a mother's love for her child, for example (1159a27–1159b1).

[17] At *Theaetetus* 209b, Socrates complains that the conditions introduced so far for distinguishing something in one's thought will not in fact distinguish Socrates' thought of Theaetetus from his thought of Theodorus, or of "the remotest Mysian." The phrase suggests literal remoteness, and also a certain psychological distance or even contempt; John MacDowell in his translation (Oxford, 1973) translates "the remotest peasant in Asia" to convey this. (Mysia was an area in northern Asia Minor.) The Anonymous Commentator on the *Theaetetus* (see below, footnote 28) introduces the remotest Mysian into an ethical discussion in his comment on an earlier passage in the dialogue, and I have taken this up.

[18] Stoic ethical theory is complex in structure, and I am simplifying considerably (but not, I hope misleadingly) in giving just this one aspect of it.

[19] The idea sounds unnecessarily odd in English because we have no single word which answers well to *oikeiōsis*. The root idea is that of being akin to, and hence of being familiar or close to. (We do have a word for its opposite, "alienation" or *allotriōsis*.)

overrides in importance the value of actually getting the things which
normally result from acting on that kind of reason. This is what we would
call recognizing the moral point of view, since the Stoics also characterize it as coming to recognize the value of virtue, and realizing that the
value of virtue is different in kind from the value of other things, and
overrides that value.[20] They do not, any more than Kant does, offer arguments for the thesis that there is a moral point of view; instead, they
are concerned to show that it is by developing as *rational* beings, rather
than in some other way, that we come to grasp it.

Our instinctive other-concern also develops in an ever more rational
way as we develop as rational beings. Purely instinctual other-concern is
seen in our attachment to our offspring, but, again, as we develop rationally we come to be able to extend other-concern beyond the scope given
by instinct, which is limited to people who, like our offspring, can be seen
as extensions of ourselves. As we become more rational, we extend other-
concern to particular people to whom we are related or have a particular
commitment.[21] What is striking about the Stoics is that they insist that
philia, the boundaries marked by particular commitments, is not a significant stopping-place; as rational beings, we will come to see that there is
no defensible stopping-place until we come to have concern for every human just as a human being. "It should be that one human does not find
another human alien, precisely because of being human."[22] The claim is
not, of course, that we should treat others with equal concern in all ways,
but rather that from the moral point of view the virtuous agent would
treat all relevant people with equal concern, even though she may have
ties of kinship or affection to some of them. One way in which the idea
is expressed is by saying that each agent is at the center of concentric circles, which contain the people to whom she is bound by increasingly
weak ties of affection or commitment, until the final circle contains all
other humans. The goal is eventually to get everybody—absolutely everybody—into the same circle. The importance of *philia* is not denied, but it
is no longer an ethically significant boundary.[23]

[20] This is a very brutally abbreviated account, since what I focus on in this essay is not
the first aspect of Stoic *oikeiōsis* but the second. To fully understand the first aspect of Stoic
ethics, one would have to expand on the connection the Stoics find between rationality and
virtue, and their reasons for holding that the value of virtue is not straightforwardly com-
mensurable with the value of other kinds of things.

[21] We have the instinct to love our offspring as soon as we are born, though of course it
cannot come into play until much later, when we have already formed attachments of other
kinds. This aspect of Stoicism attracted a certain amount of ridicule; see, for example,
Plutarch, *de St. repugn.* 1038b.

[22] Cicero, *de Finibus* III 63.

[23] The image of the concentric circles comes from Hierocles, a popularizing Stoic of
(probably) the second century A.D., who wrote an *Elements of Ethics* of which we possess a
long papyrus fragment, and also some passages preserved in Stobaeus. For the text of both
see *Hierokles: Ethische Elementarlehre*, ed. H. von Arnim and W. Schubart, *Berliner Klassikertexte*, vol. IV (Berlin, 1906).

Since this result, of extending one's other-concern to everybody, is an achievement of reason, one way of putting it is that the agent will, when morality requires it, be concerned only with rationally defensible differences between people. The fact that someone is a remote Mysian rather than my father, say, is not a rationally defensible difference from the moral point of view. It seems reasonable to describe the conclusion of the process of extension as one in which the agent achieves impartiality from the moral point of view. There is no one Greek word or concept which answers to impartiality, but we seem to have convergence on the important points. For impartiality surely requires that from the moral point of view the agent (1) not weight his own interests merely because they are his own and (2) not weight his own particular attachments and commitments merely because they are his own. And this is surely what Stoic ethical theory requires.[24]

Once the Stoics had introduced into ethics this idea — that the rational development of our natural tendency to other-concern ends up requiring impartiality, not just the far less demanding *philia* — we find interesting reactions. On the one hand, we find that the idea finds acceptance; some ethical philosophers agree that once the demand for impartiality has been made, it seems obvious that this and no less is what a moral theory must provide.[25] Thus, we find ethical theories which consciously present themselves as being in the Aristotelian tradition, which nonetheless assume that we reach the moral point of view in the way that the Stoics think we reach it (namely by the rational development of our natural instincts to self-concern and other-concern) and which accept the Stoic point that other-concern requires us to become equally "familiarized" to every rational human. Predictably, such theories have problems, which I shall pass over here, in making this account of morality coherent with the Aristotelian approach.[26]

---

[24] It might be objected that the Stoics have shown only that impartiality is demanded by our promoting part of our nature, namely the rational part, which still leaves problems with happiness, which must satisfy all of our nature. (This is the objection of Antiochus of Ascalon; see Cicero's *de Finibus* IV. The objection was rediscovered independently by Shelly Kagan, one of the contributors to this volume.) But other aspects of Stoic ethics avert this conclusion. Very sketchily: for the Stoics, rationality is not a distinct part of our nature, but a way in which our nature as a whole can develop. We are led to impartiality because rationality properly developed recognizes the special nature of virtue, granting it an overriding role in our lives because of the kind of thing which it is, not because it outweighs other values. Thus, promoting the aspect of ourselves which recognizes the force of impartiality can lead to *eudaimonia*, because our nature as a whole is both rational and able to recognize the special force of reasons that spring from virtue.

[25] Hence it is not true, as is sometimes claimed, that virtue ethics as such implies a meritocratic or inegalitarian perspective. Some versions of eudaimonism (those in the Aristotelian tradition) do have the implication that from the moral point of view some agents count more than others. But the Stoic and Stoic-influenced versions are committed to a moral egalitarianism which, although not as thorough as Kant's, is nonetheless reminiscent of it in some ways.

[26] The most important "hybrid" theories are those of Antiochus in Cicero's *de Finibus* V, and the Aristotelian account of ethics in Arius Didymus; on these, see part 3, chapter 3, sec-

On the other hand, however, we find objections to the claim that morality does require this kind of impartiality in the area of other-concern,
objections which are interestingly reminiscent of some modern protests
against the demand for impartiality in ethics.[27] One passage in particular is worth giving in full, with some comment, because of its intrinsic interest. It comes from the Anonymous Commentator on Plato's *Theaetetus*,
probably from the first century B.C.[28] It takes off from Socrates' comment
in the dialogue that he cares more for the people in his home town of
Athens than for the people at Cyrene.

> [Socrates] cares for the Cyreneans also [as well as the Athenians] and
> by the same principle for all humans whatsoever, for we have been
> familiarized with members of the same species. However, he has
> been more familiarized with his own fellow-citizens, for familiariza-
> tion is more or less intense. So if those [the Stoics] who derive jus-
> tice from familiarization are saying that someone has it equally with
> himself and with the remotest Mysian, then given this assumption
> justice is preserved—but it is not agreed that it *is* equal. For this goes
> against what is evident, and our self-awareness.
>
> For familiarization with oneself is natural and nonrational, while
> familiarization with one's neighbors, while itself natural also, does
> not happen without reason.
>
> Thus if we condemn the wickedness of some other people, we not
> only blame them but are also alienated from them; but when people
> go wrong themselves, they do not accept the opposing claims (?)[29]
> but cannot come to hate themselves. Thus the familiarization is *not*
> equal with oneself and with anyone else.
>
> Indeed, even with the parts of ourselves we are not equally famil-
> iarized. We do not stand in the same relation to an eye and to a fin-
> ger, not to mention nails and hair, since as regards their loss we are
> not alienated in the same way, but more or less.
>
> But if they [the Stoics] say themselves that the familiarization can
> be intensified, then there will indeed be benevolence (*philanthrōpia*),
> but they will be refuted by circumstances . . . where it is necessary

tion 3, of my forthcoming book, *The Morality of Happiness*, and my "The Hellenistic Version
of Aristotle's Ethics," *The Monist*, vol. 73, no. 1 (January 1990), pp. 80–96.

[27] See, in particular, Bernard Williams's classic essay "Persons, Character, and Morality,"
in *The Identities of Persons*, ed. A. Rorty (Berkeley: University of California Press, 1976),
pp. 197–216.

[28] For the text, see *Anonymer Kommentar zu Platons Theaetet*, ed. H. Diels and W. Schubart,
Berliner Klassikertexte, vol. II (Berlin, 1905). The translation is mine. For arguments that the
commentator belongs to the first century B.C., see H. Tarrant, "The Date of Anonymous *In
Theaetetum*," *Classical Quarterly*, vol. XXXIII (1983), pp. 161–87.

[29] The papyrus reading is uncertain at this point, but the general sense of the sentence
is clear.

that only one of them be saved; and even if these circumstances do not arise, they are nonetheless in a position to be refuted.[30]

The initial complaint is that we are, in fact, partial to certain groups of people, not impartial to all. (This is, of course, the basis for *philia* and for political association.) This complaint, like all Anonymous's charges in this passage, is firmly based on common sense and our intuitions — "what is evident." The Stoic response would fairly clearly be that even if we are not in fact impartial to all, but favor some groups more (and if, further, this is "evident"), the Stoics were not intending to deny this, but rather to claim that we *ought* to be impartial, at least where this is morally required.

We should note, incidentally, that we do not have a simple conflict of theory versus intuition. The Stoics do not despise what is evident; they claim indeed that their theory is supported by our intuitions. They mean, however, that the theory *as a whole* answers to our intuitions, not that every individual thesis does. Since the theory contains several very counterintuitive theses, it answers to our intuitions only when our intuitions have been very considerably modified. Thus, if a Stoic thesis turns out to be hopelessly counter-intuitive, this is a count against it, but not necessarily a fatal one.

Anonymous persists with the charge that the Stoic theory is in hopeless conflict with what we find evident. In three ways, he claims, my concern for myself is fundamentally different from my concern for others. Firstly, self-concern is "nonrational" while other-concern is not. That is, I do not come to feel concern for myself on the basis of reasons; I just do feel concern for myself — whereas I do not feel concern for others until I have, and can appreciate that I have, reason to do so. Technically, this misfires as an objection to the Stoic view, which is that self-concern and other-concern are both instinctual, and both develop rationally. But Anonymous clearly has in mind a perennial kind of objection which could be more defensibly posed: that there is something *more* natural and basic about self-concern than about other-concern. I will have self-concern, the thought goes, regardless of what reasons I do or do not have for acting, whereas other-concern rests entirely on recognizing the force of certain reasons; and what does not rest on reasons is more basic and powerful as a form of motivation than what does.

The Stoic reply to this is obvious: why be so pessimistic about the force of reasoning? In a mature rational adult, do instincts in fact have greater motivational force than reasons, or attitudes based on reasons? Further, suppose that in a particular agent they do; are they therefore regarded as having more justificatory weight? Faced by a sudden danger to herself and to another, an agent may well yield to instinct and act to preserve

[30] *Anonymer Kommentar zu Platons Theaetet*, col. 5.14–6.29.

herself, even while knowing that she should have tried to save the other. But this does not in itself justify her action, either to others or to herself.

The second way Anonymous claims that self-concern differs fundamentally from other-concern is alleged to lie in our reaction to wrongdoing and, again, is clearly intended to show the less-fundamental nature of the latter. We feel alienated by the wrongdoing of others, he claims, but do not similarly hate ourselves for our own wrongdoing. There is a correct point here: we know, each in her own case, that we do not in fact regard ourselves as *just* one among others; it is basic common sense that there is a self/other asymmetry; each of us has a special perspective on her own actions, and we cannot feel towards our own actions in the way we feel towards those of others.

Does this, however, show that my own point of view is always a self-*favoring* point of view? The Stoics can reply that we do not in fact always *excuse* ourselves for wrongdoing, and even if we did, we would not regard this as justified. Intuitively, we both recognize the distinctive perspective that we each have on our own actions, and feel that this special perspective does not, in itself, justify or privilege me in what I do. Anonymous thus seems wrong in his claim. He appeals to common sense, but common sense does not support him.

Thirdly, Anonymous points out that nature has made familiarization to our own bodies a matter of degree: hair and nails matter less to us than eyes and fingers do. But if our self-concern naturally turns out to be a matter of degree, then surely other-concern will also. Thus, familiarization will not serve to produce in the agent *equal* concern for all including himself. This is an argument from analogy, and as such is distinctly weak.[31] It is strengthened, however, if we suppose there to be a hidden premise: in the case of self-concern it is clearly *rational* to care less about your hair than about your eyes; thus, there are at least some cases where it is rational for familiarization to be a matter of degree, and it seems that it can be rational to care less about human beings as such than about your own family and country. The claim is, then, that common sense supports the idea that it is a rational requirement on a moral theory that you have *some* concern for others, proportionately to your degree of attachment to them, but not that you have *equal* concern for all.

Can the Stoics meet this point? It is stronger than the other two, since here Anonymous is right: common sense does not demand equal concern for all as morally required, but allows that some count for more than others with the agent, consistently with the demands of morality. On the other hand, it does not support favoring oneself against others, either. Does common sense then favor Anonymous's view, which represents a kind of compromise? This is a difficult point to settle. Intuitively, it seems

---

[31] Unless, as has been suggested to me, the argument is supposed to be a claim, based on inductive surveys of familiarization, to the effect that this process is not one which could lead, as the Stoics want it to lead, to *equal* concern for all.

that common sense does not have a definite view on this point; it rejects both extremes, but does not itself contain a firm view on a definite alternative. If so, then common sense is radically incomplete in this area; theories produce firm views, but cannot support them by appeal to common sense, for in this area they simply go beyond it. As a criticism, then, this charge is neutralized. The Stoics can show that, while their own demand for impartiality is not supported by common sense, neither is either of the claims Anonymous rests his objections on: that we feel justified in favoring ourselves, and in favoring others proportionately to our degree of personal attachment to them. Anonymous can show, at most, that the Stoic demand for impartiality is not directly supported by common sense; he has not shown that it is counter-intuitive and ridiculous.

Finally, Anonymous concedes for the sake of the argument that the process of rational development of other-concern can be "intensified"; he concedes, that is, that we could feel benevolence, a concern broader than concern for ourselves or for particular other people. Even if this is so, he says, self-concern will win out. He uses an example destined to have a long history. In a shipwreck two people struggle for life. At this point the papyrus gives out, but we know the situation from another source, a passage in the third book of Cicero's *De Officiis* where we get a list of textbook examples in Stoic ethics. There are two passengers and only one plank on which to float to safety. Which should have it? The Stoic solution is: the morally worthier one should, and if they are equal in this respect then they should use a fair random procedure.

> "If there is only one plank and two shipwrecked men, both of them [Stoic] virtuous men, would each try to seize it for himself, or would one cede it to the other?" "One would cede it, and it would go to the one whose life is of more value to himself or his country." "What if there is nothing to choose between them on this point?" "There will be no struggle; one will cede to the other as though the loser by lot or in a game of chance."[32]

It seems fairly clear that Anonymous's objection was going to be that this is absurd, since in fact anyone in such a position would fight for the plank himself. It would be not only more interesting, but more in keeping with the stress here on *philanthrōpia* (benevolence), if the example were of someone wanting to save not himself but some other particular person to whom he is committed. In a similar discussion, Bernard Williams uses the example of a man in a shipwreck saving not himself but his wife. And failure to be impartial is displayed just as much in favoring one's spouse or friends as in favoring oneself. However, we do seem to have the same situation as before: concern for my own welfare versus concern for the welfare of others. The Stoic reply would be the familiar

[32] Cicero, *De Officiis* III 90.

one: it is not, in fact, obvious or "evident" that we do favor ourselves in situations like these, and, even if we do, it is far from "evident" that we regard such partiality as morally justified. Thus, Anonymous's objection fails again: he has not shown that the Stoic view is absurd or grossly counter-intuitive. Once again, common sense is indecisive on the matter: it does not demand impartiality as something morally required, but neither does it endorse self-favoring as morally acceptable.

Anonymous's objections, as already noted, are very like those that have been brought against the role of impartiality in modern theories such as Kantianism and consequentialism. The question is simply whether morality requires impartiality. The special features of virtue ethics do not come into the argument at all. Anonymous urges that any reasonable person would find the Stoic claim absurd; at no point does he suggest that the Stoics are flouting, or even likely to have trouble with, any formal feature of an ethical theory based on virtue and the agent's final end. Nor is there any sign from any other ancient critic of the Stoics that a problem was felt in demanding impartiality within a eudaimonistic theory.

Eudamonism is thus seen as a type of theory which can accommodate stronger or weaker demands on other-concern. The eudaimonistic framework includes hedonistic theories which have a problem accommodating other-concern; Aristotelian theories which assume that some degree of other-concern, namely *philia*, is required in the agent's life; and Stoic theories which demand an equal degree of impartial other-concern towards everybody.[33] Eudaimonism is plainly seen as being equally compatible with strong demands on other-concern as with weak ones. Thus, the felt problem about scope turns out to be illusory; eudaimonism as such sets no limits on the scope of other-concern.

Just this point about scope, however, may raise anew the second felt problem, the problem of status. For the way we reached the above conclusion underlined the fact that the demand for impartiality is not an essential part of the eudaimonistic framework — just because *no* particular demand about other-concern is part of it. Does this not, however, revive the worry that the interests of others do not have the right kind of status within eudaimonism? It is no part of the eudaimonist framework itself that one should give the interests of others any particular weight.

Is this a problem, however? The problem of status arose from the thought expressed above that "in a eudaimonistic theory, the agent's own view of his life is not only the entry-point but the perspective of ethics," and from the consequent suspicion that the interests of others seemed doomed to have a status which is in some way secondary or less serious than the agent's own interests. But the investigation about scope ended in showing that the agent's own view of his life did not in itself put any

---

[33] And, of course, hybrid theories which aim to combine features of the Aristotelian and Stoic types.

substantial restrictions of a self-interested kind on the content of *eudaimonia*. When we realize that eudaimonism is compatible with a number of theses about other-concern, some of them very demanding, we see that the status question rests upon an incomplete or defective understanding of eudaimonism. Put perhaps rather crudely: if eudaimonism is thought of as a kind of theory which embodies substantial self-interest, then there is indeed a status problem; but once we see that it is a kind of theory which, as such, involves no such substantial self-interest, then the status problem dissolves.

It might be claimed that this dissolution is premature; surely problems of principle remain, at least with the ancient theories which make strong demands on other-concern. Impartiality, surely, fits more awkwardly into a eudaimonist theory than into other forms. The whole point of a eudaimonist theory was that ethical reasoning begins from the agent's point of view, and aims to render the agent's priorities coherent and organized, but how is this compatible with accepting a strong view of the requirements of rationality which impose impartiality on the agent? How can morally required detachment from one's own point of view fail to be in conflict with the rest of a theory which starts from one's own point of view? By now this objection can clearly be seen as superficial. If one takes it, as the Stoics do, that humans are rational creatures and that the development of our nature leads us to see the force and importance of acting on certain sorts of reasons, then there will be nothing strange in the fact that the rational agent will organize her life in ways which give priority to the impartial viewpoint. There is here an analogue with utilitarianism. It has seemed to many paradoxical that a theory which begins from the importance of maximizing welfare (in some form) should demand of the agent that she detach herself from her own welfare and devote her life to producing the maximum of welfare, no matter whose it is.[34] The familiar reply is that this seems strange only if we fail to stress the importance, to rational agents, of appreciating and acting on what rationality requires.

Another objection which is often made is that there *must* be a deep tension between impartiality and eudaimonism, just because impartiality may, on occasion, require you to sacrifice your own happiness. Even if your happiness figured at the start of the reasoning that led you to this conclusion, how can it without paradox be said to be functioning at the point when you are required to do this? This problem, however, springs entirely from confusion between the comparatively rigid way that happiness functions in modern moral theories, and the different role it has in ancient theories. For all ancient theories, the fundamental notion is that of the agent's final good; happiness is regarded as a weak and unspecific characterization of this, one which is very differently specified (as, for example, pleasure, virtue, and so on) in the different theories. Thus, when I begin from the idea that my final good is happiness, this is so under-

---

[34] Of course, utilitarians make moves to defend their theory at this point.

stood that when, with the help of one or other available theory, I specify my final good as, say, virtue, the result is that happiness, correctly
understood, consists simply in virtue. One implication of this may per-
fectly well be that happiness, as specified by the theory, demands that I
sacrifice happiness as I understood it before I started to adopt the theory
(in terms of money, health, and so on). There is no paradox here, because
happiness was taken to be a thin conception of the good from the start.
Philosophers accustomed to modern moral theories may well still find the
conclusion unacceptable, but this simply reflects the greater rigidity of our
conception of happiness (and, thus, the limits we should bear in mind
when thinking of *eudaimonia* as happiness).[35]

On the view I have put forward, what is contentious, and contested,
in ancient ethical theory is the extent of the demands made by rationality in one's ethical thought. What is not contentious, and indeed what nobody bothers to contend, is that ethical thought is eudaimonist in form.
The entry-point for ethical thought is reflection on one's life as a whole;
this is reflection on how to achieve *eudaimonia* and on the place of morality, in the shape of the virtues, in a life which does achieve *eudaimonia*.
These are clichés. But there are disagreements over the nature of the demands of other-concern in the agent's life, and these spring from a different source, namely disagreement as to what rationality requires.

Of course, I am aware that "what rationality requires" is itself a large
and difficult topic, and needs further work to make it clear. I have here
simply tried to show two things. One is that eudaimonism as a type of
theory is not committed to any particular view about the extent of other-
concern which is morally demanded. I have concentrated on the Stoics
in order to show that eudaimonism is in fact compatible with an extreme
view about other-concern, but the wider message is that eudaimonism,
as such, does not require any particular level of demandingness as far as
other-concern goes. The second point is that, once eudaimonism is properly understood as a type of theory which is formally self-centered but assumes no substantial self-interest, there is no problem of principle with
the fact that some forms of eudaimonism make stringent moral demands
on the agent in the name of the interests of others. In particular, forms
of eudaimonism which make virtue central to one's *eudaimonia* can be
seen as raising exactly the same problems as modern theories of morality which make morality very demanding, even though the answers
which they give are rather different.

Philosophy, Columbia University

---

[35] This paragraph deals in a necessarily rather abrupt way with a point of great interest,
which marks the greatest conceptual divide between ancient and modern theories. The point
is dealt with in more detail, with reference to several ancient theories, in parts 4 and 5 of
my forthcoming book (see footnote 6).

VIRTUE AS LOVING THE GOOD

By Thomas Hurka

In a chapter of *The Methods of Ethics* entitled "Ultimate Good," Henry Sidgwick defends hedonism, the theory that pleasure and only pleasure is intrinsically good, that is, good in itself and apart from its consequences. First, however, he argues against the theory that virtue is intrinsically good. Sidgwick considers both a strong version of this theory—that virtue is the only intrinsic good—and a weaker version—that it is one intrinsic good among others. He tries to show that neither version is or can be true.

Against the strong version of the theory, Sidgwick argues as follows. Virtue is a disposition to act rightly, and right action is identified by the good it promotes. (He believes the second, consequentialist premise has been justified by his lengthy critique of nonconsequentialist moralities in Book III of *The Methods of Ethics*.) But this means that treating virtue as the only intrinsic good involves a "logical circle": virtue is a disposition to promote what is good, where what is good is itself just a disposition to promote what is good.[1] Virtue turns out to be a disposition to promote virtue.

As Hastings Rashdall notes in a commentary on Sidgwick, one can accept many of this argument's premises yet reject its conclusion. One can agree that right action is identified by its consequences but still hold that virtue is the only intrinsic good. One can do this if one denies that the relevant consequences are good. This is the Stoic view: certain states are "preferred," and thus supply the criterion of right action, but are not themselves intrinsically good. As Rashdall continues, however, the Stoic view is "paradoxical."[2] How can it be right to produce certain consequences if those consequences are not good? If the consequences must be good for the action to be right, Sidgwick's conclusion follows: virtue cannot be the only intrinsic good.

Against the weaker view that virtue is just one intrinsic good among others, Sidgwick's argument is, by his own lights, less conclusive. It is also more difficult to reconstruct, but it seems to start from the same premises. If virtue is a disposition to promote what is good, it is by definition something instrumentally good. And, Sidgwick writes, "it seems difficult to conceive any kind of activity or process as both means and

---

[1] Henry Sidgwick, *The Methods of Ethics*, 7th ed. (London: Macmillan, 1907), p. 392.

[2] Hastings Rashdall, "Professor Sidgwick's Utilitarianism," *Mind*, old series, vol. 10 (1885), p. 207.

149

end, from precisely the same point of view and in respect of precisely the same quality."[3] If virtue is essentially instrumentally good, in other words, it cannot be intrinsically good.

As Rashdall also notes, one can reject this conclusion, and not just on a Stoic basis. Following Rashdall, I will develop an account of the goodness of virtue that does so. The account accepts all of Sidgwick's premises, and therefore accepts his first conclusion. It agrees that virtue must be defined by relation to the good and therefore cannot be the *only* intrinsic good. It maintains, however, that virtue is *an* intrinsic good. The core of the account is an iterative or recursive characterization of the good, which identifies some intrinsic goods by their relationship to others.

This account is important theoretically. It is widely assumed that consequentialist moralities cannot treat virtue as intrinsically good, and it is instructive to see that they can. I believe the account is also intuitively appealing. Some may say that, even if virtue *can* be intrinsically good, it is not: what is good is only pleasure, or happiness, or the items on a list that does not include virtue. Many of us do not share this view. We believe that in assessing the goodness of a life (for example, our own when we look back on it) we should give some consideration to its responsiveness to moral values. My recursive account captures this view and gives it a satisfying rationale. In doing so, it assumes a certain picture of what virtue is, one that accepts Sidgwick's premises and is therefore consequentialist. As I shall argue, however, the account honors many traditional claims about virtue and should be widely acceptable as describing at least part of what virtue involves.

I. Loving the Good and Hating the Evil

The recursive characterization of the good begins by identifying some states other than virtue as intrinsically good. Let us imagine that it affirms:

(1) Pleasure, knowledge, and the achievement of difficult goals are intrinsically good.

It then adds a recursion clause about loving what is good, or more specifically, about loving it for itself:

(2) If x is intrinsically good, loving x for itself is also intrinsically good.

By "loving x" I mean having a positive affective or conative relationship to x. This takes three main forms: desiring or wishing for x when it is not present, actively pursuing x to make it present, and taking pleasure in x

---

[3] Sidgwick, *The Methods of Ethics*, p. 396; see also p. 393.

when it is present. By loving x "for itself" I mean loving it apart from its consequences, that is, loving instances of x because they are instances of x. One may believe that x is good and love it for that reason or, without any thoughts about goodness, feel a simple emotional attraction to x. Either way, if one's love does not depend on x's consequences, one loves x for itself. Given clause (2), if other people's pleasure is intrinsically good, then desiring, pursuing, and taking pleasure in their pleasure for itself are also intrinsically good. Likewise, if knowledge is good, then desiring, pursuing, and taking pleasure in knowledge for itself are good.

From this beginning, the recursive characterization can be extended. Clause (2) makes it good to love for itself what is intrinsically good. It is a natural extension of this to affirm:

(3) If x is instrumentally good, loving x as a means is intrinsically good.

If it is intrinsically good to love other people's pleasure, it should also be intrinsically good to love the means to that pleasure; if it is good to love knowledge, it should be good to love what increases knowledge.[4] The love of instrumental goods presupposes the love of intrinsic goods and can only be an addition to it; it cannot stand on its own. It is, however, a morally appropriate addition: responding fully to the good requires loving intrinsic goods for themselves and instrumental goods as means.

The recursive characterization can go further if it affirms the existence of intrinsic evils, states that not only lack positive value but have negative value. Imagine that it affirms:

(4) Pain, false belief, and the failure to achieve a difficult goal are intrinsically evil.

It can then add:

(5) If x is intrinsically evil, loving x for itself is also intrinsically evil.

If others' pain is evil, then desiring, pursuing, and taking pleasure in their pain for itself is evil.

There can also be clauses about hating x (desiring or pursuing x's destruction, being pained by x's presence):

(6) If x is intrinsically good, hating x for itself is intrinsically evil.
(7) If x is intrinsically evil, hating x for itself is intrinsically good.

[4] The love of what is instrumentally good is often itself instrumentally good, if it encourages one to promote what is good. But this is a matter of empirical fact, not of moral principle. Clause (3) says that loving what is instrumentally good is good intrinsically, that is, good apart from its effects, because it is an appropriate response to one kind of good.

These make it evil to be pained by others' pleasure and good to feel for their pain. Finally, there can be instrumental versions of clauses (5)–(7), making it, for example, intrinsically evil to hate as a means what is instrumentally good.

Given the many clauses in the foregoing characterization, the same state can be the object of different (and even conflicting) good attitudes. Imagine that someone has a painful experience that increases her self-knowledge. We may hate the experience for being painful but love it for promoting knowledge; we may regret it when we consider it on its own but approve it as a means. Which attitude is stronger should depend on what is greater: the evil in the experience or the good in its results.

This recursive characterization allows an account of the intrinsic goodness of virtue. It does so, obviously, if we define virtue as loving the good, or, more precisely, as loving the good and hating the evil as they are good and evil. (From now on I shall use "loving the good" to mean both "loving for itself what is intrinsically good" and "loving as a means what is instrumentally good," with a parallel use for "hating the evil.") This definition of virtue as loving the good assumes a certain picture of virtue, but, if we accept that picture, we can combine it with the recursive characterization to construct a recursive account of the goodness of virtue. If virtue is loving the good—if it consists in desiring, pursuing, and taking pleasure in the good—then to affirm the goodness of loving the good is to affirm the goodness of virtue.

This recursive account is not novel. It or partial statements of it appear in Rashdall, who affirms "the intrinsic worth of promoting what has worth,"[5] and in Aristotle, G. E. Moore, W. D. Ross, and Robert Nozick. Consider Aristotle's view of pleasure:

> Since activities differ in respect of goodness and badness, and some are worthy to be chosen, others to be avoided, and others neutral, so, too, are the pleasures; for to each activity there is a proper pleasure. The pleasure proper to a worthy activity is good and that proper to an unworthy activity bad; just as the appetites for noble objects are laudable, those for base objects culpable.[6]

For Aristotle, pleasure in itself is neither good nor bad; its value depends on that of its object. If contemplation is good, pleasure in contemplation is good, and contemplation accompanied by pleasure is better than contemplation without pleasure. If gluttony is bad, pleasure in glut-

---

[5] Rashdall, *The Theory of Good and Evil*, vol. 1 (London: Oxford University Press, 1907), p. 59; see also pp. 63–67, and "Professor Sidgwick's Utilitarianism," pp. 207–8.

[6] Aristotle, *Nicomachean Ethics*, trans. David Ross (Oxford: Oxford University Press, 1980), 1175b24–30. The connection with virtue is that "moral virtue and vice are concerned with pleasures and pains" (*ibid.*, 1152b5–6; see also 1104b8–1105b13).

tony is bad, and gluttony accompanied by pleasure is worse than gluttony alone.

A fuller version of the recursive account is found in Moore's *Principia Ethica*.[7] Moore counts as intrinsic evils, not only pain, but the enjoyment or admiring contemplation of what is evil and the hatred of what is good. Moore also recognizes "mixed" goods: for example, the hatred of what is evil. Not all of Moore's theory follows the recursive line. He thinks one intrinsic good is the admiring contemplation of what is beautiful, where to call something beautiful is not to say that it is itself good, but to say that a whole containing it is good. Thus, the love of x is sometimes good when x is not. Since the love itself is good, however, the recursion clauses apply to it. Another intrinsic good, then, is the admiring contemplation of other people's good qualities, which include their contemplation of beauty.

Ross holds that there are three intrinsic goods: pleasure, knowledge, and virtue. An important part of virtue, however, is action springing from (a) "the desire to bring into being something good" or (b) "the desire to produce some pleasure, or prevent some pain, for another being."[8] Since pleasure is itself something good, desire (b), no less than desire (a), involves a positive relation to something good.[9]

Finally, the recursive approach is explicitly discussed in Nozick's *Philosophical Explanations*. Nozick uses the phrase "*V*-ing value" where I use "loving the good," but we mean the same thing. Nozick makes a very strong claim: he says that the truth of the recursion clauses must follow from the initial or base characterization of the good. Given the content of clause (1), clauses (2)–(7) must be true.[10] I will not discuss this claim here, but Nozick states, in its full generality, the same recursive view suggested by Rashdall, Aristotle, Moore, and Ross.

The view these philosophers share involves a certain perfectionism. It holds that at least one thing, virtue, is good regardless of whether anyone wants, cares about, or takes pleasure in it. (Virtue involves people's caring about other goods, but its value does not depend on whether they care about *virtue*.) These particular philosophers make other perfectionist claims. In the base clauses of their recursive accounts, Aristotle, Rashdall, and Ross hold that knowledge is intrinsically good; Moore holds that

---

[7] G. E. Moore, *Principia Ethica* (Cambridge: Cambridge University Press, 1903), ch. 6.

[8] W. D. Ross, *The Right and the Good* (Oxford: Clarendon Press, 1930), p. 160.

[9] Desire (a) must be read opaquely, as the desire to bring into being something *because it is good*. This is both evident from the context (see *ibid.*, esp. p. 161) and necessary to prevent desire (b) from falling under desire (a). But this reading of desire (a) leaves a lacuna in Ross's account. If it is good, and an exercise of virtue, to desire pleasure for itself without thinking it good, why is it not also good to desire knowledge and virtue for themselves without thinking them good? The special status (if any) of the desire for things *as good* is discussed in Section V below.

[10] Robert Nozick, *Philosophical Explanations* (Cambridge: Harvard University Press, 1981), pp. 429–33.

the contemplation of beauty is intrinsically good; and Nozick holds that organic unity is intrinsically good. But their shared view is compatible with anti-perfectionism about other goods — and, at the extreme, with hedonism about other goods. The base clause of a possible recursive account might hold only that pleasure is good and pain evil, and the recursion clauses might apply only to these two feelings. Loving pleasure and hating pain would then be the only second-level goods, and their opposites the only second-level evils.

Even in this restricted form, the recursive view has many attractive features. First, it gives a unified account of what virtue is. In its various manifestations in desire, action, and feeling, virtue always involves a positive orientation toward what is good or a negative orientation toward what is evil. Second, the account honors traditional understandings of virtue. Virtue is thought to be a matter of character, of the dispositions and motives behind a person's acts. This is captured by the account's references to pursuits and desires. Virtue is also thought to involve feelings; this is reflected in the account's talk of pleasures. Finally, the account is, in my view, intuitively appealing, both in itself and for its consequences. The general idea that a positive relation to the good is good, is attractive by itself; and, when combined with hedonism about first-level goods, it corrects hedonism at just those points where hedonists should most agree it needs correcting.

Imagine two possible worlds.[11] In the first world, natural conditions are benign and, because of this, people live very pleasantly. But they are all self-concerned: they do not desire or pursue each other's pleasure, and their hearts are cold to any enjoyments not their own. In the second world, resources are more scarce and there is some disease, but people are more altruistic. They care about each other's happiness and are pleased when it is attained. This altruism increases their happiness, but not enough to overcome their natural disadvantages. Despite their mutual concern, people in the second world enjoy less pleasure overall than those in the first.

Hedonism says that the first of these worlds is better, because it contains more pleasure. But many of us would reverse this ordering: if we could bring either world into existence, we would prefer the second, the one with more altruism. Hedonists should feel pressure to join in this preference. People in the second world have more of the attitude toward pleasure — valuing it everywhere — that hedonists think is proper. Should this not be reflected in the hedonists' judgments of the values of the two worlds? (There is no logical compulsion here, but the move seems natural.) The recursive account captures the intuition that the second world is preferable. By caring about each other's pleasure, the people in the second world manifest more virtue, and the value of their regard for one another can outweigh their shortfall in pleasure.

---

[11] See Ross, *The Right and the Good*, pp. 134–35.

The recursive account of virtue also corrects a more familiar weakness in hedonism. If someone who causes another person pain (for example, a torturer) takes pleasure in his activity, hedonism says that this makes the situation intrinsically better than if he were indifferent about his action or, worse, pained by it. Most of us cannot accept this. We think the torturer's pleasure, even apart from any bad effects it may have on victims, makes the torturing worse. Again, the recursive account explains why. In enjoying his victim's pain and his own role in causing it, the torturer loves intrinsic and instrumental evils. This is morally vicious, and has negative moral worth.

These implications of the recursive account bear on issues of self-sacrifice. Imagine that a person foregoes pleasure for himself to promote it for others. If the pleasure the others gain is greater than the pleasure he loses, his action may, on balance, be right. But must it involve a sacrifice of his own good? Must he be, on balance, a loser? The recursive account may allow us to say no. A plausible principle is:

(8) If x is intrinsically better than y, loving x for itself is intrinsically better than loving y for itself.

By pursuing the greater pleasure of others, the person manifests more virtue than if he loved just his own pleasure. Whether this entirely makes good his loss of pleasure depends on how much weight virtue has relative to other goods (see Section IV). If virtue has great weight, his action involves no sacrifice; even if it does not, his sacrifice is less than if virtue were not valuable.

The account's attractive consequences are extended if its base clause is not hedonistic, but affirms perfectionist goods such as knowledge and achievement. Many great intellectual figures (for example, Aristotle in his career as a physicist) did not achieve much knowledge. Despite the brilliance of their thought, most of their explanatory theories about the world were false. Similarly, many inspiring political actors do not achieve the noble goals they seek. Does this mean that their lives contain little intrinsic value? The recursive account lets us say no. By desiring and seeking knowledge he did not have, Aristotle showed exemplary love of knowledge, and the value of this love may compensate for his false beliefs.[12] In the same way, someone who pursues noble goals shows a love of achievement. It would be best if this love led to real achievement, but even alone it has some worth.

As a final attractive feature, the recursive account captures the difficult status of virtue as both a dependent and an independent moral concept. Since virtue consists in the right response to other moral considerations,

---

[12] More generally, the recursive account captures the view shared by many that there is special value in the search for knowledge, as opposed to the mere possession of knowledge; see Ross, *The Right and the Good*, p. 152.

it requires the existence of other considerations and cannot be morally foundational. At the same time, it is not reducible to other considerations; it is of separate moral significance. Both points are captured in the recursive account: virtue is a response to other considerations but, as this response, is separately good.

In the particular way it captures these points, the account satisfies the premises of Sidgwick's arguments and is consistent with moral consequentialism. The account makes virtue intrinsically good, and, as good, virtue can be something that it is morally right to promote. (It can usually be promoted only indirectly, but when it can be so promoted, it should be.) More importantly, the account defines virtue by reference to the good. "Good" is the central explanatory concept in consequentialism; therefore, an account framed in terms of the good uses consequentialist materials. It defines virtue in a way consistent with consequentialist moralities.

Of course, some philosophers reject these moralities. They hold that, although there is some duty to promote the good, there are other duties that can conflict with it. These philosophers should not abandon the recursive account; they should expand it. This is what Ross does. He is not a consequentialist; he affirms several duties other than a duty to promote intrinsic good. This is reflected in his account of virtue: for him, virtue consists, not just in acting from the desire for something good or for other people's pleasure, but also in acting from the desire to do one's duty.[13] Ross believes that this additional form of virtue can conflict with the other two and, when it does, should outweigh them. Imagine that someone refrains from breaking a promise even when doing so would most promote others' pleasure. He shows less love of others' pleasure than he might, but if his motive is to do what is right, then his motive, according to Ross, is the best possible in the circumstances. Philosophers who are hostile to consequentialism can follow Ross's line. They can agree that the recursive account gives part of the truth about virtue, the part concerning virtuous responses to good and evil, but not the whole truth. It supplies an attractive initial picture of virtue—one that would be complete if consequentialism were true, and is a large part of the picture even if consequentialism is false.

II. VIRTUE AND SELF-SUFFICIENCY

The three main forms of virtue are desiring the good when it is not present, pursuing it to make it present, and taking pleasure in it when it is present. How do the different values of these three combine to make up complete virtue?

---

[13] *Ibid.*, pp. 157–60.

Three different views are possible. A very generous view says that any one form of virtue is sufficient for complete virtue. If you desire a certain good, your virtue with respect to that good will not be greater if you also pursue and take pleasure in it. A very restrictive view says that all three forms are necessary for any virtue—lack one and the other two are valueless. Finally, an intermediate view says that each form has some value, but that complete virtue requires them all. The overall value of one's response to a good is something like the sum of the values of one's desiring, pursuing, and taking pleasure in it.

Deciding among these views involves deciding to what extent virtue is self-sufficient, that is, something each person can attain on his own, without external aids. Desiring the good seems possible for anyone in any circumstances; no matter how bad one's lot, one can always wish it were better. Thus, the generous view that requires only one form of virtue makes virtue entirely self-sufficient: it can be attained by anyone anywhere. On the restrictive view, however, virtue is not at all self-sufficient. To pursue the good actively, one must believe one has a chance of achieving it, which is not possible in all circumstances. To be pleased by it, one must have it present to contemplate. (If the good is not present, one can take pleasure in imagining it, but the love of imaginary goods is less good than the love of real ones—see Section III.) The intermediate view, which I favor, makes virtue only partly self-sufficient. The value of desiring the good can be achieved by anyone; the further values of pursuing and enjoying it cannot.

The same issue arises when we try to specify the second form of virtue, pursuing the good. Some philosophers hold that virtuous action is better when it is competent, when the manner of its execution allows a justified belief that it will achieve its goal.[14] Others hold that pursuit of the good is better when it is successful, or does achieve its goal. Aristotle, for example, holds both views. He thinks that complete virtue requires practical wisdom, which involves not just aiming at the right mark but choosing the "right means" and actually "hitting" the mark.[15] These claims further diminish the self-sufficiency of virtue. Competence in action requires experience and training, which not everyone receives, and even given competent action, success requires the absence of bad luck. Whatever external aid is needed to pursue the good, more is needed to do so competently and successfully.

For some philosophers, virtue essentially involves a disposition, a stable tendency to respond in morally appropriate ways. As Aristotle puts it, a virtuous act "must proceed from a firm and unchangeable character."[16] To be morally interesting, this view must concern the value of a

[14] Philippa Foot suggests this view in the title essay of her *Virtues and Vices* (Berkeley: University of California Press, 1978), pp. 4–5.

[15] Aristotle, *Nicomachean Ethics*, 1144a8, 1144a26.

[16] *Ibid.*, 1105a34.

stable disposition. It must claim that a loving response to the good is better, or is good only, when it is part of a continuing series of similar responses. I do not believe this moral claim is correct. Someone who has a virtuous disposition will have a better life overall than someone who does not, because he will have a greater number of good desires, acts, and feelings. When we set this fact aside, however, I see no reason to value his individual response to some good more highly than a similar response from someone who is not stably disposed. (We might even prefer the second, out-of-character response, since it was achieved against greater obstacles.) Nonetheless, Aristotle's view can be accommodated within the recursive account. We can say that instances of loving the good have more value, or value only, when they are preceded and followed by similar instances issuing from the same disposition. This view, again, diminishes the self-sufficiency of virtue. Whether I achieve virtue now depends on facts about my acts and feelings in the past and future, facts that are not presently under my control.

It is widely recognized that first-level goods such as pleasure and knowledge are not self-sufficient, but virtue is often thought to be different. One possible view (the generous view that finds complete virtue in desiring the good) does leave virtue entirely under a person's control, but others make its full attainment depend on numerous external factors.

III. LOVING IMAGINARY GOODS AND EVILS

On an initial reading, clauses (2)–(7) concern the love and hatred of real goods and evils, that is, real instances of knowledge, pain, and the like. But one can also have attitudes toward imaginary goods and evils; one can have such attitudes while falsely believing that the goods and evils are real or while knowing that they are not (as occurs in fantasies). The account of virtue should be extended to cover these attitudes.

To illustrate one sort of case, consider Aristotle's love of knowledge. He demonstrated this love partly by seeking knowledge he did not have and partly by taking pleasure in knowledge he thought he had. He thought his explanatory physical theories were true, and he was pleased to have such theories. In fact, of course, his theories were false. This does not prevent his pleasure in them from being virtuous, or even from having the same value as pleasure in real knowledge. If we compare Aristotle's attitude toward his imagined knowledge with a similar attitude toward real knowledge, there is no reason to value the former less.

A parallel point holds for imagined evils. In well-known psychological experiments, subjects inflict what they believe is intense pain on another person. If a subject enjoys his imagined inflicting of pain, this is surely just as vicious as if the pain were real. Pleasure in what one falsely believes is pain, is just as bad as pleasure in the real thing.

The more complex case is where the imagined good or evil is self-consciously imagined, that is, where it is known not to be real. This occurs in fantasies and horrors. Fantasies and horrors are self-conscious imaginings that are affectively colored: with pleasure, for fantasies; with pain, for horrors. Both of these imaginings involve a content and a response to that content: one knowingly imagines a state or event and either takes pleasure in it or is caused pain. In either case, the response may concern the state only as imagined: someone who fantasizes evil may have no desire to cause real evil and no capacity to be pleased by it. Nonetheless, if he enjoys the evil as imagined, his imagining qualifies as a fantasy.

Consider a specific fantasy with an evil content, say, that of committing a violent rape. Unlike other theories, such as hedonism, the recursive account says that this fantasy is intrinsically evil. The fantasy may also be instrumentally evil, and will be if it encourages real rape. Even if it does not, even if the fantasy prevents rape by drawing off the energies behind it, it is intrinsically regrettable. People who can only avoid real violence by such morally dubious means are depraved.

Loving fantasized evils may be less evil than loving real ones. Someone who enjoys only imaginary rapes may be less depraved than if he relished actual rapes. If so, there is a difference between fantasy and the earlier case of false belief. In this earlier case, loving what one believed was pain seemed just as bad as loving real pain. In both cases, however, the love of imaginary evils is, if sometimes a lesser evil, still an evil.

In making these claims, the recursive account avoids the difficulties faced by other views about imaginings. A traditional view holds that rape fantasies involve not evils (undesirable states of affairs) but sins (undesirable acts), more specifically, "sins of the heart." This switch from notions of good and evil to notions of right and wrong, from judgments about states of affairs to judgments about acts, is problematic. We normally think wrongness requires voluntariness, that an act can only be wrong if a person could have prevented it, but the disturbing elements in fantasy are often not voluntary. For some people, once a violent rape is imagined, their pleasure in it cannot be blocked. Moreover, although sometimes their imagining is voluntary (as when they rent a pornographic video) often it is not; the whole fantasy, content and response, may appear unbidden in their minds. How, then, can it be wrong?

Faced with this difficulty, adherents of the traditional view use desperate measures. Aquinas describes the sin in evil fantasy as that of "consent to delectation," as if there were in every fantasy a conscious choice to enjoy it.[17] Robert M. Adams denies that wrongness requires voluntariness.[18] But why take either route when we can evaluate imaginings

---

[17] St. Thomas Aquinas, *Summa Theologica*, trans. Fathers of the English Dominican Province (Westminster, Maryland: Christian Classics, 1981), Ia–IIae, question 74, article 8.

[18] Robert M. Adams, "Involuntary Sins," *The Philosophical Review*, vol. 94 (1985), pp. 3–31.

using the theory of good and evil? Pain and false belief are, on this theory, evil and regrettable even when they are not chosen, and the same can hold for vicious fantasies. They can make a person's life less valuable and can be something he should strive against even when they are not presently under his direct control.

A more difficult question concerns virtuous fantasies. The recursive view implies that, if fantasizing evils is evil, fantasizing goods should be good, but it is not clear that we believe this conclusion. Do we believe that imagining pleasure, knowledge, or acts that promote them, and being pleased by what we imagine, is intrinsically good? Do we think people should fill their empty hours with virtuous fantasies? We may believe that if a person imagines an intrinsic good, it is better to take pleasure in it than not. Regarding evil fantasies, we have the stronger view that imagining the evil and enjoying it is worse than not imagining it at all, but it is not clear that we have the parallel view about virtuous fantasies. If we do not, our attitude suggests a further difference between this case and the earlier case of false belief. In the earlier case, falsely believing a good to be real and taking pleasure in it did seem positively good. If the parallel claim about imagined goods is not plausible, our account may have to be modified. It may have to say that, although fantasizing evils is evil, fantasizing goods is not good, or at least not good to the same degree that fantasizing evils is evil.

IV. How Good Is Virtue?

If virtue is intrinsically good, how great a good is it? How does its value compare with that of other intrinsic goods?

Some philosophers make very strong claims about this. Ross says that virtue is infinitely better than any other good, that is, infinitely better than pleasure or knowledge.[19] Rashdall's view is less extreme, but still makes virtue the (finitely) highest good.[20] Against both views, I will argue that virtue is a lesser good, one whose value is a smaller function $[f(x) < x]$ of the other goods to which it relates.

Consider, first, Ross's view that virtue is infinitely better than other goods. Applied to the two worlds of Section I, this view says that the second world is better even if the people in it are only slightly more altruistic and, because of terrible natural conditions, far less happy. This is surely not what we believe. In judging the two worlds, we do not look only at the pleasure they contain, but we do give it some weight. Even if we disagree about exactly how much pleasure makes good a loss in virtue, surely some amount of it does.

[19] Ross, *The Right and the Good*, pp. 149-54.
[20] Rashdall, *The Theory of Good and Evil*, vol. 2, p. 37.

Consider a second example.[21] Someone pondering a career as a nurse may know that in this career she will do much to relieve others' pain; at the same time, she may rightly fear that nursing will harden her character. The constant exposure to suffering will change her from someone who feels deeply for others' pain to one who is untouched by it, who handles it efficiently but without much emotion. If virtue were infinitely better than pleasure, it would be wrong for this person to become a nurse. But few would agree with this. Perhaps small benefits to others do not justify hardening one's character, but large ones surely do.

These arguments are compatible with Rashdall's view that virtue, though not infinitely better than other goods, normally outweighs them. However, if virtue normally outweighed other goods and evils, it would be better if one person suffered pain and another sympathized with his pain than if the first had no pain at all. This is unacceptable: the second person's sympathy manifests virtue and is intrinsically good, but it cannot be so good that it outweighs the pain. As Moore argues, the theodicy that justifies evil on the ground that it permits virtuous responses to evil is untenable.[22] Pain conjoined with sympathy is better than pain alone, but it must still be on balance evil. The same holds generally for evils and virtuous hatings of them. Arguments are sometimes advanced that seem to deny this: Aristotle praises private property because it allows charitable acts by the rich;[23] I have heard contemporary neoconservatives condemn the welfare state because it discourages charity. The argument these remarks suggest—that it is good that there are poor people, because the rich can act generously toward them—is odious. Even if generosity is virtuous and a proper response to poverty, it can never make poverty desirable.

This argument suggests the following principle:

(9) If x is intrinsically evil, hating x for itself, though intrinsically good, is not as intrinsically good as x is intrinsically evil.

This principle ensures that any combination of an evil and someone's virtuous response to it is on balance evil. It also suggests the following generalization:

(10) If x is intrinsically good or evil, loving or hating x for itself, though intrinsically good or evil, is not as intrinsically good or evil as x is intrinsically good or evil.

---

[21] *Ibid.*, p. 47.

[22] Moore, *Principia Ethica*, pp. 219–20.

[23] Aristotle, *Politics*, trans. Benjamin Jowett, in *The Basic Works of Aristotle*, ed. Richard McKeon (New York: Random House, 1941), 1263a25–b14. Aristotle is criticizing Plato's proposals about communal property in the *Republic*, but in doing so he mentions only the effects on those who will be rich under a system of private property, and never the effects on those who will be poor.

Principle (10) does not follow from (9). One can affirm (9) about hating evils, yet hold, for some virtue of loving, that loving x has more value than x. I am inclined, however, to affirm (10). This is partly for reasons of theoretical simplicity. If a comparative claim is compelling for one virtue, it seems natural to extend it to all virtues and vices. Moreover, the extension has several attractive consequences.

Imagine that one person, through virtuous action, augments the pleasure or knowledge of another. What should we be more pleased by: the new pleasure or knowledge, or the virtue that brought it about? I think we should care more about the pleasure or knowledge; it is, after all, the point of the exercise. (This is especially so if the gain has been substantial.) This means, however, that the pleasure or knowledge must also be better than the virtue that brought it about. By principle (8), it is better to love what is intrinsically better, and here it is better to love the product of virtue than the virtuous act itself.

There is a subtler consequence. A recursive account iterates indefinitely, finding value not only in the love of pleasure but also in, for example, the love of the love of the love of pleasure. Is this third-level attitude really a significant good? I believe it has some intrinsic value, but the world would not be significantly poorer if it did not exist. Treating virtue as a lesser good captures this view. If the value of loving x is always smaller than the value of x, the value of higher-level attitudes steadily diminishes and may eventually become infinitesimal.

Finally, principle (10) reflects virtue's status as a dependent moral concept. Sidgwick argues that, if virtue is defined by relation to other goods, it cannot be more than instrumentally good. This strong argument fails, but in my view its premises do support a weaker conclusion. If virtue is defined by its relation to other goods, it cannot be a greater good than they. Its value must be a smaller function $[f(x) < x]$ of the other goods that its existence requires.

Let us agree, then, that virtue is a lesser good. This has one important consequence and creates two difficulties.

The consequence concerns self-sacrifice. If a person foregoes pleasure for himself to promote the greater pleasure of others, does this involve a sacrifice of his good? If virtue is a lesser good, the answer is: sometimes yes, sometimes no. Imagine that the value of loving x is one half the value of x. If the person gives up three units of pleasure for himself to promote ten units for others, he gains five units of virtue, making up for his loss in pleasure. If he creates only four units in others, he does not make up for his loss. Sometimes benefiting others makes one's own life better; sometimes it does not.

Of the two difficulties, the first concerns the torturer who takes pleasure in his torturing. If vice is a lesser evil, the torturer's pleasure is less evil than his victim's pain. Considered apart from other consequences, this conclusion seems right: if we witness the torturing, we should care more about what happens to the victim. But the same conclusion can have an unfortunate consequence. If the torturer's pleasure, which has some disvalue as vice, has positive value as pleasure, then it can, if sufficiently intense, be on balance desirable. Its presence can make the overall situation better. Perhaps some can accept this conclusion, but most of us cannot. To avoid it, we have two options. One is simply to deny that pleasure is a first-level good. If the value of pleasures felt toward good objects is affirmed in the recursive account of virtue, there is less need to value pleasure on its own. This is an extreme step; it would force us to maintain that pleasures with morally neutral contents (for example, the pleasures of suntanning) have no value. To avoid this result, we might take a second option: to maintain only that pleasures with evil contents have no value as pleasures. Whichever option we take, we deny that the torturer's pleasure contains any good to offset its evil.

The second difficulty concerns numbers. As I have formulated it above, principle (9) compares one person's sympathy with another person's pain. But what if many people sympathize with one person's pain? On the one hand, we want to say that more sympathy is better, and nondiminishingly better: the fact that you already sympathize with someone's pain does not make it any less appropriate for me to do so. (We may think the value of extra sympathizers diminishes if we think of sympathy instrumentally, as helping to console the victim. But we do not think this if we consider it by itself.) On the other hand, I do not think we believe that any number of sympathizers can outweigh the pain. A situation involving one person in pain and a hundred sympathizers is not better than one person without any pain at all. But these two beliefs contradict each other: if more sympathy is better, and nondiminishingly better, must it not eventually outweigh the pain?

V. LOVING THE GOOD BECAUSE IT IS GOOD

Loving the good for itself is loving it apart from its consequences. One can do this either from a simple emotional attraction—one just wants or enjoys knowledge or pleasure—or because one believes it is good. In the second case, one's love is mediated by thoughts about intrinsic value: it is love of the good *as good*.

Some philosophers hold that the second kind of love is better than the first. Loving what is good from simple emotion has some value; loving it as good has more.[24] A stronger view holds that only love based in beliefs about the good is of value.

---

[24] See, for example, Loren Lomasky, *Persons, Rights, and the Moral Community* (New York: Oxford University Press, 1987), p. 253.

How we assess these views depends partly on whether we are moral realists, who hold that moral beliefs are objectively true or false, or moral anti-realists, who reject this claim. Some forms of moral anti-realism identify the belief that x is good with an emotional attraction to x — perhaps one with formal features such as universality. On these views, the question of whether the two kinds of love differ in value does not arise, for they are not distinct. Other forms of anti-realism equate the belief that x is good with a qualitatively unique attraction to it. They are more favorable to the view that loving the good as good is better, but they are not as favorable to this view as moral realism. By treating moral beliefs as objective, moral realism draws the sharpest possible distinction between (a) the belief that x is good, and (b) an emotional attraction to x. Since the views before us require this distinction, I shall assume in this section that moral realism is correct.

Assuming moral realism, is loving the good from simple emotion less good than loving it as good? I do not believe that it is. If our first-level goods include knowledge, the second kind of love may have more intellectual value. It involves, as emotional attraction need not, the awareness of a moral truth. This aside, however, there seems no moral reason to prefer loving the good as good, to loving it out of simple emotion. Each is a positive response to what is good; each is directed at an appropriate object. It is true that someone who loves the good only emotionally lacks something valuable, namely love of it as good. But it is likewise true that someone whose love derives only from beliefs about the good lacks the value of a direct emotional attraction. Complete virtue seems to require both kinds of love: simple attraction and love of the good as good. But each on its own has some value, and neither has more or less than the other.

The case is similar to that of motives for right action. One can help others just because one wants to, or because one thinks helping them is right. To act only from emotion is to lack a valuable motive, but there is likewise something missing if one acts only from duty, with no fellow-feeling. With the good as with the right there seem to be two good motives, neither better than the other and each of separate worth.

VI. SELF/OTHER ASYMMETRIES?

In this final section I shall consider some possible counterexamples to the recursive account, cases where it may seem that loving something good is not good. All the counterexamples involve possible "self/other asymmetries,"[25] situations in which loving or hating a state in oneself may seem less good than loving or hating the same state in others.

---

[25] The phrase is Michael Slote's; see his *Common-Sense Morality and Consequentialism* (London: Routledge & Kegan Paul, 1985), ch. 1.

Consider, first, the love of pleasure. Desiring, pursuing, and taking pleasure in other people's pleasure, it may be argued, are virtuous and good, but loving one's own pleasure is not. If someone feels a second-order pleasure when he contemplates his own pleasure, this may be good insofar as it increases his aggregate pleasure. It is not, however, a manifestation of virtue, nor is desiring or pursuing one's own pleasure.

One response to this argument is suggested by Ross. He believed that there is no moral duty to seek one's own pleasure, and in *The Foundations of Ethics* he explained this by saying that, from each person's point of view, his own pleasure is not intrinsically good.[26] If we adopted this view, we could accommodate the alleged asymmetry without altering the recursive structure of our account. We could say that the love of others' pleasure is good because their pleasure is good, but the love of one's own pleasure has a valueless object.

A second response is to deny the asymmetry. If innocent pleasure (for example, in a relaxing vacation) is good, is further pleasure in it not an appropriate response? Wouldn't *not* feeling this pleasure be a failure of appreciation? What is most troubling is the *exclusive* or *predominant* love of one's own pleasure, but this can be handled by a strengthened version of principle (8). Principle (8) states that, if x is better than y, loving x is better than loving y. A strengthened version would state that, if x and y are equal (or nearly equal) in value, loving x much more than y is evil, or at least not positively good: it violates a due proportion. Given this strengthened principle, loving one's own pleasure much more than other people's is not virtuous and may be vicious. The test case for the revised account is a person who takes pleasure in his own pleasure, but no more than in the similar pleasure of others. This person's pleasure does not seem evil; on the contrary, it seems good.

An analogous counterexample concerns pain in response to one's own pain. Again, it may be said, although pain in response to others' pain is virtuous, pain in response to one's own pain is not. If someone is unfortunate enough to feel this extra pain, this only makes his condition worse.

Here Ross's move is not plausible. We cannot say, and Ross never suggests, that from each person's point of view his own pain is not intrinsically evil. Perhaps for this very reason, however, the second asymmetry seems more open to challenge. In this case, some other forms of hating evil do seem to be virtuous: if a person who suffers pain wants or strives to be free of it, his efforts, even if unsuccessful, do seem intrinsically good. This suggests that the third form of hating pain, namely feeling pain in response to it, should also be good. Pain in response to one's own pain may not be so obviously good as pain in response to others', but if one's own pain really is evil, feeling pain in response to it should be good.

[26] W. D. Ross, *The Foundations of Ethics* (Oxford: Clarendon Press, 1939), pp. 271–89.

The most important asymmetry, and the greatest challenge to the recursive account, concerns the love of virtue. Loving other people's virtue is clearly virtuous and good, but is it also good to love one's own virtue — for example, to take pleasure in the fact that one takes pleasure in others' pleasure?

Aristotle thinks it is. He says that a virtuous person takes pleasure in virtuous acts,[27] and his portrait of the "proud" person is precisely of someone who is virtuous, knows he is virtuous, and revels in this knowledge.[28] Nevertheless Aristotelian "pride" has seemed repellent to many commentators. Ross says that the description of it "betrays somewhat nakedly the self-absorption which is the bad side of Aristotle's ethics."[29] Others may say that it involves smugness, or what Bernard Williams calls "moral self-indulgence."[30] They may conclude, contrary to the recursive view, that while it is usually good to love what is good, it is not good to love one's own virtue.

Again, we cannot make a Rossian move in answering this argument. We cannot say that, from each person's point of view, his own virtue is not good. We can, however, deny the supposed asymmetry between valuing the virtues of others and valuing one's own. When the love of one's own virtue is unattractive, it is not valued by the recursive account; when it is valued, it is positively good.

One unattractive feature of Aristotle's proud person is his concern to be more virtuous than other people. He likes conferring benefits but not receiving them, "for the one is the mark of a superior, the other of an inferior." If done a favor, he does a greater one in return, to place the other person in his debt.[31] This concern for one's rank among the virtuous is inconsistent with a genuine love of virtue. It can make one envious about virtue, so one prefers having two units of virtue when others have only one, to having three units when others have four. This envy is not valued under the recursive account.

Without being envious, one can care more about one's own virtue than about others' virtue, and the proud person clearly does this. But his attitude is condemned by the strengthened version of principle (8). This principle states that loving one of two equal goods much more than the other is evil, or at least not good. In greatly preferring his own virtue to others' virtue, the proud person violates this principle.

Finally, the love of one's own virtue must respect the idea that virtue is a lesser good. Principle (10) states that the value of loving x is always

---

[27] Aristotle, *Nicomachean Ethics*, 1104b5–6.

[28] *Ibid.*, 1123a33–1125a35.

[29] Sir David Ross, *Aristotle* (London: Methuen, 1949), p. 208.

[30] Bernard Williams, "Utilitarianism and Moral Self-Indulgence," in *Moral Luck* (Cambridge: Cambridge University Press, 1981), pp. 40–53.

[31] Aristotle, *Nicomachean Ethics*, 1124b9–12.

less than the value of x. Combined with the strengthened principle (8), this implies that a person's love of his own virtue must always be less strong than the love of first-level goods that constitutes his virtue. His pleasure in his pleasure in others' pleasure, for example, must always be less intense than his pleasure in their pleasure. Otherwise he will be responding more to what has less value.

If this last condition is satisfied, the love of one's own virtue avoids self-indulgence. A person is morally self-indulgent, Williams writes, if his motivation "focuses disproportionately upon the expression of his own disposition,"[32] rather than on the effects his disposition will produce. "Disproportionately," for Williams, means "more." To call a utilitarian self-indulgent is to suspect "that what the agent cares about is not so much other people, as himself caring about other people. He has an image of himself as a virtuous utilitarian, and this image is more important in his motivation than any concern for other persons."[33] These remarks allow a virtuous person to have some love of his own virtue, though this love takes a subordinate position. He can be motivated partly by the desire to act virtuously, so long as he is motivated more by the desire to help others. He can take some pleasure in his virtuous act, so long as he takes more pleasure in the benefits it produces for others.

For a fair test of the recursive view, we must imagine a person whose love of his own virtue is not envious, is not much stronger than his love of others' virtue, and is less strong than his love of the first-level goods that are the virtue's object. In this restricted form, the love of one's virtue does seem intrinsically good. As Williams emphasizes, the virtuous person is focused primarily on goods and evils outside his acts and dispositions. This is compatible with having, as a secondary accompaniment, some desire for and pleasure in those acts and dispositions. To lack these attitudes, in fact, would be to fail to respond appropriately to something intrinsically good.

VII. CONCLUSION

Let me summarize the main claims of this essay. I have argued, against Sidgwick, that consequentialist moralities can treat virtue as intrinsically good. They can do this if they have a recursive characterization of the good, one that makes loving the good — desiring, pursuing, and taking pleasure in it — also intrinsically good. If virtue is defined as loving the good, the recursive characterization gives virtue intrinsic value.

I have also argued that the recursive account is attractive. It captures intuitions many of us have about the intrinsic value of moral action and

---

[32] Williams, "Utilitarianism and Moral Self-Indulgence," p. 47.

[33] *Ibid.*, p. 45.

feeling, and gives them a unifying rationale. Its definition of virtue, though specifically consequentialist, honors many traditional claims about virtue and should be widely acceptable as describing at least part of what virtue involves. Beyond this, I have considered some issues arising from the account, and some applications of it. I have discussed the moral evaluation of fantasies, the relative weight of virtue compared to other goods, and some possible self/other asymmetries. These further discussions have clarified the recursive account and underscored its intuitive appeal.

Philosophy, The University of Calgary

THE LIMITS OF WELL-BEING

By Shelly Kagan

I. The Dialectic

What are the limits of well-being? This question nicely captures one of the central debates concerning the nature of the individual human good. For rival theories differ as to what sort of facts directly constitute a person's being well-off. On some views, well-being is limited to the presence of pleasure and the absence of pain.[1] But other views push the boundaries of well-being beyond this, so that it encompasses a variety of mental states, not merely pleasure alone. Some theories then draw the line here, limiting well-being to the presence of the appropriately broadened set of mental states. But still others extend the limits of well-being even further, so that it is constituted in part by facts that are not themselves mental states at all; on such views, well-being is partly constituted by states of affairs that are "external" to the individual's experiences.

In this essay, I want to explore some of this debate by focusing on a particular stretch of the dialectic. That is, I want to think hard about a particular connected series of arguments and counterarguments. These arguments—or, at least, the concerns they seek to express—emerge naturally in the give and take of philosophical discussion.[2] Together they make up a rather simple story, whose plot, in very rough terms, is this: first there is an attempt to push the limits of well-being outward, moving from a narrow to a broader conception; then comes the claim that the resulting notion is too broad, and so we must retreat to a narrower conception after all.

Giving the plot with greater care requires first a bit of machinery. In what is rapidly becoming the traditional classification, there are three basic types of theories of well-being. First, there are *mental state* theories, which hold that an individual's well-being consists solely in the presence of the relevant kinds of mental states. Hedonism is, of course, the most familiar theory of this sort, claiming that well-being consists in the presence of pleasure. But as already noted, one might accept a broader mental state theory according to which, even though being well-off was a

---

[1] Hereafter I will focus only on the *goods* of a given theory of well-being (e.g., pleasure); for simplicity, I will not discuss the *bads* (e.g., pain).

[2] Examples are to be found in James Griffin, *Well-Being* (Oxford: Oxford University Press, 1986), chapter 1, and in Derek Parfit, *Reasons and Persons* (Oxford: Oxford University Press, 1984), appendix I. Although I will not be concerned with the specifics of either of these discussions, I have obviously learned—and taken—a great deal from both of them.

matter of having the right mental states, the direct relevance of a given mental state need not be exhausted by its pleasantness.

Second, there are *desire* or preference theories, which hold that being well-off is a matter of having one's (intrinsic) desires satisfied. What is intended here, of course, is "satisfaction" in the logician's sense: the question is simply whether or not the states of affairs that are the objects of one's various desires obtain; it is irrelevant whether or not one realizes it, or whether one gets some psychological feeling of satisfaction. (Some desire theorists restrict well-being to the satisfaction of the desires one would have if fully informed and rational, but for our purposes these refinements will not matter.)

Finally, there are *objective* or objective list theories, which hold that various things are objectively good for a person to have, whether or not he realizes it, and whether or not he desires it. Being well-off is simply a matter of one's having the various objective goods. These might include not only pleasure, but also, for example, friendship, fame, knowledge, or wealth. The list of objective goods is, of course, a matter of dispute, but there is no obvious reason to think it would be restricted to kinds of mental states.

One effect of the discussion to follow will be to call into question whether this classificatory scheme is in fact the most illuminating way to divide the terrain. But it will do to get us started.

Here, then, is the stretch of the dialectic to which I want to draw our attention. It begins with hedonism. And it challenges the hedonist to offer an account of what all pleasant mental states have in common. After all, it is not as though "pleasure" designates a single *kind* of mental state. The experiences of taking a hike, thinking about moral philosophy, and eating chocolate can all be pleasant ones, yet they are obviously quite different in their content. Nor does it seem as though there is an identifiable ingredient or "component" that they share that we are prepared to label as the pleasure. But if pleasure is neither a single kind of mental state, nor a single component of mental states, what then is it for a mental state to be a pleasant one?

The answer that gets offered to the hedonist is this: a mental state is pleasant if it is desired. And to say that one mental state is more pleasant than another is to say that the former is preferred to the latter.

Perhaps this is not, on reflection, an altogether satisfactory analysis of pleasure. But it doesn't really matter, for no better analysis is forthcoming. It is the best the hedonist can do, and if she is not to abandon her position altogether, she will have to make do with it. Given this account of pleasure, then, hedonism becomes a theory of well-being that might with equal justice be called *preference mental statism*: I am well-off to the extent that I have the various mental states that I desire.

But once we have gone this far — the argument goes — it is hard to avoid going further. Recasting hedonism as preference mental statism allows us to see that it is really *preference* that is doing the work. One mental state is more valuable than another — makes a greater contribution to our welfare — by virtue of the fact that we prefer it. But it is obvious enough that our desires are not *limited* to matters involving our mental states. We want various "external" states of affairs to obtain as well. Indeed, sometimes we prefer that some such external state of affairs obtain even if that means that we will be subject to some undesirable mental state. Yet if satisfaction of preference is sufficient to ground well-being when it is a matter of preferences *between* mental states, why shouldn't it be sufficient to ground well-being *regardless* of the object of the desire?

In this way we seem pushed toward a pure or unrestricted desire theory. What makes one well-off is the satisfaction of one's desires, period. The restriction to desires concerning one's mental states falls away as unmotivated. No doubt people typically do have desires concerning their own mental states, and these are often among their most central desires. But well-being is simply a matter of the satisfaction of one's desires, and these will usually include desires concerning external states of affairs as well.

Unfortunately, the move to the desire theory brings its own difficulties. For in pushing outward from hedonism to the desire theory, we seem to have pushed too far. There are many cases where it seems altogether implausible to suggest that the satisfaction of the relevant desire affects the person's level of well-being. Suppose I meet a stranger on a train.[3] He tells me his story, and I form the desire that he succeed in his projects. We then part, and I never hear of him or even think of him again. If he does in fact succeed, then my desire has been satisfied. According to the desire theory, then, this makes me better off. But this is intuitively an absurd claim. Obviously my level of well-being is not affected *at all* by the success of the stranger. The success of the stranger has nothing to do with *me*.

This suggests that the unrestricted desire theory is hopelessly broad. A theory of well-being must explain which facts constitute my being better off. So they must be facts about *me*. Since my desires can range over facts that have nothing whatsoever to do with me, the satisfaction of such desires cannot constitute my well-being. If we are to preserve a desire theory at all, we will have to move to some sort of restricted desire theory, according to which my well-being consists in the satisfaction of the appropriately restricted subset of my desires. The trick, of course, is to provide some plausible specification of the restriction.

From this perspective, the position of mental statism no longer seems so arbitrary. At least it seems to keep the content of well-being within reasonable bounds, for facts about my mental states are certainly facts about me. In contrast, it is far from clear whether anything external to my mind

---

[3] The example is Parfit's, from *Reasons and Persons*, appendix I.

can count as well, that is, can count as — in the relevant sense — facts about me. If not, then the limits of well-being must be drawn at the limits of our minds.

This is the stretch of argument and counterargument which I propose to examine more carefully. Please note that I have not yet endorsed any of it. Now in point of fact, I am inclined to think that much of the argument is mistaken, although I also suspect that some of the conclusions can be supported for all that. But with regard to other portions of the argument I am rather uncertain as to where the truth lies. So the discussion that follows is indeed a genuine exploration: everything is rough, and everything is tentative.

II. Hedonism

Let us begin again at the start of the argument, with the challenge to the hedonist to disclose what it is that pleasant mental states have in common. It does seem correct to me to note that 'pleasure' does not pick out a single kind of mental state or experience, or a single shared component of all pleasant experiences, or even a kind of component. But it is, I think, too quick to conclude from this that the best that can be said by the hedonist is that a mental state is pleasant if it is desired.

An alternative move is to identify pleasantness not as a component of experiences, but rather as a *dimension* along which experiences can vary.[4] As an analogy, consider the loudness of auditory experiences — that is, sounds. It is obvious that loudness or volume is not a *kind* of sound. And it seems plausible to insist that loudness is not a single kind of component of auditory experiences. Rather, volume is a dimension along which sounds can vary. It is an aspect of sounds, with regard to which they can be ranked. Recognition of the qualitative differences between the sounds of a symphony, rain falling, and a bird chirping, does nothing at all to call into question our ability to identify a single dimension — volume — with regard to which these and other sounds can be ranked.

Similarly, then, pleasure might well be a distinct dimension of mental states, with regard to which they can be ranked as well. Recognition of the qualitative differences between the experiences of hiking, listening to music, and reading philosophy, need not call into question our ability to identify a single dimension — pleasure — along which they vary in magnitude.

Once we have a picture like this in mind, we might in fact be prepared to insist that there *is* a sense in which pleasure is an ingredient common to all pleasant experiences. For it seems to me that there is a sense in

---

[4] I am here influenced by unpublished work by Leonard Katz. See his forthcoming book, *Hedonism: A View of Mind and Value.*

which a specific volume is indeed an ingredient of a given sound, along with a particular pitch, and so forth. (Similarly, intensity or saturation is an ingredient of colors, along with hue.) Thus, pleasantness might well be considered an ingredient of (conscious) mental states in general, albeit an ingredient that we will only notice if we "chop up" experiences in some nonstandard ways. But whether or not pleasure can be helpfully viewed in this way as an ingredient of experiences, the possibility remains that it is a single, specific dimension along which experiences vary.

Of course, even if this is granted, the challenge might still be raised to identify the particular dimension which pleasure is. Mental states can presumably vary along a number of dimensions, and we would like to have some illuminating way to characterize the particular dimension with which discussion of pleasure is concerned.

It is not at all clear to me whether it would be objectionable if this new challenge could not be met. Suppose there were no interesting way to identify the pleasure dimension except ostensively—drawing someone's attention to different experiences which varied significantly and saliently in terms of this particular dimension. I do not see how this would threaten the intelligibility of the various claims the hedonist wants to make concerning pleasure.

Of course, this is not to say that there is no more theoretically satisfying way to identify the pleasure dimension. After all, the connection between pleasure and desire is a striking one. We may well be able to use the latter notion to help fix the referent of the former. Indeed, the original proposal to analyze pleasure as desired mental states can be seen as a friendly suggestion along these lines.

But we can do better. More sophisticated accounts have been offered. No doubt, pleasant experiences are desired, but they seem to be desired in a particular way and for particular reasons. A more plausible account might look something like this:

An experience E that occurs at time t to a person P is pleasant if and only if:

(1) P has a desire at t that E occur at t

(2) P's desire is an immediate response to E's occurrent phenomenal qualities (i.e., its qualia).

Clause (1) brings out the fact that one likes pleasant experiences while they are occurring. Clause (2) brings out the fact that one likes pleasant experiences because of how they *feel*. This means, roughly, that one's desire is a direct, immediate response to the phenomenal qualities of the experience—and only to those properties of the experience. It is not mediated by further beliefs. In particular, the desire cannot be a response to recognition of the instrumental (or evidential, or moral) properties of the experience. We often are glad to have a given experience when we know it will lead to certain other experiences, but that doesn't make the first experience pleasant in itself.

I certainly do not mean to suggest that this improved account will do as it stands. Clause (2) in particular needs considerable refinement. But if an account anything at all like this is correct, it allows us to raise certain questions.

So suppose that something like this improved account is correct. How does this connect to our earlier suggestion that pleasure is a particular dimension along which mental states vary? One possibility is this: A mental state is pleasant if it is the object of the appropriate sort of immediate desire. Mental states can be ranked according to whether or not they generate this kind of desire, and if so, the strength of the desire. The stronger the desire, the more pleasant the mental state.

In effect, we have identified a dimension along which mental states can vary — strength of the generated immediate desire. And if something like the improved account is correct, then this dimension varies in lock step with the dimension of pleasure. But this is still subject to two possible interpretations. One could hold the "reductionist" view, according to which the two dimensions are not genuinely distinct ontologically, but are one and the same. Pleasantness simply *is* strength of immediate desire. Alternatively, one could hold the "nonreductionist" view, according to which the two dimensions remain ontologically distinct. We may use the desire dimension to help us identify the pleasure dimension, but pleasure remains a psychological reality distinct from immediate desire. Presumably on this nonreductionist view, it is the presence of this distinct psychological magnitude that helps to *explain* the presence of the corresponding desire.

I will not attempt to adjudicate between these two interpretations here. Let us consider the implications of each. Suppose, first, that we adopt the reductionist approach. Then for a mental state to be pleasant simply is for it to be the object of the appropriate sort of immediate desire. Now when the hedonist claims that well-being consists in the presence of pleasant mental states, she is presumably claiming that it is the pleasantness of the pleasant mental states that makes me better off. So on the reductionist approach the hedonist is claiming that when I am well-off, I am well-off by virtue of the fact that various mental states for which I have the right sort of immediate desires do in fact obtain.

This does seem to be a version of the desire theory. Perhaps not all desires are such that their satisfaction contributes to my well-being, but for an important subset of my desires — the immediate desires — their satisfaction is constitutive of my being well-off. I am well-off by virtue of the fact that desires of the relevant kind are satisfied. I belabor this point because I am not completely convinced of it, although it seems correct. If I am well-off this is because I have the right kinds of mental states, namely, pleasant ones. But these states only count as pleasant by virtue of the fact that I have the appropriately immediate desires for their occurrence. If the mental states themselves occurred in the absence of the immediate desires (admittedly, something that might not be causally possible), they would not be pleasant states, and I would not be the better off for their occurrence. So if I am better off, this is only because the immediate desires do in fact exist and are satisfied (that is, the immediately desired mental states do obtain). So it is the satisfaction of the right kind of desires that grounds my well-being. This, as I say, seems to be the implication of adopting the reductionist stance.

In contrast, if the hedonist is a nonreductionist, she is not similarly forced to adopt a version of the desire theory. According to the nonreductionist approach, pleasure is a specific psychological magnitude that we can identify through attending to appropriately immediate desires, but the pleasantness is nonetheless distinct from the desiredness. So when the hedonist claims that being well-off is a matter of having pleasant mental states, she need not claim that when one is well-off this is by virtue of the fact that various desires are satisfied. Of course, since pleasant mental states are immediately desired, it is in fact the case that when one is well-off one has immediate desires and they are indeed satisfied. Nonetheless, the hedonist can insist that it is not by virtue of *this* fact that one is well-off. Rather it is by virtue of the fact that one's mental states exhibit the specific and distinct psychological magnitude — pleasantness — to a significant degree. Even if one did *not* have any desire at all for the occurrence of the pleasant mental states (again, something that admittedly might not be causally possible), one would still be well-off to the extent that one had the pleasant mental states themselves.

On this approach, what the hedonist is endorsing appears to be a version of an objective theory. There is a particular kind of good, namely pleasure, that it is objectively good for a person to have. Its goodness is not at all founded in the fact that the person happens to desire it. In effect, the hedonist is offering an objective list theory with a very short list. Pleasure is an objective good, and it is the *only* such good.

It seems then, that the nonreductionist hedonist need not embrace any version of the desire theory. She can instead adopt an objective approach. But this is not to say that the nonreductionist hedonist *cannot* endorse a desire approach. As far as I can see, it is completely open to the nonreductionist to insist that even though pleasantness is a distinct psychological dimension from that of strength of generated immediate desire, pleasant mental states are indeed valuable by virtue of the fact that they are the object of this sort of desire. That is, even the nonreductionist can hold that when I am well-off, this is by virtue of the fact that the right sorts of desires are satisfied.

In short, it seems that the hedonist must choose between accepting a version of the desire theory (an option open to both the reductionist and the nonreductionist) and accepting a version of the objective list theory (an option that seems to be open only to the nonreductionist). Insofar as the original dialectic with which this essay began assumed that the hedonist must appeal to some version of the desire theory, it seems to be in error. There is also the possibility of objective hedonism.

Nonetheless, some hedonists will indeed prefer to embrace the desire theory sketched above, according to which well-being consists in the satisfaction of the appropriate sort of immediate desires. And for these hedonists, at the very least, it does seem that we can push a line of attack similar to that given in the original dialectic. For what these hedonists do is identify a particular kind of desire—immediate desires of the right sort—and hold that for this kind of desire alone is its satisfaction constitutive of my well-being. This is doubtless a consistent position to hold, but it is difficult to see how it is to be motivated. Why shouldn't there be other desires whose satisfaction contributes to my well-being as well—desires which admittedly fail to be immediate in the relevant sense?

Consider the first of the two conditions used to characterize pleasant experiences: an experience is pleasant only if the individual has a desire *at the time of its occurrence* for the occurrence of that experience. This seems a reasonable condition to place on what is to count as pleasant: one likes pleasant experiences while they are occurring. But what could possibly explain why only desires that meet this condition are such that their satisfaction leaves me better off?

Suppose there were a kind of experience such that while it was occurring, the person had *no* desire that it occur at that time, but immediately after its conclusion the person was spontaneously glad that he had had the experience. His desire or "pro attitude" toward the earlier experience might still be immediate in the sense intended by the second of the two conditions—it is a direct response to the immediate phenomenal qualities of the experience, unmediated by cognitive concerns such as the instrumental value of the experience. But the desire occurs later rather than concurrently with the experience.[5]

If there were such experiences, they would not be labeled as pleasant by the improved account. So the hedonist would not count them as contributing to one's well-being. But why shouldn't they count? What could possibly explain why the satisfaction of a desire should count toward my well-being when the obtaining of its object is concurrent with the existence of the desire, but not count when the obtaining of its object is not concurrent?

Similar questions arise if we focus instead on the second of the two restrictions. Pleasant mental states are desired in an immediate—that is, not cognitively mediated—response to their phenomenal qualities. But sup-

---

[5] Are there any such desires? Their logical possibility suffices to make my point, but I am intrigued by the empirical question as well. Perhaps certain meditative experiences are too "empty" to allow for the desire at the same time; other experiences might be too "full" or consuming to allow for the concurrent desire, crowding it out.

pose there were some mental states that were intrinsically desired, but in a nonimmediate manner. The occurrence of the given mental state might be desired at the time of its occurrence, but only because the person had one or another belief concerning some of the properties of that state. That is, one might find various mental states intrinsically attractive, but only as a result of reflection.

Once more, if there were such experiences, the hedonist would not view them as pleasant, and thus would not count them toward my well-being. But why shouldn't they count too? There is, of course, a difference between desiring a mental state solely in response to its phenomenal qualities and desiring a mental state at least in part because of one's various other beliefs. But what could possibly explain why it is only the satisfaction of the former sort of desires that counts toward my well-being, and never the satisfaction of the latter sort of desires?

It seems that the hedonist has two options. She might concede the theoretical point, and admit that *if* one had desires of these various kinds, then their satisfaction too would contribute to one's well-being. Or she could simply insist that even if one did have desires of these kinds, one's well-being would be completely unaffected by their satisfaction.

On the first option, the hedonist is conceding that well-being is a matter of the satisfaction of one's various desires concerning one's mental states. She could, of course, go on to argue that, as a matter of empirical fact, one never does have intrinsic desires for mental states except in the case of the kind of immediate desires that ground pleasures. (Or perhaps: one *would* not, if one were fully informed and rational.) But even if such an empirical claim were plausible, the point would still remain that the hedonist would indeed have been forced to accept preference mental statism. I am well-off to the extent that I have the mental states that I desire. If the only states I desire are pleasant ones, so be it. But even if this is so, the differences between pleasantness and other aspects of mental states are of no fundamental significance to the theory of well-being. What would be fundamental would be the theory of preference mental statism.

If the hedonist did take this option, then it also seems right that she could be pushed further still. Why should it be that only preferences concerning my mental states are relevant to my well-being? Up to this stage of the dialectic, it is indeed difficult to see how the hedonist can justify restricting the set of relevant desires. Of course, the hedonist might try to argue that, in fact, I have no intrinsic desires concerning matters other than my mental states (or would have none were I rational and fully informed). But whether or not this empirical claim is true, the underlying position now does seem to be an appeal to an unrestricted desire theory.

This is what happens if the hedonist concedes that *if* someone had desires other than the appropriate kind of immediate desires, then they would indeed be relevant to well-being. But the hedonist might prefer the other option, holding that *only* immediate desires would be relevant to well-being. As I have already noted, this is a consistent position, but it is an unsatisfactory one philosophically. Why exactly is it that only the one sort of desire contributes to well-being?

The hedonist might, I suppose, attempt to defend her position by appeal to an inspection of cases. Perhaps we will agree that—inexplicable as this may be—well-being is affected in all and only those cases where immediate desires are at stake. But nonhedonists are likely to disagree about the results of this survey, and it leaves the hedonist's position seeming rather vulnerable. And even those who agree with the hedonist about the results of her survey should find it philosophically unsettling to lack any account of why the various distinctions to which she appeals matter.

However, none of this amounts to a proof that the various restrictions and distinctions cannot be defended. Indeed, in the next section of this essay we will turn to the second half of the dialectic and consider an argument for the view that well-being must be solely a matter of having the right sorts of mental states. If such an argument were successful, then the hedonist's rejection of an unrestricted desire theory would not be unmotivated. The restriction to preference *mental statism* would have some foundation. Similarly, then, there might be additional arguments justifying the hedonist's further restriction to *immediate* desires. As I have already indicated, I do not currently have any plausible suggestions for arguments along these lines, and I am strongly inclined to doubt that any such arguments would succeed. But it seems to me premature to conclude that there are no such arguments.

Up to this point we have been considering the implications of the hedonist's adopting a version of the desire theory. But I noted the possibility of the hedonist preferring an objective theory, and I want to consider the implications of this approach as well. Here, however, I can be more brief. For it seems to me that the objective hedonist faces difficulties that closely parallel those that trouble the hedonist who insists upon the fundamental significance of immediate desires.

Of course, if the hedonist does take an objective approach, then to the extent that immediate desires are especially significant, this will simply be because of the special significance of the objects that are uniquely picked out by such desires. That is, the hedonist will no longer need to argue for the intrinsic significance of certain distinctions within a desire theory. Instead, the defense of hedonism will require arguing for the uniquely valuable nature of the mental states such immediate desires pick out. The hedonist must insist that it is simply a fact that certain mental states, namely the pleasant ones, are objectively good for the person to have.

But it is obvious that this leaves the hedonist with a great deal to explain as well. Even if we put aside the difficulty of arguing that pleasure *is* an objective good, there is the significant difficulty of arguing that it is the *only* such good. Why is it that of all the various aspects of mental states, it is only this particular dimension that contributes to a person's well-being? What explains the unique significance of *pleasure* as distinct from the various other aspects of mental states for which they might be valued? There is, no doubt, a strong temptation to appeal to the fact that only pleasure involves being immediately desired—but this would push the hedonist back in the direction of the desire theory. Yet what else could explain why this should be the only aspect of mental states that contributes to being well-off?

Once the hedonist is engaged in offering arguments for the objective value of pleasure, the possibility emerges that other aspects of mental states might be shown to have objective value as well. These might well be aspects whose value can only be recognized upon reflection, given the appropriate beliefs. As such, they will differ from the aspect of pleasure, whose value is apparently recognized immediately. But is is difficult to see why the only objective goods should be ones whose value is recognized directly and immediately.

In this way even the objective hedonist can be pushed toward the possibility of a more general mental statism. Even if well-being were limited to the presence of the right mental states, it might well be that the relevance of a given mental state is not limited to its pleasantness. And of course, once we are this far, it seems that we can again push further still. Why should the objective goods that contribute to well-being be limited to the possession of the right sorts of mental states? Once the possibility of objective goods is recognized, it seems an open question whether they include goods external to the individual's mind.

Of course, as should also be obvious, none of this amounts to a refutation of the hedonist's position. We are about to turn to an argument that well-being must be limited to having the proper mental states. Should this argument—or another to the same effect—be successful, then clearly it is not ad hoc for the hedonist to restrict her attention to mental states. And there might well be other, additional arguments that pleasure is the sole aspect of a mental state that can contribute to its value. Once more, I do not currently know what these further arguments might look like, but it seems premature to assume that none could succeed.

To summarize quickly, I think the first half of the dialectic is correct in claiming that there is a certain kind of philosophical pressure that can be put upon the hedonist, pushing outward from hedonism to a more general mental statism, and then further still. But I think it too hasty to conclude that this pressure cannot be resisted. On this point, I think, the verdict may still be out. At any rate, even if the hedonist must eventually succumb to this pressure, the position that emerges need not be the unrestricted desire theory. If the hedonist should start as a proponent of an objective theory, then the position that eventually emerges might well be objective as well, but with a richer and longer list of objective goods.

III. Restricting the Limits

The second half of the dialectic argued that if we move to an unrestricted desire theory, we have moved too far. For there are desires the satisfaction of which intuitively contributes nothing at all toward my well-being. Recall the example of the stranger on the train. Even though I wish him success, I never hear of him or even think of him again, and so the question of whether or not he does succeed seems simply irrelevant to the level of my well-being. The moral seems to be that the unrestricted desire theory is hopelessly broad. The desire theorist must claim that it is only a certain subset of desires whose satisfaction can contribute to well-being. If a desire theory of well-being is to be plausible at all, it must be a suitably restricted desire theory.

Now I have been at some pains to argue that even if the hedonist must eventually succumb to the pressure to push the limits of well-being outward, this need not result in any version of the desire theory at all. So even if the argument of the second half of the dialectic is correct, and the only plausible version of a desire theory will be a restricted version, the overall significance of this conclusion might still be doubted, since it seems to have no implications for objective theories. I believe this appearance is incorrect, however, for I think that once we move beyond the striking example itself, and attempt to extract a general argument, the result is an argument relevant to objective theories as well as to desire theories.

Why is it that it seems so clear that the success of the stranger does not contribute to my well-being, even though his success satisfies one of my desires? The answer does not seem to turn on the fact that by the time the stranger succeeds, my desire for his success has faded and been forgotten. For even if I continued to wish the stranger success, so long as I did nothing about it and never heard of his success, it *still* seems as though his success contributes nothing at all to my well-being. Why not?

The irresistible answer is that the stranger's success has no effect on *me*. I remain exactly as I was before. I am not altered at all by the fact of the stranger's success. But if something is to make a difference to my level of well-being it must make a difference to *me*. The facts that constitute my being well-off must be facts about me.

Presumably your level of well-being is not a free-floating fact about you; it supervenes on various natural facts. You are well-off by virtue of the fact that the relevant natural facts obtain. But individual well-being is a state of the individual person. So it seems plausible to insist that differences in individual well-being must supervene on things that constitute differences in the individual person.

The point can be summarized this way: changes in well-being must involve changes in the person. It is because the stranger's success does not involve a change in me, that it cannot involve a change in my level of well-being.

This still leaves open the issue of what exactly does constitute a change in the person. One could, of course, decline to tackle this question. We might simply concede the point that the desire theory must be restricted to desires concerning the state of the person, without attempting to further specify what states are indeed states of the person.

But at this point the mental statist may well want to seize the initiative. Boldly insisting that persons are simply the right sort of collections of mental states—that is, minds—the mental statist is now in a position to argue for the necessity of a mental state theory of well-being.

The argument she puts forward has two premises:

(1) Changes in well-being must involve changes in the person.

(2) A person simply is a collection of mental states.

These two premises seem to yield the desired conclusion that changes in well-being of a person must involve changes in the mental states of that person. Nothing can make a difference to my well-being that does not make a difference to my mental states. My being well-off just is a matter of having the right mental states.

What are we to make of this argument? When I first began to think about it, I thought it fairly clear that the problem was with the second premise. No doubt we all have our moments in which we are drawn to the thought that we are indeed simply our minds. But typically this is not our considered view of the matter. Generally, we are quite prepared to insist that we have bodies as well as minds. Surely no one of naturalist or physicalist inclinations should want to endorse (2).

Perhaps I am too hasty in thinking this. It has been suggested to me that certain contemporary theories of personal identity—namely those that appeal to a psychological criterion of identity—imply that persons are minds.[6] Since these theories are available to physicalists, the second premise, or at least something very much like it, may well be a part of a robust physicalist point of view.

I am not yet convinced that this is so. But it now seems to me that the issue is something of a red herring. The really central question is whether the *first* premise is to be accepted. To see this, suppose that we agree to modify the second premise. Whatever it is that people are, presumably a given person is nothing more than a body and a mind. So suppose we insert a suitable revision of the second premise, keeping the first as it is:

[6] The suggestion was made by Tim Snow, with whom I have discussed this argument with benefit; he has in mind theories like that put forward by Parfit in Part III of *Reasons and Persons*.

(1) Changes in well-being must involve changes in the person.

(2′) A person simply is a collection of mental states.

These two premises seem to yield the conclusion that changes in a person's well-being must involve changes in either the person's body or his mind.

This obviously will not satisfy the mental statist, since it allows for the possibility that some changes in my body that make no difference to my mental states might nonetheless affect my level of well-being. But the conclusion seems a strong and surprising one nonetheless. I find myself strongly inclined to think it must be in error. Yet the second premise is now unexceptionable,[7] so the question is whether the first is correct. (This assumes, of course, that the conclusion does follow from the premises.)

This much at least seems clear. If the first premise is true, it is not as an instantiation of the following generalization: Changes in the value of an object must involve changes in that object. For a simple example seems to suffice to disprove this more general claim. A car is presumably just a (properly organized) collection of metal, rubber, and so forth. So one might put forward the thesis that changes in the value of the car must involve changes in the metal, or the rubber, or what have you. But this is obviously incorrect. For example, if other cars of the same model are destroyed, the original car may become rare, and hence more valuable. But there will have been no changes in the metal or rubber.

No doubt one should hesitate before saying this. There are changes and there are changes. In some sense, the metal and the rubber have changed, since they have changed some of their relational properties — in particular, properties having to do with their coexistence in a world with other cars of the same model. One could preserve the general claim that change in value of an object must involve changes in that object if one were prepared to count such merely relational changes.

But the mental statist or the defender of our modified argument had better not be prepared to count such merely relational changes as potentially sufficient to ground a change in well-being. After all, when the stranger on the train later succeeds, this too alters my relational properties. So if something like the argument we are evaluating is to explain our intuition that my well-being cannot be affected by the stranger's success, the first premise must be understood to exclude merely relational changes. It is only nonrelational, or intrinsic, changes that are to count.

---

[7] In contrast, it is not nearly as plausible to assert that a person's *life* is comprised solely of facts about that person's body and mind. This raises the intriguing — and generally overlooked — possibility that it might be one thing for a person to be well-off and quite another for that person's life to go well. Unfortunately, I cannot explore this fascinating question here; in this essay, I am considering only the nature of the individual *person's* well-being.

Understood in this way, then, the general claim is false. The car undergoes changes in its merely relational properties, but none in its intrinsic properties. Yet its value does increase. So not all changes in the value of an object must involve (intrinsic) changes in that object.

What this means is that if the first premise is true, this must be because of something about the particular type of value that well-being is. Not all values depend solely on intrinsic properties, but some class of values does, and well-being is a member of this class.

Further reflection on the car example may seem to indicate how this more narrow class of values is to be identified. When the value of the car varies, it is its economic or market value that changes. But economic value is clearly an example of *instrumental* value; what varies is the car's usefulness in acquiring various other goods. And it should hardly surprise us that instrumental value will depend in part on merely relational properties.

But even if well-being does sometimes take on instrumental value, this clearly does not exhaust its significance, nor is this even where its primary significance lies. Well-being has intrinsic value; we desire it for its own sake. When my level of well-being varies, something of intrinsic value varies. And unlike instrumental value, intrinsic value can plausibly be thought to be something that must depend solely upon intrinsic properties.

So the claim that changes in well-being must involve intrinsic changes in the person can be defended as an instance of the more general thesis that changes in the intrinsic value of something must involve changes in the intrinsic properties of that thing.

Is this more general thesis true? It has about it the air of an analytic truth. Surely—one might think—intrinsic value must depend solely upon intrinsic properties.

Yet I think this appearance of being a truism is illusory. I think it trades upon two different senses of 'intrinsic value'.[8] One concept of intrinsic value is that of the value an object has independently of all other objects. It is the value an object has "in itself"—the value it would have even if it were the only thing existing in the universe. If anything does indeed have intrinsic value in this sense, then it seems clear that such intrinsic value must depend solely upon the intrinsic properties of the object. After all, since its intrinsic value is had independently of all other objects, it cannot depend upon its various relational properties; so its intrinsic value must depend solely upon its intrinsic properties.

But this first sense of 'intrinsic value' should not be confused with a second sense, according to which an object has intrinsic value when it is desired (or deserves to be desired) "for its own sake." Typically one goes

---

[8] Compare Christine Korsgaard, "Two Distinctions in Goodness," *Philosophical Review*, vol. 92 (1983), pp. 169–95.

on to contrast intrinsic value in this sense with instrumental value. Although I think this further contrast problematic, its familiarity should help fix this second sense of 'intrinsic value'. In this second sense, an object has intrinsic value to the extent that it is valuable as an end.

On the face of it, there is no reason to assume that what has intrinsic value in this second sense — value as an end — must have this value solely by virtue of its intrinsic properties. What is valued for its own sake might well be valuable in part because of various relational properties. Or so it seems. One might think, for example, that something's uniqueness contributes to its intrinsic value. Yet uniqueness is clearly a relational property; it is not a property that an object has independently of whatever else exists in the world. So here we have at least one possible view according to which something's intrinsic value in the second sense is not a matter of its intrinsic value in the first sense.

More generally, one might consistently hold that absolutely nothing has intrinsic value in the first sense, while still insisting that many things have intrinsic value in the second sense. One might, for example, hold a radically subjectivist conception of value, according to which nothing would be valuable as an end in the absence of there being some creature who values it. Given that there *are* creatures who value some objects as ends, some things do have intrinsic value in the second sense, but since being valuable in this way depends upon the relational property of being valued, nothing has intrinsic value in the first sense.

Thus, as a matter of logic, at least, being intrinsically valuable in the second sense does not entail being intrinsically valuable in the first sense. These points are important for the argument we are evaluating in the following way. We were looking for reason to believe that well-being must depend solely upon the intrinsic properties of the person. This seemed plausible in light of the thought that well-being is intrinsically valuable, and the further thought that intrinsic value must depend solely upon intrinsic properties. The difficulty is that the first of these two thoughts seems obviously correct only if it is the second sort of intrinsic value that we are ascribing to well-being, while the second of these two thoughts seems obviously correct only if it is the first sort of intrinsic value that is at issue.

I am certainly prepared to grant that well-being has intrinsic value as an end. But this does not suffice to show that this value depends solely upon the person's intrinsic properties, since intrinsic value in the second sense does not entail intrinsic value in the first sense. What is still needed, then, is some reason to believe that well-being is an intrinsic value in the *first* of our two senses.

Now one might try to argue that all value as an end must be a matter of intrinsic value in the first sense — value "in itself." As we have seen, this would have to be a substantive claim about the nature of value, rather than some trivial entailment. But if this general claim could be defended, then we would indeed be in a position to conclude that well-being must depend solely upon intrinsic properties of the person. However, once the distinction between the two senses of 'intrinsic value' is kept firmly in mind, I see no good reason to think that this general claim is true.

This still leaves the possibility of arguing with regard to well-being in particular that it is intrinsically valuable in the first sense. But now it becomes increasingly difficult to see just how this particular claim is to be defended. Admittedly, if well-being is an intrinsic value in the first of our senses, then it must depend solely upon the person's intrinsic properties. But why should we believe that it is, in fact, intrinsically valuable in this sense? The assertion amounts to little more than a begging of the question.

Given that I am hostile to the conclusion of the argument—that is, to the claim that changes in well-being must involve changes in the body or the mind of the person—I wish the matter could simply be left here. But it now seems to me that there is a further move that must be considered.

A theory of well-being attempts to specify in general terms the set of facts that comprise the good for the individual. An adequate theory of well-being would have to meet several conditions. One condition—one that we have, in effect, been exploring—is that the specified facts must be about the person. We might call this the *content* condition. A second condition—the *value* condition—is that there must be a plausible account of why it is good that the specified facts obtain. But there is a third condition—the *benefit* condition—that must be met as well: the specified facts must be good *for* the person who is well-off; the well-off individual must *benefit* from being well-off.

Meeting the first two conditions need not guarantee meeting the third as well. For all that the first two conditions guarantee is that the relevant facts are good *concerning* the given individual; they do not guarantee that they are good *for* him. For example, suppose one held a retributivist view of desert, according to which it is a good thing (other things being equal) if the wicked suffer. Here is Abdul, an unrepentantly evil individual, being forced to undergo misery and pain as punishment for past crimes. If one holds a sufficiently extreme version of the desert view, then one will claim that it is a good thing that Abdul suffers. The fact of Abdul's suffering surely constitutes a fact about Abdul, and on the view being considered it is a good thing that this fact obtains. So both the content and the value condition appear to be met. But for all that, one might well want to insist that Abdul is not well-off: however well deserved his suffering may be, it is not good for *him*.

The point, of course, is not that I want to endorse this view of desert, but that an adequate account of well-being will have to meet the third condition as well as the first two: the specified facts must be good for the person, not merely good concerning him.

Consider then one further claim: What is of benefit to a person must involve the person's intrinsic properties. Now if we include merely instrumental benefits, this is certainly false. But well-being is an intrinsic benefit; it is the payoff itself, and not a mere means to the payoff. So let us restrict our attention to final, or ultimate, benefits, and understand the claim accordingly: If something constitutes an (ultimate) benefit to a person, it must involve the person's intrinsic properties.

If this claim is correct, then the argument we have been considering goes through. Increasing well-being is providing an intrinsic, ultimate benefit to the person; thus, it would have to involve altering the person's intrinsic properties. Since a person just is a body and a mind, changes in well-being would have to involve changes in the person's body or mind.

But is the claim correct? Much to my dismay, I find myself strongly inclined to think that it *is*. If something is to be of genuine (ultimate) benefit *to* a person, then it must *affect* the person; it must make a difference *in* the person. That is, it must affect the person's intrinsic properties. Changes in merely relational properties cannot be what is of ultimate value *for* the person.

I certainly have no argument for this claim. It is simply that I find it overwhelmingly plausible. What benefits the person must make some intrinsic difference in the person. Otherwise there would be nothing in it *for him*.

Now it is easy enough to reject this claim on the grounds that it must be false or else we are led to the undesirable conclusion that well-being can only be affected by intrinsic changes in the body or the mind. But that doesn't make it any easier for me to maintain the dismissal of the claim when it is considered in its own right.

Similarly, one might point to some intuitively plausible example where one is strongly disposed to claim that something affects well-being even though it does not affect the person's body or mind. Take your favorite example, say, someone who has been deceived into thinking that she is loved and successful. Surely — I want to say — this person is not as well-off as she would have been had she genuinely been loved and successful. So it must be false that what benefits someone must affect her intrinsically.

But when I reconsider the claim once more I find myself unable to maintain this rejection. How could something be of genuine benefit *to* the person, if it never "touches" her, if it never alters the person at all?

At best, then, I find myself with a set of mutually inconsistent beliefs. (1) What benefits someone must affect her intrinsically. (2) Were the person genuinely loved rather than deceived she would be better off. (3) The deception does not affect the person intrinsically. Presumably, the set can be rendered consistent by rejecting any one of the members. But that gives us no guidance in choosing which member to reject.

In fact, however, the situation in my own case is not nearly so symmetrical. I wish I could comfortably reject the claim that what benefits someone must affect her intrinsically. But before I can do this, I need some sort of account that would precisely locate and diagnose the error in the thought that benefit must make an intrinsic difference — as opposed to merely rejecting this thought despite its intuitive appeal. In the absence of such an account, I currently find myself more inclined to think that it is the standard examples that are mistaken. They appear to be cases where well-being is affected, but they must not be, for they cannot be.[9]

As I hope I have made clear, I am not at all happy with this result. I remain open to a persuasive diagnosis of the error. But for the time being, it seems to me that the argument for severely restricting the limits of well-being may well be sound. The limits of well-being may be the limits of the person.

IV. CLASSIFICATORY CONCERNS

Suppose the argument of the last section were correct. This would not yet establish the truth of mental statism. For the argument would only establish that well-being must be a matter of the appropriate intrinsic states of the body or the mind. As I have already noted, this leaves open the possibility that certain changes in the body might affect well-being even though they involve no changes in one's mental states.

Of course, if it could be shown that a person is indeed just a mind, then the argument would support a mental state theory. But I myself remain convinced that people are bodies as well as minds.

However, this does not yet close off all hope for the mental statist. Even if people are bodies as well as minds, all that the argument shows is the *possibility* that certain nonmental bodily changes might affect well-being. It is still open to the mental statist to argue that, in fact, no nonmental bodily change *does* affect well-being. And this does not seem an altogether implausible claim.

Nonetheless, at this point the possibility still remains that there are certain goods of well-being that are not a matter of one's mental states. Perhaps, for example, certain dispositions or abilities are themselves partly constitutive of well-being independently of their effect on one's mental states. I cannot here explore this possibility.

But one thing that does seem to emerge fairly clearly is the inadequacy of dividing theories of well-being into mental state, desire, or objective theories. This gets things wrong for three reasons.

First, it places mental state theories on the side, as though they were removed from the choice between desire and objective theories. We saw that this was mistaken when we realized that even hedonism could be given either an objective interpretation or a desire theory interpretation. It seems to me more illuminating to say that theories of well-being divide

---

[9] Alvin Goldman has helpfully characterized my argument as being: "Yes, yes, I've heard that example before."

on the question of the source of the value of well-being. There are subjective theories (most saliently, desire theories) and there are objective
theories. And this choice between subjective and objective is one that
arises within mental state theories as well as within a second cluster of
theories that draw the limits of well-being more broadly.

The second shortcoming is that the trichotomy—mental state, desire,
objective—fails to provide any kind of label for this second cluster of theories, that is, theories (whether objective or subjective) that hold that
well-being can involve facts that go beyond facts involving mental states.
There is a distinction to be drawn that roughly corresponds to that between mental state theories and all other theories, and we need a name
for it.

But this points to a third, related shortcoming, which is that to the limited extent that the trichotomy seems to recognize this second distinction
at all, it mistakenly suggests that the fundamental divide is between mental state theories and all other theories. But in fact, the more fundamental distinction seems to be between theories that limit well-being to
intrinsic facts about the person and theories that allow for relational facts
to directly contribute to well-being as well. Mental state theories may be
the most well-known or the most plausible examples of the former type
of theory, but they do not exhaust the class. Perhaps this second division
should be labeled as the division between intrinsic theories and relational
theories (or intrinsic theories and extrinsic theories), but I myself am
drawn to a slightly different set of labels: some theories restrict well-
being to facts *internal* to the person; other theories allow for the direct relevance of facts *external* to the person as well.

These two distinctions—subjective/objective and internal/external—cut
across each other. Thus, there are four basic types of theory, not three,
and the traditional classification fails to properly demarcate any of them.

Rather than pursue these classificatory concerns any further, let me
turn to one final point. Suppose the argument of the previous section
were correct. Then a variety of "external" goods that are often taken to
be constitutive of well-being are actually irrelevant to it. I am distressed
to think that this may be so, but for the time being at least I find myself
pulled in this direction. But even if this is so, this does not at all show that
the various external goods are not genuine goods. Indeed, they may well
be more significant than well-being itself. We will still care deeply about
the presence of these external, relational goods. And nothing suggests
that we are mistaken to do so.[10]

Even if they are external to well-being, there will remain an important
sense in which these external goods are *personal*, in that their value lies

[10] Having a life that goes well may plausibly turn out to be one of these goods (or a function of them)—if the quality of my life is indeed distinct from my level of well-being (see
note 7).

in their relation to the given person. From a moral point of view, we may still have weighty reasons to promote the existence of these goods. Admittedly, promotion of these external goods may do nothing at all to benefit the person, but we may still be obliged to promote them out of *respect* for the person.

If this is right, then the importance of well-being may be less than we often take it to be. In many cases, the pursuit of the external personal goods will be far more important than the pursuit of the internal goods that happen to comprise well-being. The more narrowly we understand well-being, the more likely that this is the case.

If well-being is limited in its extent, then it may also be limited in its significance.

Philosophy, University of Illinois at Chicago

LEGALISM AND HUMANKIND*

By Frank I. Michelman

I. Introduction

Prescriptive political and moral theories contain ideas about what human beings are like and about what, correspondingly, is good for them. Conceptions of human "nature" and corresponding human good enter into normative argument by way of support and justification. Of course, it is logically open for the ratiocinative traffic to run the other way. Strongly held convictions about the rightness or wrongness, goodness or badness, of certain social institutions or practices may help condition and shape one's responses to one or another set of propositions about what people are like and what, in consequence, they have reason to value.

It is this two-way exchange between high-level theories and underlying views of human nature and the human good that will occupy us here, especially its reciprocating movement *from* high-level theory *to* human nature. I begin with an example taken from contemporary jurisprudential debate. Next comes a short, general account of the two-way exchange in normative argument at large and jurisprudence in particular. Drawing on that account, I then ask what, if anything, is required of human nature by a certain widely shared, prescriptive notion of law and legality. Finally, I shift the focus from jurisprudence to moral theory, and use the idea of the two-way exchange to raise some questions for Kantian deontology.

II. Personality to Politics, Politics to Personality

We begin with an example of the two-way exchange, drawn from controversy over the work of Roberto Unger. Unger urges constitutional reform to the end of "disentrenchment" of social arrangements, including constitutions themselves; a legal constitution ought to reflect and advance the ideal of a social life that "makes available, in the course of ordinary politics and existence, the instruments of its own revision."[1] For Unger, the constant aim of constitutional practice is to loosen "frozen politics" and "fixed orders" in society by prying them open to "collective conflict

---

* For helpful criticisms and suggestions, I am especially indebted to James Boyle, Thomas Scanlon, Judith Jarvis Thomson, and Steven Winter.
[1] Roberto Unger, *The Critical Legal Studies Movement* (Cambridge: Harvard University Press, 1986), p. 105.

and deliberation."[2] His constitution would be designed to honor claims to "disrupt[ion of] established institutions and forms of social practice that have achieved the insulation and have encouraged the entrenchment . . . that the entire constitution wants to avoid."[3] To that end, it would establish in the government a special "destabilization branch." Modeled in part after judicial interventions into public education systems (in the era of the Warren Court), this branch would, unlike the conventional judiciary, "have at [its] disposal the technical, financial, and human resources required by any effort to reorganize major institutions and to pursue the reconstructive effort over time." It would have a roving license to intervene wherever politics are "frozen," extending not just to "every function of all the other powers of the state," but to "every aspect" of social life and every "major institution" in it.[4]

Unger connects his argument for institutionalized disentrenchment to a particular view of human personality—a philosophic anthropology—according to which a human being's "dignity" or "infinite quality" resides in the human capacity for self-revision or self-transcendence.[5] He contends that only a constitution committed to disentrenchment can "do justice" to people's self-transformative capacities[6] or "enable the self to experience in ordinary life its true freedom."[7] Given that we all always find ourselves within "formative contexts" of social relationships and practices, and culturally mediated constructions of experience, the capacity for self-revision must encompass, Unger says, "the power of the self eternally to transcend the limited imaginative and social world that it constructs."[8] There arises, then, a corresponding ideal for a legal constitution, in part because a legal constitution is itself a formative context conditioning our self-understandings.

There are many conceivable ways to mount resistance against such an argument. Resisters might question the workability or coherence of Un-

---

[2] See, for example, ibid., p. 23.

[3] Ibid., p. 39.

[4] See Roberto Unger, False Necessity (Cambridge: Cambridge University Press, 1987), pp. 452–53.

[5] See, for example, Unger, Critical Legal Studies Movement, pp. 22–23, 94. See also Roberto Unger, Passion: An Essay on Personality (New York: Free Press, 1984), p. vii, where Unger advises that he aims to

> reconceive and reconstruct the ancient and universal practice of attributing normative force to conceptions of personality or society so that this practice can better withstand the criticisms that philosophy since Hume or Kant has leveled against it.

[6] Unger, Critical Legal Studies Movement, p. 23.

[7] Ibid., p. 105.

[8] See, for example, ibid., p. 26. In Passion, pp. 88–89, Unger gives two reasons for working toward "a . . . way of living in the present . . . as people not wholly defined by the current forms of their existence." These reasons are, "first, because this is the kind of being we really are and, second, because by living in this fashion we empower ourselves individually and collectively." Unger then adds that the two reasons really reduce to one: "they state the same thesis under different names."

ger's prescriptions for political and constitutional practice,[9] or the co-
gency of his arguments connecting anthropology with politics.[10] None of
this would yet be to reject the *value* of institutions geared to disentrenchment, assuming that any such could be satisfactorily designed. But of
course there are many who do strongly question this value. Some find it
disconsonant with something else that they value highly, such as, for example, the ideal of the rule of law. Such a stance would give a critic reason to question, as well, the anthropological underpinnings of Unger's
argument. I do not mean to suggest that there is anything amiss in being
thus prompted to question a premise by unease about its apparent implications. In the clearest case, the critic would argue not only that Unger's
underlying notion of plasticity-as-the-human-essence is wrong, but that
among the considerations suggesting that it is wrong is its correspon-
dence with a high-level normative political theory whose prescriptions the
critic also feels to be almost certainly wrong or ill-advised.

Now, in fact, Unger's attribution of plasticity to human nature is relatively guarded and moderate, at least by comparison with some spirited
postmodernist accounts of personality as absolutely fluid and ungrasp-
able.[11] A part of Unger's view is that we are dependent for personal
freedom on our "contexts" of personal relationships, social practices, laws
and institutions, languages and cultures. Formative contexts enable a relative fixation of the self and hence a self-possession prerequisite to moral
agency; they provide the field of resistance against which self-revision-
ary moral agency is exercisable.[12] Moreover, Unger's constitutional proposals, which include provisions for property rights and "immunity
rights," do plainly "[rely] to a considerable degree on the rule of law to
regulate public and private powers."[13]

Even so, one gathers from many critiques of Unger a sense — perhaps
abetted by Unger's sometimes-paradoxical formulations ("structure-revis-

---

[9] See, for example, Martin Stone, "The Placement of Politics in Roberto Unger's *Politics*,"
in *Law and the Order of Culture*, ed. Robert Post (Berkeley: University of California Press,
1991), pp. 78–108; Cass Sunstein, "Routine and Revolution," *Northwestern University Law
Review*, vol. 81 (1987), pp. 869–93, esp. pp. 881–93.

[10] See, for example Sunstein, "Routine and Revolution."

[11] See, for example, Duncan Kennedy, "A Cultural Pluralist Case For Affirmative Action
in Legal Academia," *Duke Law Journal*, vol. 1990, pp. 705–57, esp. pp. 743–46.

[12] Unger's view here resembles Michael Sandel's view of agency as dependent on the
"situated" character of the self. See Michael Sandel, *Liberalism and the Limits of Justice* (Cambridge: Cambridge University Press, 1973), pp. 152–73. As James Boyle says:

> In the place of . . . total denial [of limits], Unger offers us a chastened brand of
> modernism — one that accepts the inevitability (and even the desirability) of the limi-
> tations imposed by the cultural context in which one is embedded, yet insists none-
> theless on the possibility of self-realization, the assertion of the infinite within the
> confines of the finite.

James Boyle, "Modernist Social Theory: Roberto Unger's *Passion*" (Book Review), *Harvard
Law Review*, vol. 98 (1985), p. 1079.

[13] Andrew Altman, *Critical Legal Studies: A Liberal Critique* (Princeton: Princeton University Press, 1990), p. 170.

ing structure"; "destabilization rights")—of strained relations between Unger's philosophic anthropology and cherished notions of legal ordering. One sees doubts about the anthropology commingled with objections to its apparent jurisprudential implications (or qualms about them), in ways suggesting that it may be those implications, as much as Unger's picture of personality in itself, that drive the critiques.

Consider Cass Sunstein's fine critical essay on Unger's *Politics*.[14] Sunstein strongly disapproves of the idea that a constitution ought to be designed to foster constant destabilization. He does so, in part, because of that idea's association with a "pluralist" style of politics, in which "political outcomes represent an equilibrium point among hostile forces" and what are called laws can only, therefore, be "naked transfers of wealth or exercises of power," arbitrarily shaped by particular interests and not by a common good.[15] Sunstein holds to a contrasting ideal for lawmaking. He envisions, ideally, a process geared to perception and recognition of "common interests," and also to "the virtues [of] the rule of law: stability, checks on discretion and caprice, and predictability over time."[16] Such a process, Sunstein says, would have to be itself already framed by higher laws entrenching "rights" sufficiently "broad" to block factional political struggle from destroying the life prospects of political losers. In addition, it would have to engage faculties of "dialogue," "deliberation," and "empathy" to "filter out" objectionably particularistic motivations from lawmaking.[17] But these attributes of legality and mutuality are, Sunstein says, largely alien to Unger's vision of politics.[18]

Sunstein also enters objections against Unger's conception of personality, in which he finds "Christian notions of self-transcendence" linked with "existential approaches" that seem to equate freedom with "breaking through fixed roles, whatever their content may be."[19] This Christian-existentialist view of personality is, Sunstein says, inimical to "the formation of character."[20] Moreover, its "Faustian" celebration of "self-creation" smacks too much of "erasure of the mother"—a phrase that seems to speak not only of "separation and self-assertion rather than community and compassion,"[21] but of denial of human commonality expressed as the siblinghood of humankind.

[14] Sunstein, "Routine and Revolution," pp. 869–93. I choose this example in part because, among critiques of Unger's vision proceeding from a stance that is closer than Unger's to a conventional, liberal appreciation of legal ordering, Sunstein's critique exceptionally keeps its own distance from the conventional view, and contains its own sophisticated appraisal of that view's vices and virtues.
[15] *Ibid.*, pp. 885–86.
[16] *Ibid.*, pp. 887, 891.
[17] *Ibid.*, pp. 886–88.
[18] *Ibid.*
[19] *Ibid.*, pp. 885, 892.
[20] *Ibid.*, p. 885.
[21] *Ibid.*

Sunstein's objections to Unger's philosophic anthropology are distinct from his objections to the pluralist character of the politics of disentrenchment. Yet the two sets of objections collaborate in Sunstein's argument against Unger. Sunstein finds Unger's "Faustian" vision of personality conducive to acceptance of " 'conflict', 'struggle over the mastery of power', and 'fighting' [as] the principal determinants of social outcomes," in contradistinction to a process of law-creation — of politics — that would be cognizant and supportive of human commonality. He holds Unger's anthropology partly accountable for what he sees as inattention on Unger's part to "substantive arguments" addressed to problems of discrimination and poverty, and more broadly, to the cultivation of a politics of dialogue, deliberation, and practical reason.[22]

III. "Naturalism" in Normative Argument

A. The structure of naturalistic argument

By "naturalism" in moral and political argument I do not mean the claim that knowledge of what is good or right for us is reducible to knowledge of humanity's physical and psychical constitutions. Rather, I mean the use of propositions regarding the human condition and, correspondingly, the good for humankind to help justify propositions about how persons ought to act or ought to be governed. Argument is "naturalistic" when it explicitly shuttles between propositions of these two sorts.[23] (Such argument need not assert claims about humankind timeless and universal. It may refer to the humankind of "our" civilization as we are able to know it and willing to take it as fixed for our purposes.) Implicitly, if not always explicitly, such argument requires us to distinguish between humanity's essence and its accidents; it makes us separate conceptually a human being's contingent states and changes in states from the constitutive structures and attributes that render it the kind of being it is, namely, human. Thus, to say that X, a human being, is suffering, or that X is in a state of heteronomy, is to speak of contingent states. To say that human beings are vulnerable to suffering, or that human beings have the capacity for moral self-government, is to speak of constitutive structures.

---

[22] See *ibid.*, pp. 885–86.

[23] Not every self-contained piece of normative argumentation exhibits this form. A given piece of moral argumentation, for example, may confine itself to analysis and elaboration of socio-ethical data consisting of moral vocabularies and intuitions. Such argumentation is not, as far as it goes, naturalistic in form, and I do not here inquire whether it must depend on unspoken naturalistic premises for whatever prescriptive force it may exert. I do take up below some arguments of prescriptive jurisprudence that analogously proceed by analysis and elaboration of the concept of law as it occurs in ordinary legal thought, and I do suggest that these arguments always implicitly appeal to unspoken naturalistic premises.

The point of naturalistic normative (moral or political) argument is to evaluate acts, practices, rules, and institutions by tracing correlations between them and certain contingent states of human beings;[24] it is to pronounce the act, practice, rule, or other arrangement in question good or bad (right or wrong) depending on whether its correlative human-state contingencies do or do not bear a certain kind of approved relation to the structures and attributes deemed constitutive for beings of the human kind. Perhaps we ask whether the correlative human-state contingencies are "in the interest of" such beings. Perhaps we ask whether the rules or arrangements would, in light of their expected correlative human-state contingencies, be "rationally chosen by" beings of our kind.[25]

For present purposes, I want to define the requisite kind of relation very broadly and loosely, so that it also includes such relations as "expresses (or fulfills) the nature of," "manifests the flourishing of," and "is becoming (or suited) to" beings of such-and-such a kind (as, for example, the state of conforming-its-conduct-to-moral-law may be said by some Kantians to fulfill the nature of human being *qua* human).[26] Common to all the species of this genus of relations is that they signify consonance of some kind between a being's states/changes-in-states (or arrangements affecting those) and the being's "nature." Since nothing in what follows depends on which species of this genus of relations is in play, we can refer to them all generically (and evasively) as the relation-genus "right-for beings of that kind" or, for short, $RF[x]$, where x designates the kind of being in view.[27]

---

[24] I choose the vague term "correlation" in order to avoid binding my account of naturalistic moral argument to *causal* linkages between acts, institutions, etc., on the one hand, and human-state contingencies on the other. I want language that allows us to classify (say) "being involved in affectionate relationships" or "acting autonomously" as states of human beings that may or may not occur, and further allows us to propose that institutions such as the family or a libertarian political constitution "correlate" with occurrences of such states, without having to sort out the senses (if any) in which the institutions may be said to cause the occurrences.

[25] I mean to include both "would be rationally chosen by" us in any circumstances imaginable, given our constitutive attributes, *and* "would be rationally chosen by" us, given our constitutive attributes, in hypothetically specified circumstances (an "original position").

[26] For Unger's analogous gestures, see *supra* notes 5 and 8.

[27] Understanding always that "right-for" may be defined in terms of "good-for."

Humean critics of naturalistic argument—that is, of such argument's allegedly outrageous elision of the gap between facts and values—may well see the choice of a content for the *RF* relation ("preserves the life of," "fulfills the excellence of," etc.) as the point where naturalistic argument levitates itself across the gap. As James Boyle explains the Humean critique, "an opponent of one's theory can [always] claim that it links . . . description to political prescription by means of an arbitrary assumption." See James Boyle, "Modernist Social Theory," p. 1072. Evidently, the arbitrary assumption Boyle has in mind is the choice of content for *RF*. He makes this explicit in his comment on Unger's two linked reasons for cultivating negative capability in our lives (namely, this corresponds with how "we really are," and this is how "we empower ourselves"; see *supra* note 8): "I do not object," says Boyle, "to the conjunction of these [two] reasons, but when Unger [adds] . . . that both of them 'state the same thesis under different names' . . . it becomes hard to differentiate his argument from the Aristotelian one" that Hume skewered.

B. Two-way traffic

Consider how much high-level liberal political theory has been justificationally linked to a philosophic anthropology found in Part I of
Hobbes's *Leviathan*,[28] including both that anthropology's methodological
individualism and its motivational mechanics of self-preservation, imagination, and power-lust.[29] Naively, it may seem as though argument in
this model is unidirectional, running always "upward" from a more ele-
mentary anthropological proposition to a more intricate political one –
from (1) the nature of human being, to (2) the goodness (or badness) for
beings of the human kind of certain states, and on to (3) the goodness (or
badness) for humankind of certain rules and other institutions judged
conducive (or not) to such states. In the actual practice of much moral and
political argument, however, the traffic runs both ways, and RF[*human
being*] serves as a two-way switch. Strongly fixed intuitions about what
is required or permitted in the way of actions or institutions can prompt
anthropological contentions and motivate adjustments or clarifications of
anthropological belief.[30]

Take as an example this interesting argument of David Gauthier's.[31]
Gauthier points out that a Hobbesian justificatory (rational-choice) argument for unquestioning submission to sovereign authority requires that
individuals be "rule egoists," meaning they are disposed to "perform
nonegoistic *actions* in . . . situations in which the egoistically best *rules*
would require that [one] do so."[32] He further points out that in order to
justify a political arrangement by the criterion of rational choice, one must
show more than that choice of the arrangement would be rational for all

---

[28] Thomas Hobbes, *Leviathan: On the Matter, Forme and Power of a Commonwealth Ecclesi-
astical and Civil* (New York: Collier Books, 1962), pp. 21–128.

[29] See, for example, John Rawls, *A Theory of Justice* (Cambridge: Harvard University
Press, 1971), p. 240; Elizabeth Mensch and Alan Freeman, "A Republican Agenda for
Hobbesian America?" *University of Florida Law Review*, vol. 41 (1989), pp. 581–600.

[30] That is, disconsonance between currently held beliefs at either end of the logical traffic
may motivate a process of reflective equilibrium. See Rawls, *A Theory of Justice*, pp. 48–51.

[31] David Gauthier, "Taming Leviathan," *Philosophy and Public Affairs*, vol. 16 (1987),
pp. 280–98. Michael Sandel's *Liberalism and the Limits of Justice* provides another choice example. It is because of the two-way flow of the traffic between high-level institutional prescription and low-level attributions to human nature that Sandel can comfortably, in one
and the same work, both (1) argue against John Rawls that an alleged mistake of philosophic
anthropology (conceiving the self as radically "unencumbered" or prior to its ends rather
than as constitutively "situated") undermines the conception of justice as the priority of the
right over the good (see *ibid.*, pp. 7–59); and (2) argue against Ronald Dworkin (in the reverse direction) that Dworkin's concrete stance in favor of race-conscious affirmative action
logically commits him to a communitarian as opposed to a Kantian-individualist conception
of the self (see *ibid.*, pp. 135–47). Compare Richard Rorty, "Habermas and Lyotard on Post-
modernity," in *Essays on Heidegger and Others* (Cambridge: Cambridge University Press,
1991), p. 165: "[W]e find French critics of Habermas ready to abandon liberal politics in order to avoid universalistic philosophy, and Habermas trying to hang on to universalistic philosophy . . . in order to support liberal politics." Rorty's essay criticizes this tendency to
think that espousal of a "politics" commits one to a "philosophy" and vice versa.

[32] Gauthier, "Taming Leviathan," p. 287 (emphasis added).

agents, supposing they all assume that all will really keep the commitments entailed by their choice and by the argument for its rationality. One must further establish, Gauthier explains, that the agents, given their natures, are psychologically able to keep those commitments. From these two perceptions, Gauthier deduces, in effect, the need for Hobbesian theorists to attribute to humankind a natural psychology that is not strictly egoistic but only qualifiedly (or, as Gauthier says, "predominantly") so, in the sense that it allows for some degree of disposition to act nonegoistically, even if all human action is ultimately driven by self-interest.[33]

IV. NATURALISM IN LEGAL ARGUMENT

A. Jurisprudence

Deeply insinuated in all of legal disputation as we know it are arguments linking propositions about what we human beings are like with propositions about what, accordingly, serves our good (would be rational for us to choose, befits our natures, manifests our flourishing, etc.) and how, accordingly, we ought to treat each other. I intend a strong claim here. By "legal disputation" I mean disputation among lawyers directed to "object-level" questions of law[34] — questions about what is the applicable law as distinguished from questions about what manner of stuff or idea law is. Disputation about what law is I will call "jurisprudential" rather than "legal."

My claim may well strike you as not just controversial but cavalier. You may think of classic and ever-lively debates — jurisprudential debates — over this very question of the separation of object-level legal disputation from the discourse of morality. Such debates do certainly go on. Separationist stances (I will be sketching some just below) are energetically defended by theorists,[35] and we sometimes see such stances strenuously assumed by judges in their opinions.[36] These facts of legal life are, however, entirely consistent with the fact (I claim it is a fact) that every object-level legal claim or defense urged by every legal controversialist, and every object-level legal judgment rendered by every judge, is justificationally connected — proximately or remotely, explicitly or implicitly — with

---

[33] See *ibid.*, pp. 285, 297–98: "[A]n alienation contract [resting on rule egoism] would be each person's best option [only if] . . . the psychology of Hobbesian persons were to permit it. . . . But . . . the best rule for a rule egoist to adopt may require her to be sincerely nonegoistic in some circumstances."

[34] I adapt the term "object-level" from Judith Jarvis Thomson, *The Realm of Rights* (Cambridge: Harvard University Press, 1990), p. 30.

[35] See, for example, Charles Fried, "The Artificial Reason of the Law or What Lawyers Know," *Texas Law Review*, vol. 60 (1981).

[36] See, for example, *Cruzan v. Missouri Dept. of Health*, 110 S. Ct. 2841, 2859, 2863 (1990) (Scalia, J., concurring).

some set of propositions about the nature and, correspondingly, the good of humankind. There is a reason why this is so, one that is as easy to state as it may be perplexing to explain. The reason is simply that jurisprudential controversy itself, including controversy over the separability of object-level legal disputation from considerations of morality, has no known discourse of justification save appeal, sooner or later, to the kinds of propositions about human nature and need, and corresponding good, that underlie moral and political argument. Jurisprudential debates over the separation of (object-level) law and morals are, after all, *debates*, in which the separationist positions require justification.

I advance this as an empirical claim about jurisprudential debate, not as a claim about the necessary character of such debate. Full support of the empirical claim would require an exhaustive survey of all known separationist jurisprudential arguments together with their apparently strongest justifications in the face of challenge. Here I offer only a glance at such material — enough, I hope, to establish the plausibility of my empirical claim. For present purposes, that ought to suffice.

Some separationist jurisprudential arguments are analytical (later I will also call these "legalist" arguments); they say that the independence of questions of law from questions of value (of the "right-for" human being) derives from the very notion of law, or from what we mean by the word and its cognates — legal, legality, (legal) right — as we actually use them. Some separationist jurisprudential arguments are pragmatic or prudential; they stress the desirability, for some reason, of keeping object-level legal disputations clear of questions of value.

Let us glance first at some pragmatic arguments. I said that these all stress the desirability *for some reason* of keeping legal disputation clear of moral considerations. What reason? Won't any cogent reason itself have to refer to some conception of value?[37]

Some pragmatic separationist arguments are what we may call allocationalist arguments. Allocationalist arguments recommend that we distinguish questions of law from questions of value by regarding law as a principle or rule for allocating competence or authority over questions of value. There are many of these arguments. Libertarian allocationalist arguments say that law ought to be understood and judicially elaborated as (perhaps among other things) a complex rule for reserving questions of value for individuals (or for spontaneous social formations such as families and religious communities) to resolve without constraint from other persons or from any encompassing, solidary "community" or "society" organized as the state.[38] Democratic allocationalist arguments say, rather

---

[37] See Margaret Jane Radin and Frank Michelman, "Pragmatist and Poststructuralist Critical Legal Practice," *University of Pennsylvania Law Review*, vol. 189 (1991), pp. 1019–58.

[38] See, for example, David Richards, *Toleration and the Constitution* (Oxford: Oxford University Press, 1986).

to the contrary, that law ought to be understood and elaborated as the duly expressed will of the organized political society; that we ought to see the fact of some directive's democratic-institutional provenance, and not the quality or validity of whatever moral reasoning went into it, as what makes that directive into law.[39] Different still are conventionalist arguments that recommend distinguishing questions of law from questions of value by treating law as a rather different kind of objective social fact: a fact not of willed decision or formal enactment but of circumstantial commitment or experiential social learning — of custom and tradition, organically grown practice, perhaps even natural selection.[40]

How is controversy among such clashing jurisprudences — each in its own way calling for exclusion of considerations of value from object-level legal disputation and judgment — to be resolved? What counts as argument on behalf of one of them against its competitors? It must be obvious that all cogent arguments on this field of controversy regress eventually on one or another set of ideas about what people are like and what, correspondingly, is "right-for" them. Of course, disputants may say murky things. Someone may say, for example, that "we" are "committed," just by reason of finding ourselves in an ongoing community already thus committed, to live in accordance with the social ordering (or basic structure for a social ordering) dictated by contemporary retrievals of the common-law tradition or of the original understanding of the ratifiers of the Constitution. But such a declaration is not yet an argument; it only waves towards some argument still waiting to be made. It intimates values of community and commitment. A persistent interrogation of those values must finally yield, in effect, a deep essay in moral anthropology.[41] How else might the arguments conceivably go?

B. Prescriptive legalism: The rule of law

It is always possible that someone tries to argue analytically rather than naturalistically. Someone can always start an argumentative sentence with something like: "Whoever understands what law is can be brought to see. . . ." If that means asking us to decide whether law "is" the principle of institutional respect for duly expressed political will, or "is" the principle of institutional respect for conventional normative wisdom, or "is" the principle of institutional respect for personal autonomy, the re-

---

[39] See, for example, Robert Bork, "Neutral Principles and Some First Amendment Problems," *Indiana Law Journal*, vol. 47 (1971), pp. 1–35.

[40] See, for example, Friedrich Hayek, *The Fatal Conceit* (Chicago: Chicago University Press, 1988), ch. 1; Hayek, "Epilogue: The Three Sources of Human Values," in *Law, Legislation, and Liberty: The Political Order of a Free Society* (Chicago: Chicago University Press, 1979), pp. 153–76.

[41] For an example of what such an essay might be like, see Alasdair MacIntyre, *After Virtue* (Notre Dame: Notre Dame University Press, 1981), pp. 190–209.

sult will be *nil* — not because there is not, among us, *anything* that law just "is," but because there is not anything *like those principles* that it just "is." On this field of contestation, contestants can only argue about what way of understanding law would be most conducive to value.

The case is not, however, that there is *nothing* that interlocutors all tend to think that law is, or that analytic argument to separationist conclusions is for that reason out of the question. Indeed, I believe the contrary is true. Here are some things that law notionally is, according to ordinary legal understanding: Law is *other*, it is *given*, and it is *one*. Law is *other*: that is, it is constraint. Law is *given* antecedently: that is, it binds not just prospectively but already. Law is *one*: that is, it is determinate in principle (questions of law have right answers), and it is in that sense a rule (the rule of law);[42] it is consistent across its subdivisions; it is general over the population of agents subject to it.

Law in ordinary legal understanding is ideally a determinate principle or force that antecedently binds the will. *Nomos* cannot be immediately and identically *autos*. Law may be willed and be a product of will, but law is not will. Law may be "self-given" (and only in light of this is "autonomy" not the father of all oxymorons), but law is not self. (The stuff that binds Odysseus to the mast is there, binding him, by his own stroke. But that stuff is not Odysseus, and it is not his will, either.)

Law in ordinary legal understanding is ideally one; it is *the* law, unitary and whole; legality is a kind of integrity.[43] Insofar as there is law relative to a population, then it is ideally one and the same law for all the population's members. If there are different working rules applicable to different subpopulations, then that difference in working rules is, ideally, justificationally referable to some (set of) higher-order rule(s) — even if, for a limiting case, it is only the rule of unquestioning adherence to some designated ruler's dictates; and that higher-order rule is either identical with the rule used to reconcile other pluralities of working rules found elsewhere in the system, or else there is some still higher-order rule that reconciles *their* differences; and so on. It is the reconciling, unifying rule(s) in which the "lawness" consists. If irreconcilable normative pluralities appear on the scene, then the conclusion is that true law, legality, is absent from that scene.

A normative notion of law as unitary, determinate, and always-already binding can certainly motivate analytic arguments to the effect that law is distinct from morality, especially given the highly subjectivistic and plu-

---

[42] As I use the term "rule" in this discussion, a rule may consist of several principles and standards, as long as a competent lawyer, judging in good faith, can experience their combination as compelling a determinate decision. See Duncan Kennedy, "Freedom and Constraint in Adjudication: A Critical Phenomenology," *Journal of Legal Education*, vol. 36 (1986), pp. 518–62.

[43] See Ronald Dworkin, *Law's Empire* (Cambridge: Harvard University Press, 1986), pp. 151–67.

ralistic accounts of morality that such arguments tend to adopt.[44] For purposes of this essay, the point in which I am chiefly interested is that even such sternly legalist arguments for the separation of law from morals, even such arguments built closely on analysis of the very notion of law, are ratiocinatively connected with considerations of human nature and corresponding human good. A familiar litany of legalist virtues that are prudentially associated with the givenness and determinancy of the law — the intelligibility, performability, calculability, and reliability of institutionally sanctioned obligations and permissions — obviously appeals to such considerations.[45]

C. Two-way traffic:
Human-natural correlates of prescriptive legalism

Propositions about the law's content and "nature," I have contended, all sooner or later seek their justifications in ideas about the human condition and corresponding human good. The converse is that any set of ideas about the nature and content of law will be differentially receptive to various conceptions of human good and human being. It is tempting to press the point to a purely formal conclusion. From the notion of law as constraint and as unitary it evidently follows, by the logic of naturalistic argument, that there is — must be — *something* that we *qua* human are, some thing or some way that we *qua* human have in common, to which law *qua* constraint and *qua* unified can possibly bear the relation $RF[human\ being]$. By the logic of the relation-genus $RF[x]$, to deny a robust commonality of human nature is to deny the possibility of (morally justifiable) law. (By "robust," I mean to exclude propositions such as that what human beings have in common is only their "diversity," their being each one a unique individual.)[46] Denial of law-independent, robust human commonality would seem tantamount to denial that law, being what it

[44] See, for example, Bork, "First Amendment Problems"; compare *Michael H. v. Gerald D.*, 109 S. Ct. 2333, 2344 n. 6 (1989) (Scalia, J.).

[45] See, for example, Margaret Jane Radin, "Reconsidering the Rule of Law," *Boston University Law Review*, vol. 69 (1989), pp. 781–819, esp. pp. 787–89.

[46] By contrast, the commonality adduced by Judith Jarvis Thomson as a "source" of our having claims — the fact (accepting that it is a fact) that human beings are creatures whose *interests* are "inherently individual" — seems quite robust enough to contribute support or explanation for a notion of unitary and constraining law. See Thomson, *The Realm of Rights*, pp. 218–23, discussed below.
     I do not here consider whether the ordinary idea of law as constraint allows for a human commonality that we construct by our very acts of law-creation and participation in legal culture. See, for example, Andrew Fraser, *The Spirit of the Laws: Republicanism and the Unfinished Project of Modernity* (Toronto: University of Toronto Press, 1990), pp. 284–87; Robert Gordon, "New Developments in Legal Theory," in *The Politics of Law: A Progressive Critique*, ed. David Kairys (New York: Pantheon Books, 1990), pp. 413–25, esp. pp. 418–21. The question is whether positing that human commonality is completely constructed by — and purely reflexive with — legal culture contradicts law's otherness vis-à-vis human agency, law's attribute of constraint or resistance.

notionally is — unitary and constraining — can possibly be RF[*human being*]. For just that reason, we may expect such denials of human commonality to meet resistance in legal thought. Given what law notionally is, those who tend to think it a good thing that there should be law are likely also to believe (as they may do on independent grounds) that there are robust commonalities of need and condition among members of the society whose law it is.

Which returns us, finally, to Unger and his critics. Recall that Unger links his political program of disentrenchment to a plastic conception of humanity, in which the human essence lies in each person's capacity for self-revision or self-transcendence. Suppose you thought that this sort of capacity is the sum and substance of "human nature."[47] Would that provide you with a sufficiently robust commonality of human being to support (in the manner we have just been discussing) the legalist notion of law as unitary and constraining? Or might the difficulty of squaring plasticity as the human essence with the legalist ideal provide, for some who find great value in that ideal, one reason for raining on plasticity's parade?

You might wonder whether it truly is all that hard to square plasticity-as-human-essence with the legalist ideal. Do we not easily conjoin the *form* (or "notion") of law as abstract and general (that is, as unitary) with conceptions of the self as prior to its ends, or with other ideas about human open-endedness and infinite possibility? The generality of law is, after all, a part of the rule-of-law ideal that has been thought to mark institutions hospitable to liberty. Michael Oakeshott, to take a striking example, is construed as extolling that ideal's hospitality to a conception of human agency as the capacity to "interpret [one's situation] in an indefinite number of particular ways" in determining what it is that one will do and who it is that one will thereby become.[48]

Our problem, however, is not to understand how legal *form* can be RF[*human being* qua *plastic*]. Rather, it is to understand how *law* can be RF[*human being* qua *plastic*]. *Law* is not the abstract legal form of generality; it is definite prescriptive content *in* that form. The problem is to understand how *that* can possibly be RF[*human being* qua *plastic*]. Surely there is a real problem there.

Might this problem help prompt resistance, on the part of thinkers strongly attached to the political virtues of legal ordering, to Unger's conception of personality? That inference may be too hasty. It imagines readers taking Unger's argument to be one that purchases human-natural universality (that is, the universality of plasticity or infinitude) at the price of giving up on any *substantial* human-natural commonality on which de-

---

[47] As James Boyle puts it, in Unger's argument "the only noncontingent phenomenon is contingency itself, and 'infinite personality' appears to be contingency clad in the robes of human nature." See Boyle, "Modernist Social Theory," pp. 1069–70.

[48] The characterization is David Mapel's. See Mapel, "Civil Association and the Idea of Contingency," *Political Theory*, vol. 18 (1990), p. 393.

terminate law, as putatively *RF*[*human being*], can possibly fix. I doubt, though, that Unger's astutest and best critics do read him that way, because he does not write that way. Unger's depiction of personality does not rest with pure infinitude. It attaches infinitude to something more substantial although still highly abstract—that is, the idea of sociality as essential to humanity and, more specifically, the idea of subjectivity as a fragile achievement wrought out of encounters with others in which the subject must constantly risk itself in order to confirm and recreate itself.[49] This may provide just enough substance to inspire or support a normative theory of social relations and politics.[50] The vision of personality forging itself in dialectic might, then, be perceived as sponsoring the everything-always-up-for-grabs vision of politics. For those to whom such a vision of politics appears to be dangerously undercapitalized with human commonality, so too, perhaps, will the parallel vision of personality.

V. LEGALISM AND NATURALISM IN KANTIAN MORAL ARGUMENT

The question remains of how much and how far the vision of human plasticity has to yield to the demand for human commonality, before legalist law can possibly qualify as *RF*[*human being*]. For example, suppose it is an attribute of human nature that (by contrast with what we may conceive about ants and bees) our lives are individually separate and we have "inherently individual" interests.[51] Would that be enough? And if that is not quite enough, then suppose we add in something like a natural human faculty of law-abidingness, such that beings of the human kind derive or produce value just by exercising the faculty. Enough?

Much modern deontology rests, in part, on a "Kantian idea":[52]

Given that

(1) human beings are by nature capable of conforming their conduct to moral law,

then

(2) human beings ought to conform their conduct to moral law.

---

[49] Thus, Unger develops a normative theory of human passions as containing and expressing—"ring[ing] the changes on"—"the relations between our reciprocal and infinite longing for one another and our reciprocal and infinite terror." See Unger, *Passion*, p. 100.

[50] James Boyle, having remarked that, in Unger's argument, "the concept of infinite personality seems to allow us to skirt relativism," adds that the argument would also skirt contentlessness if it could succeed in deriving from a pure, unadulterated notion of human personal infinitude a normative theory of intersubjective relations and an attendant theory of human passions. Boyle denies that any such derivation is possible as a matter of logic. See Boyle, "Modernist Social Theory," p. 1073. At the same time, though, he also urges that Unger's linkage of politics to personality can nevertheless work if we take it as an appeal not to logic but experience—"a dispatch from the front and not a treatise on war." See *ibid.*, pp. 1075–76, 1080–83.

[51] See Thomson, *The Realm of Rights*, pp. 212–24, discussed below.

[52] *Ibid.*, p. 215.

We easily perceive some kind of connection between these two propositions, and yet we may puzzle over just what the connection is. What is
it that is supposed to make (2) follow from (1)?

One possibility (I do not say the only one) is that we find in human beings what I will call a legalist propensity. By "legalist," I mean a propensity to conform one's conduct to requirements and prohibitions derivable
from strongly generalizable principles. By "propensity," I mean a capacity
whose exercise is considered to be a form of human flourishing or fulfillment. Do judgments such as (2) ever rest, in any degree, on attributions
of legalist propensities to human nature? What basis might we have for
such attributions? Where might they come from?

It will be useful to have before us an example of moral argument that
brings such questions to mind. Judith Jarvis Thomson's argument in *The
Realm of Rights* does so in an exceptionally engaging way.

Thomson offers an account of moral rights, specifically rights of the
kind she calls "claims." A "claim," in Thomson's explication, consists in
its being the case that there is something that someone ought (not) to do
or let happen.[53] Thus, to say that X has such and such a claim against Y,
or to say more generally that people have claims, is to express a moral
judgment. For Thomson, it is also to say that claims and their correlative
constraints are operative—our having them is manifest—in moral data
consisting in our (that is, your, the reader's) strong and confident judgments about what people ought (not) to do or let happen in various
classes of cases.[54] Out of a deftly plotted array and rigorously executed
examination of moral data, Thomson develops her account of what a
claim is and of what claims we have.

At the same time, and in support of her account, Thomson inquires as
to the "sources" of its being the case that we have these claims. A source
is a consideration supportive of our having claims, something that helps
"make true" the judgment that we have them.[55] To identify a source of
(our having) claims is to respond in some way to the question of why we
do have them.[56]

Not every sort of consideration that helps explain or support a moral
judgment is, in Thomson's usage, a source of such a judgment's being
true. Some supportive considerations are, rather, what she calls "explan-

----

[53] "X's having a claim against Y that such and such be the case consists, centrally, in its
being the case that other things being equal Y ought not to let such and such fail to be the
case." *Ibid.*, p. 214.

[54] Thomson presents some, but not nearly all, such judgments as necessary truths, statements of what simply cannot fail to be the case. For example, given what pain is,

Other things being equal, one ought not to cause others pain.

is both a moral datum and a necessary truth. See *ibid.*, p. 18.

[55] See, for example, *ibid.*, p. 31.

[56] See, for example, *ibid.*, p. 33.

atory moral judgments."[57] By helping knit together the moral data, explanatory moral judgments illuminate and satisfy. However, explanatory moral judgments do not get all the way to what one seeks, when one seeks to know what makes for the truth of such a sweeping moral judgment as the judgment that we have claims.[58] Thomson, at any rate, wants in addition to find moral explanation flowing from *nonmoral* considerations — sources — consisting of *facts* about the world and us in it. She holds that moral judgments ultimately must reach down to sources that "consist in some feature of *us*."[59]

Thomson argues at length that one of these sources of our having claims is the fact about human beings that we have inherently individual interests.[60] More precisely, her argument is that this fact about us explains why we should expect that any moral law pertaining to us — any moral law by which we as human are bound — will contain the particular kinds of constraints on conduct that claims represent. Thomson recognizes, however, that this fact leaves unexplained why we as human are bound by any moral law at all.[61] Thus, her argument requires for its completion an additional source for our being so bound. In order to provide this, Thomson looks to a "Kantian idea" (which she does not undertake to investigate further) that we, as human, ought to conform our conduct to moral law because we, as human, are capable of doing so.[62]

---

[57] In what Thomson seems to propose as their standard form (see *ibid.*, p. 30), these are two-clause conjuncts in which the first clause is the moral judgment we are concerned at the moment to explain or support, which Thomson calls an "object-level moral judgment," and the second embeds a moral judgment providing a major premise for an argument yielding the first. For example (see *ibid.*):

Capital punishment is wrong because it is intentional killing of those who pose no threat to others.

is an explanatory moral judgment relative to the object-level moral judgment,

Capital punishment is wrong.

[58] See *ibid.*, p. 31. The major premise embedded in the second (*explicans*) clause of an explanatory moral judgment — in our example in note 57, it would be "intentional killing of those who pose no threat to others is wrong" — is itself also waiting its turn to be focalized as an object-level moral judgment and *explicandum*.

[59] *Ibid.*, p. 212. Thomson distinguishes between two classes of extramoral sources, which we may call conventional and natural. A conventional source of our having claims would be the fact that we were given them by acts of promising or lawmaking. But, Thomson says, there are claims, such as the claim that others not intrude on our bodies, that we have regardless of there having been any such acts. No conventional source could possibly explain our having claims of that sort. Thomson very plausibly says that any source of such transconventional claims — in effect, natural human rights — has to consist in some fact, or facts, of human nature.

[60] See *ibid.*, pp. 212–24.

[61] See *ibid.*, pp. 214–15.

[62] "What I have in mind is a Kantian idea, and surely a very plausible one, that the capacity to conform your conduct to moral law is a necessary and sufficient condition for the moral law to apply to you." *Ibid.*, p. 215.

In this way, Thomson's account of moral rights falls back on the line of argument that draws a connection between

> (1) human beings are by nature capable of conforming their conduct to moral law;

and

> (2) human beings ought$_1$[63] to conform their conduct to moral law.

But what, precisely, is this connection? Clearly, (1) is something like a necessary condition of (2); "ought" implies "can." However, (1) standing alone does not immediately present itself as a sufficient condition of (2); certainly it is not true in general that we *ought* to do something just in virtue of the fact that we *can* do it. If we want the sovereignty of moral law to be true in virtue of facts of human nature, then we have to find something, in addition to (1), to say about human nature — or, perhaps, about moral law — that helps make (2) be true. But what might that be?

Perhaps the answer is simple. Perhaps it is that this additional something is already contained in the very concept of moral law. Moral law already *is* what any creature, capable of complying, ought$_2$ (not) to do. That such a creature ought$_1$ to do as it ought$_2$ to do would seem to be true analytically, by transitivity between ought$_1$ and ought$_2$. I wonder, though, whether this purely analytic explication of (2) accounts for all of the persuasive force that the Kantian idea exerts in moral argument. I wonder whether we sometimes take (2) to make not just an analytic point but also a synthetic one, because we understand something different by the "ought$_1$" of (2) than we do by the "ought$_2$" of moral law. "Ought$_2$" refers to a certain kind of constraint on a creature's conduct. Perhaps "ought$_1$" refers not just to that, but also to what suits the creature, is "right-for" it, given the kind of creature it is.

More, after all, is conveyed by the idea of moral law than that there are sundry things we ought (not) to do. The idea of moral law is not simply the idea of constraint on conduct. Moral law signifies constraint on conduct by or in accordance with a *principle* that is *generalizable*, in some very strong sense of the term. Thus, Kantian moralists sometimes say that guiding one's actions by strongly generalizable principles is what we mean by rationality, or that recognition of the necessity of guiding one's actions in this way is what we mean by reason and one has no (real, enlightened) choice but to exercise one's reason and do what is rational.

But why — in what sense — no choice? It is hard to escape the sense of some deep notion of human-natural interest at work here, some notion of consonance with human nature. Perhaps the thought is that we have,

---

[63] The subscript is not a typographical error. It will play a part in the following discussion.

as human, a deep impulse to conform our conduct to requirements and permissions derivable from strongly generalizable principles, which we satisfy by acting in this way; or perhaps it is that we possess, as human, a worthy propensity—a potential excellence—that acting in this way fulfills. For reasons that should by now be apparent, I call "legalist" the idea of such a human-natural interest in its being the case that we conform our conduct to requirements and prohibitions derived from strongly generalizable principles.

I neither know nor claim that appeals like Thomson's to the Kantian idea must involve attribution of a legalist propensity to human nature. I do suggest that such appeals may often actually work that way. Insofar as they do, they invite worries along the following lines:

1. Attributions to human nature of legalist propensities may be as much the correlates or products of our intuitions about certain high-level moral or political propositions (such as propositions about our having rights) as they are the independently derived, motivating sources of such propositions or of their truth.

2. Insofar as attributions of legalism to human nature really do arise independently of prescriptive accounts of morality—for which accounts these attributions then really do serve as independent, motivating sources and partial justifications—the attributions may still be doctrine-dependent, and in a way that some may find especially disturbing. They may be corollaries of a particular political doctrine whose own origins are morally suspect, or at any rate have not yet been persuasively tied into deep moral-anthropological inquiry.

   a. The notion of law as constraint on conduct by or in accordance with strongly generalizable principle is native to legal and political thought, where it has long appeared in the political doctrine of the rule of law.

   b. The political ideal of the rule of law may take its inspirations not only from concerns about human-natural interest (in freedom, for example) but from concerns about efficient social organization as viewed from the standpoint of organizers. Some arguments say that legalism is required of any ruler who aspires to rule effectively.[64]

---

[64] Such ideas are rampant in modern jurisprudence. For Max Weber, for example, the derivability of specific prescriptive content from a formally unitizable set of preestablished general principles is (among other things) an expression of capitalist bureaucratic rationality. See, for example, Anthony Kronman, *Max Weber* (London: Edward Arnold, 1983), pp. 118–46. For Lon Fuller, the ideal of the rule of law corresponds to an "internal morality of law" that commends itself to any ruler aspiring to rule efficaciously. See, for example, Lon Fuller, *The Morality of Law* (New Haven: Yale University Press, 1969), pp. 33–94.

Rather than critiques, we might better cast these worries as interrogations:

1. Insofar as it is true that a moral theory's reliance on a Kantian "source" for our being subject to (some) moral law — and hence (for example) for our having moral rights — entails attribution to humankind of something like a legalist propensity, how confident are we that this attribution has an independent basis in anthropological inquiry, empirical or speculative?

2. How confident are we that such attributions are not leaking over to moral theory from a body of legal thought aligned with a historically particular, nonmorally inspired political doctrine?

In this essay, I have tried to suggest how the first query grows out of the two-way character of the traffic between high-level prescription and low-level attributions to human nature that we find in moral and political argument. The second query grows out of the possibility of a similar two-way flow in exchanges between moral theory and legal thought.

Law, Harvard University

INDEX

Achievement, as a good, 22, 24–25
Actions, shameful, 88–89, 92–93
Adams, Robert M., 159–60
Aesthetic value, 22, 32–33, 96
Agents, ethical, 44, 47–48
Altruism. *See* Benevolence; Virtue, other-regarding
Aquinas, St. Thomas, 159
Aristotelian principle, 16, 34
Aristotle, vii, 47–48, 138–39; on virtue, 152, 157–58, 161, 166
Autonomy, 28–29, 31

Becker, Lawrence, 77–78
Benefit, 185–86; and harm, 63–64
Benevolence, 21, 142, 145. *See also* Virtue, other-regarding
Berlin, Isaiah, 50

Chatwin, Bruce, 66
Cicero, 145
Claims, 204
Commitment (*Philia*), 137–38, 140, 141, 146
Consciousness, 19
Consensus, 52
Consequences, concept of, 118–19
Consequentialism, 120–21, 127, 129; appeal of, 115–16, 132; assumptions of, 131; definition of, 120–21, 126 n. 9; standard versus interest, 115–16. *See also* Utilitarianism
Cooper, Neil, 75
Cooperation, advantages of, 43–44
Cyrenaics, 135

Decision procedures, 123–24, 131
Desert, 64
Desire (Preference), 19; basic and derived, 81; self-regarding, 82; and well-being, 170, 174
Determinism, 30
Division of labor, 45

Education, moral, 61
Egoism, 135, 137
Ends: final, 133, 135; and means, 92–93
Ethical character, 40
Ethical diversity, 38; advantages of, 50–52

Ethics: of decency, 39; functions of, 3, 130; of righteousness, 39; of virtue, 40. *See also* Agents, ethical; Morality; Norms
Eudaimonism, 133–34, 135–36, 137, 146–47; and impartiality, 147–48
Evils, imaginary, 158–60
Excellence. *See* Perfectionism; Value, perfectionist
Experience machine, 25

Fallibilist minimal realism, 56–57
Foot, Philippa, 65, 84, 115
Friendship, 137, 138–39

Gauthier, David, 83, 196–97
Good, the, 3, 6, 41, 96, 118; and derivation of the right, 1; fundamental, 1, 13; human, 6, 127, 190, 196; intrinsic, 135, 149, 153; objective, 170; promotion of, 119, 125, 130; theories of, vii–viii, 2. *See also* Goodness; Rationality; Value
Good life: criteria of, 18–23; pluralistic and monistic (unitary) accounts of, vii–viii, 17–18, 23–35
Good signs, 100–101
Goodness, 102–3; absolute, 106–7, 108–9; derivative and nonderivative, 99–100, 103; imaginary, 158–60; intrinsic, 103–5, 107, 111, 113–15, 117, 135, 149, 153; moral, 102–3; of states of affairs, 99. *See also* Good, the; Value
Goodness-for, 96–97, 98
Goodness-from-a-point-of-view, 78, 97–98, 107
Goodness-of-a-kind, 20. *See also* Perfectionism; Value, perfectionist
Griffin, James, 26 n. 14
Gutmann, Amy, 52

Hampshire, Stuart, 50
Happiness, 147–48
Harms, and benefits, 63–64
Hedonism, 135, 149, 154–55, 169; objections to, 172; objective, 178–79; reductionist and nonreductionist, 174–75
Hobbes, Thomas, 196

Human nature, 202, 206–7; and human
    good, 190, 192, 196, 201
Hume, David, 49, 82, 195 n. 27. *See also*
    Rationality, neo-Humean

Ideal ethical agents, 44, 47–48
Ideology, 41–42
Impartiality, 141–43, 147
Institutions, social, 190–91
Integrity, 22

Jeffrey, Richard, 83

Kant, Immanuel, 48–49, 205–6
Kierkegaard, Soren, 74–75
Knowledge: as a good, 19; limits of, 128

Law: moral, 206; nature of, 200; role of,
    198–99; rule of, 207
Leviathan (Thomas Hobbes), 196
Lewis, David, 60
Lexical order, 16 n. 3
Liberty, 20; positive and negative, 29–30
Life, 17, 182 n. 7; evaluation of, 36–37;
    minimally acceptable, 69, 70–71, 72, 78,
    79
Love: mutual 21; of one's own virtue,
    166–67; of self, 21, 165, 166

Means, and ends, 92–93
Meta-ethical theories, 43
Methods of Ethics, The (Henry Sidgwick),
    149
Mill, John Stuart, 52
Moore, G. E., 108–10, 152–53, 161
Moral pluralism, 63, 65, 71–74
Moral realism, 56–57, 164
Moral systems, 42, 50, 58–59
Morality, 91, 102–3, 206; and ethics, 76–
    77; object of, 3, 130; overriding force
    of, 74, 75–76; theories of, 42. *See also*
    Ethics; Norms

Natural kinds, 7
Naturalism, in moral argument, 194–95
Neo-Humeans, 83 n. 6. *See also* Rational-
    ity, neo-Humean
Nicomachean Ethics (Aristotle), 138
Nietzsche, Friedrich, 24, 49
Norms, 130–31
Nozick, Robert, 25, 152–53

Oakeshott, Michael, 202
O'Neill, Onora, 54

Perfectionism, 24, 153. *See also* Value, per-
    fectionist

Philanthrōpia (Benevolence), 142, 145
Philia (Commitment), 137–38, 140, 141,
    146
Philosophical Explanations (Robert Nozick),
    153
Phronesis (Practical wisdom), 40. *See also*
    Rationality
Phronimos, 47–48
Plato, 23–24, 38, 45
Pleasure, 152–53, 170; as a dimension,
    172–73, 174; significance of, 179; and
    well-being, 171
Pluralism, 63, 65, 71–74
Practical wisdom, 40. *See also* Rationality
Preference. *See* Desire
Pride, 166. *See also* Love, of self
Principia Ethica (G. E. Moore), 153
Productive activity, 22
Promise keeping, 122–23, 124–25
Property, institutions of, 128–29, 130

Railton, Peter, 54
Rashdall, Hastings, 149, 160–61
Rationality, 33–35, 81; and the good, 82,
    94, 111–12; neo-Humean, 81, 84–86,
    92; practical, 40, 81; varieties of, 89–90.
    See also Reason
Rawls, John, 33–34
Realm of Rights, The (Judith Jarvis Thom-
    son), 204
Reason, 19, 72–73, 81. *See also* Rationality
Rectitude, 22
Republic, The (Plato), 45
Right: derivation of, 121; and the good,
    118, 126–27
Ross, W. D., 152–53, 156, 160, 165

Savage, Leonard J., 83
Self-command, as a good, 19
Self-esteem, 21
Selfishness, 72. *See also* Egoism
Self-sacrifice, 162. *See also* Virtue, other-
    regarding
Sexuality, 21–22
Sidgwick, Henry, 149, 162
Social life, demands of, 128
Socrates, vii, 45
Stoicism, 23, 139–41, 143–46, 149
Sunstein, Cass, 193–94

Taylor, Charles, 50
Theaetetus (Plato), 142–44
Thompson, Dennis, 52
Thomson, Judith Jarvis, 204–6
Traits of character, 41, 44–45

Unger, Roberto, 190–94, 202–3
Utilitarianism, 120–21, 125 n. 8, 130–31,
    147. *See also* Consequentialism

Value, 9, 79–80; intrinsic, 183–85; moral and nonmoral, 63–64, 65, 69–70, 77, 80; perfectionist, 4–5, 6, 8, 10, 20; prudential, 4–5, 11, 12, 26 n. 14. *See also* Good, the; Goodness
Virtue: forms of, 156–57; nature of, 149, 160–62; other-regarding, 136, 138–39, 142–44, 147; recursive account of, 150–52, 154
Virtue ethics, 133. *See also* Eudaimonism
Vocation, 30–32
Von Wright, G. H., 102

Walzer, Michael, 75
Welfare, 11; as criterion of the good, 4; as fundamental good, 13, 14; as individualistic, 12. *See also* Goodness-for; Value, prudential; Well-being
Well-being, 25, 183, 185–86; changes in, 180–81; and desire, 170, 174; theories of, 169–70, 187–89. *See also* Welfare
Will, 19; limits of, 127–29
Williams, Bernard, 35, 54 n. 23, 75, 76–77, 145, 166–67
"Wrong," senses of, 91
Wrongdoing, rectification of, 27